Lecture Notes in Computer Science 11687

Kim Guldstrand Larsen ·
Tim Willemse (Eds.)

Formal Methods
for Industrial
Critical Systems

24th International Conference, FMICS 2019
Amsterdam, The Netherlands, August 30–31, 2019
Proceedings

 Springer

Editors
Kim Guldstrand Larsen
Aalborg University
Aalborg, Denmark

Tim Willemse ⓘ
Eindhoven University of Technology
Eindhoven, The Netherlands

ISSN 0302-9743   ISSN 1611-3349 (electronic)
Lecture Notes in Computer Science
ISBN 978-3-030-27007-0   ISBN 978-3-030-27008-7 (eBook)
https://doi.org/10.1007/978-3-030-27008-7

LNCS Sublibrary: SL2 – Programming and Software Engineering

This Springer imprint is published by the registered company Springer Nature Switzerland AG
The registered company address is: Gewerbestrasse 11, 6330 Cham, Switzerland

Preface

This volume contains the proceedings of the 24th International Conference on Formal Methods for Industrial Critical Systems (FMICS 2019), which was held at CWI in Amsterdam, The Netherlands, during August 30–31, 2019. This year the conference was jointly organized with the 30th International Conference on Concurrency Theory (CONCUR 2019), and the 17th International Conference on Formal Modeling and Analysis of Timed Systems (FORMATS 2019).

The aim of FMICS is to provide a forum for researchers who are interested in the development and application of formal methods in industry. In particular, FMICS brings together scientists and engineers who are active in the area of formal methods and interested in exchanging their experiences in the industrial usage of these methods. FMICS also strives to promote research and development for the improvement of formal methods and tools for industrial applications. The topics of interest include, but are not limited to:

- Case studies and experience reports on industrial applications of formal methods, focusing on lessons learned or identification of new research directions.
- Methods, techniques, and tools to support automated analysis, certification, debugging, descriptions, learning, optimization, and transformation of complex, distributed, real-time, embedded, mobile and autonomous systems.
- Verification and validation methods (model checking, theorem proving, SAT and SMT solving and constraint solving, abstract interpretation, etc.) that address shortcomings of existing methods with respect to their industrial applicability (e.g., scalability and usability issues).
- Impact of the adoption of formal methods on the development process and associated costs. Application of formal methods in standardization and industrial forums.

This year we received 15 submissions. Each of these submissions went through a rigorous review process in which each paper received at least 3 reports. We selected 9 papers for presentation during the conference and inclusion in these proceedings. The conference also featured invited talks by Jaco van de Pol (Aarhus University, and Twente University), jointly with CONCUR, and Holger Hermanns (Universität des Saarlandes), and a special session on (commercial) formal methods in industry.

We would like to thank the ERCIM FMICS working group coordinator Jaco van de Pol (Aarhus University, and Twente University), for his counseling and support during the organization of FMICS 2019, the CONCUR general chair Jos Baeten, and the local organizers for taking care of all the local arrangements in Amsterdam. We would also like to thank CWI for the generous sponsoring of the joint events. ERCIM supported the event through the FMICS Working Group, Springer provided the best paper award, and Springer Nature produced the conference proceedings. Finally, we would like to thank the Program Committee members and external reviewers for their useful and detailed reviews and discussions, all authors for their submissions, and all presenters and attendees of the conference.

August 2019   Kim Guldstrand Larsen
                                                                                                          Tim Willemse

Organization

Steering Committee

Alessandro Fantechi	University of Firenze, Italy
Hubert Garavel	Inria, France
Stefania Gnesi	ISTI-CNR, Italy
Diego Latella	ISTI-CNR, Italy
Tiziana Margaria	LERO, Ireland
Radu Mateescu	Inria, France
Jaco van de Pol (Chair)	Aarhus University, Denmark

Program Chairs

Kim Guldstrand Larsen	Aalborg University, Denmark
Tim Willemse	Eindhoven University of Technology, The Netherlands

Program Committee

Bernhard K. Aichernig	TU Graz, Austria
Giovanni Bacci	Aalborg University, Denmark
Jiri Barnat	Masaryk University, Czech Republic
Joerg Brauer	Verified Systems International GmbH, Germany
Ana Cavalcanti	University of York, UK
Michael Fisher	University of Liverpool, UK
Wan Fokkink	Vrije Universiteit Amsterdam, The Netherlands
Maria-Del-Mar Gallardo	University of Malaga, Spain
Hubert Garavel	Inria, France
Anne E. Haxthausen	Technical University of Denmark, Denmark
Jozef Hooman	TNO-ESI, The Netherlands
Falk Howar	TU Clausthal and IPSSE, Germany
Peter Höfner	CSIRO, Australia
Jeroen J. A. Keiren	Eindhoven University of Technology, The Netherlands
Zhiming Liu	Southwest University, China
Tiziana Margaria	Lero, Ireland
Peter Ölveczky	University of Oslo, Norway
Charles Pecheur	Université Catholique de Louvain, Belgium
Matteo Rossi	Politecnico di Milano, Italy
Cristina Seceleanu	Mälardalen University, Sweden
Scott Smolka	Stony Brook University, USA
Maurice H. ter Beek	ISTI-CNR, Italy
Helen Treharne	University of Surrey, UK
Jaco van de Pol	Aarhus University, Denmark

Additional Reviewers

Davide Basile
Rong Gu
Florian Lorber
Malte Mauritz
Shouvik Roy

Abstracts

Concurrent Algorithms and Data Structures
for Model Checking

Jaco van de Pol

Aarhus University and University of Twente

Model checking is a successful method for checking properties on the state space of concurrent, reactive systems. Since it is based on exhaustive search, scaling the method to industrial systems has been a challenge since its conception. Research has focused on *clever data structures and algorithms*, to reduce the size of the state space or its representation; *smart search heuristics*, to reveal potential bugs and counterexamples early; and *high-performance computing*, to deploy the brute force processing power of clusters of compute-servers.

The main challenge is to combine a brute force approach with clever algorithms: brute force alone (when implemented carefully) can bring a linear speedup in the number of processors. This is great, since it reduces model-checking times from days to minutes. On the other hand, proper algorithms and data structures can lead to exponential gains. Therefore, the *parallelization bonus* is only real if we manage to speedup clever algorithms.

There are some obstacles: many linear-time graph algorithms depend on a depth-first exploration order, which is hard to parallelize. Examples include the detection of strongly connected components (SCC), and the nested depth-first-search (NDFS) algorithm. Both are used in model checking LTL properties. Symbolic representations, like binary decision diagrams (BDDs), reduce model checking to "pointer-chasing", leading to irregular memory-access patterns. This poses severe challenges on achieving actual speedup in (clusters of) modern multi-core computer architectures.

This talk will present some of the solutions found over the last 10 years, leading to the high-performance model checker LTSmin. These include parallel NDFS (based on the PhD thesis of Alfons Laarman), the parallel detection of SCCs with concurrent Union-Find (based on the PhD thesis of Vincent Bloemen), and concurrent BDDs and other decision diagrams (based on the PhD thesis of Tom van Dijk). This functionality is provided in a specification-language agnostic manner, while exploiting the locality typical for asynchronous distributed systems (based on the PhD thesis of Jeroen Meijer).

Finally, I will sketch a perspective on moving forward from high-performance model checking to *high-performance synthesis algorithms*. Examples include parameter synthesis for stochastic and timed systems, and strategy synthesis for (stochastic and timed) games.

Power in Low Earth Orbit. Verified

Holger Hermanns[1,2]

[1] Saarland University – Computer Science, Saarland Informatics Campus,
Saarbrücken, Germany
[2] Institute of Intelligent Software, Guangzhou, China

There is an increasing interest across the space industry in deploying large-scale Low-Earth Orbit (LEO) satellite constellations for the purpose of traffic observation, Earth monitoring, and for offering communication services across the globe. Current in-orbit technology demonstrators, such as the GomX-4A and GomX-4B satellites from GomSpace, make it obvious that the main operational bottleneck in such missions is the electric power budget.

This keynote provides a survey of past and ongoing work to master operational limitations of LEO satellites and satellite constellations using formal methods. After presenting the major technological characteristics and challenges of the LEO domain, I will discuss how optimal reachability analysis in priced timed automata [5, 7] can be combined with stochastic battery kinetics [3, 4] to best exploit a satellite's operational capabilities in orbit while keeping the risk of draining the on-board battery [1, 6] provably low. We then turn to the question how to attack the problem for constellations with dozens of communicating satellites. This requires profound support for extrapolating the electric power budget as part of the inter-satellite and satellite-to-ground communication design. I present a solution embedded in the construction process of contact plans in delay tolerant networking [2], and finally address scalability aspects of the proposed solution, important for upcoming mega constellations consisting of hundreds of satellites.

References

1. Bisgaard, M., Gerhardt, D., Hermanns, H., Krčál, J., Nies, G., Stenger, M.: Battery-aware scheduling in low orbit: the GomX-3 case. Formal Asp. Comput., **31**(2), 261–285 (2019)
2. Fraire, J.A., Nies, G., Hermanns, H., Bay, K., Bisgaard, M.: Battery-aware contact plan design for LEO satellite constellations: The Ulloriaq case study. In: IEEE Global Communications Conference, GLOBECOM 2018, Abu Dhabi, United Arab Emirates, December 9–13, 2018, pp. 1–7. IEEE (2018)
3. Hermanns, H., Krčál, J., Nies, G.: Recharging probably keeps batteries alive. In: Mousavi, M., Berger, C. (eds.) Cyber Physical Systems. Design, Modeling, and Evaluation. CyPhy 2015. LNCS, vol. 9361, pp. 83–98. Springer, Cham (2015)

This work receives financial support by the ERC Advanced Investigators Grant 695614 (POWVER) and by the Deutsche Forschungsgemeinschaft (DFG, German Research Foundation) grant 389792660 as part of TRR 248, see https://perspicuous-computing.science.

4. Hermanns, H., Krčál, J., Nies, G.: How is your satellite doing? battery kinetics with recharging and uncertainty. LITES, **4**(1), 04:1–04:28 (2017)
5. Larsen, K., et al.: As cheap as possible: effcient cost-optimal reachability for priced timed automata. In: Berry, G., Comon, H., Finkel, A. (eds.) Computer Aided Verification. CAV 2001. LNCS, vol. 2102, pp. 493–505. Springer, Heidelberg (2001)
6. Nies, G., et al.: Mastering operational limitations of LEO satellites – the GomX-3 approach. Acta Astronautica, **151**, 726–735 (2018)
7. Zhang, Z., Nielsen, B., Larsen, K.G., Nies, G., Stenger, M., Hermanns, H.: Pareto optimal reachability analysis for simple priced timed automata. In: Duan, Z., Ong, L. (eds.) Formal Methods and Software Engineering. ICFEM 2017. LNCS, vol. 10610, pp. 481–495. Springer, Cham (2017)

Contents

Modelling and Analysing ERTMS L3 Moving Block Railway Signalling with Simulink and UPPAAL SMC

Davide Basile[1,2], Maurice H. ter Beek[1(✉)], Alessio Ferrari[1], and Axel Legay[3]

[1] ISTI–CNR, Pisa, Italy
maurice.terbeek@isti.cnr.it
[2] University of Florence, Florence, Italy
[3] Université Catholique de Louvain, Louvain-la-Neuve, Belgium

Abstract. Efficient and safe railway signalling systems, together with energy-saving infrastructures, are among the main pillars to guarantee sustainable transportation. ERTMS L3 moving block is one of the next generation railway signalling systems currently under trial deployment, with the promise of increased capacity on railway tracks, reduced costs and improved reliability. We report an experience in modelling a satellite-based ERTMS L3 moving block signalling system from the railway industry with Simulink and UPPAAL and analysing the UPPAAL model with UPPAAL SMC. The lessons learned range from demonstrating the feasibility of applying UPPAAL SMC in a moving block railway context, to the offered possibility of fine tuning communication parameters in satellite-based ERTMS L3 moving block railway signalling system models that are fundamental for the reliability of their operational behaviour.

1 Introduction

The railway sector is well known for its robust safety requirements, as witnessed by the CENELEC EN 50128 standard [22] for the development of software for railway control and protection systems, which highly recommends the use of formal methods for software systems to be certified at Safety Integrity Levels SIL 3 and SIL 4. In fact, formal methods and tools are widely applied to railway systems [7,9,13,23–25,28,30]. Consequently, the railway sector is notoriously cautious about the adoption of technological innovations compared with other transport sectors. Hence, while satellite-based positioning systems are in use for some time now in the avionics and automotive sectors, current railway signalling systems still prevalently use traditional ground-based train detection systems and fixed block distancing. However, the faster trains are allowed to run, the longer their braking distance and the longer the safety distance must be, thus decreasing line capacity. A challenge in the railway sector therefore concerns the development of moving block signalling systems that are as effective and precise as possible [32]. This includes satellite-based positioning, leveraging on

© Springer Nature Switzerland AG 2019
K. G. Larsen and T. Willemse (Eds.): FMICS 2019, LNCS 11687, pp. 1–21, 2019.
https://doi.org/10.1007/978-3-030-27008-7_1

an integrated solution for signal outages (think, e.g., of tunnels) and so-called multi-paths, which typically affect satellite positioning in urban environments [12,46].

The work presented in this paper is one of the outputs of a larger endeavour of the first three authors in the context of the H2020 project ASTRail[1] (SAtellite-based Signalling and Automation SysTems on Railways along with Formal Method and Moving Block Validation) funded by the EU's Shift2Rail[2] initiative. Shift2Rail stimulates the development of safe and reliable technological advances that allow to complete the single european railway area with an ambitious aim: "double the capacity of the European rail system and increase its reliability and service quality by 50%, all while halving life-cycle costs." To this aim, it supports the transition to next generation ERTMS railway signalling systems, including satellite-based train positioning, moving block distancing, and automatic driving [8]. ASTRail makes use of a satellite-based ERTMS Level 3 moving block railway signalling scenario for two different purposes:

- First, in a reduced format, for a trial application of formal modelling and analysis to assess the usability and applicability of formal methods and tools in the railway domain. This assessment is an important issue for the successful uptake of formal methods and tools in the railway industry [7]. In [5], we presented our trial experience in modelling and (statistical) model checking a satellite-based moving block signalling scenario with UPPAAL SMC.
- Second, for modelling and validating a more detailed model as a major portion of an integrated system design of moving block signalling with automated driving technologies to provide a rigorous and verified definition of functional, interoperability, and dependability requirements. As part of the assessment, we conducted a survey with railway practitioners to identify the most mature (semi-)formal methods and tools to be used in the railway context [28]. As a result of this survey, a total of 14 tools were carefully reviewed by means of a systematic evaluation based on a set of 34 evaluation features, upon which eight tools were selected for the above mentioned trial application phase, in which we modelled principles of the moving block scenario in all eight tools. Simulink and UPPAAL were among the eight selected tools. Specifically, Simulink was considered particularly appropriate for functional requirements elicitation and animation involving domain experts, while UPPAAL was considered the appropriate choice for verification of quantitative aspects. More information is available in our contribution [28].

In this paper, we present models of the aforementioned detailed satellite-based ERTMS L3 moving block signalling system model in both Simulink and UPPAAL. The Simulink model was obtained from a requirements elicitation and refinement activity performed with the industrial partners of ASTRail, carried out to consolidate an initial set of requirements for the moving block signalling

---

[1] http://www.astrail.eu.
[2] http://www.shift2rail.org.

system into an executable specification, after which we developed a corresponding UPPAAL model. We report on and draw some lessons from this modelling experience and subsequent analyses with UPPAAL SMC. We choose to perform statistical model checking with UPPAAL SMC rather than simulation and analysis with Simulink, because we have all the monitoring infrastructure for temporal properties. However, the level of abstraction is the same in both models.

We show how UPPAAL SMC can assist in fine tuning communication parameters that are fundamental for the reliability of the model's operational behaviour. In particular, we validate that (i) the frequencies of the messages exchanged between the train and its trackside control system as well as (ii) the unit of distance that a train is allowed to proceed based on a movement authority can be set such that the probabilities of failures (like the train exceeding its movement authority, i.e., failing to brake if it lacks permission to proceed) are close to zero. While numerical constraints for (i) and (ii) were previously defined by railway experts, in ASTRail we wanted to explore to which extent UPPAAL SMC can be exploited to validate such constraints and to support sensitivity analysis on the parameters.

Related Work. We know of several other attempts at modelling and analysing ERTMS L3 signalling systems. Most notably, ERTMS Hybrid L3 systems (using virtual fixed blocks) and its RBC component have recently been modelled and analysed in [2,4,15,41,44] with Promela/Spin, mCRL2, Electrum, and Event-B. However, none of these permit quantitative modelling and analysis, which are fundamental to demonstrating the reliability of the operational behaviour of satellite-based ERTMS L3 moving block railway signalling system models.

We are also aware of attempts to model stochastic or hybrid models of ERTMS L3 (moving block) scenarios in [31,34,35,38] with Simulink, the bounded model checker HySAT, the probabilistic hybrid automata verifier Pro-HVer, UML, the symbolic model checker SMV, timed Petri nets and the timed Petri net analyser Tina, generally applying classical (i.e., not statistical) model checking.

We recognise added value in so-called *formal methods diversity*, as advocated in [42,43], according to which, inspired by code or design diversity [40], applying diverse formal methods and tools on replications or different variants of a design may increase confidence in the correctness of the analysis results. Therefore, we believe that this paper contributes to an increased confidence in the reliability of satellite-based ERTMS L3 moving block railway signalling systems. At the same time, we show how multiple formal/semi-formal tools can also play a complementary role to address different needs of the railway development process, namely functional requirements elicitation and verification of quantitative properties.

Outline. The rest of the paper is organised as follows. Section 2 introduces the industrial case study: next generation satellite-based ERTMS moving block railway signalling systems. Section 3 describes a Simulink model of the case study, developed in agreement with our industrial partners, followed by a corresponding UPPAAL model in Sect. 4. Section 5 presents an analysis of the case study with UPPAAL SMC and Sect. 6 reports some lessons learned from this modelling and analysis experience. Section 7 concludes the paper and discusses future work.

2   ERTMS L3 Moving Block Railway Signalling

The ASTRail project aims to introduce recent scientific achievements as well as cutting-edge technologies from other transport sectors, in particular avionics and automotive, in the railway sector. The project leverages formal methods and tools for careful analyses of the resulting novel applications and solutions in terms of safety and performance. One of the main focusses of ASTRail concerns the use of the Global Navigation Satellite System (GNSS) [46] for onboard train localisation. While satellite-based positioning systems have been in use for quite some time now in the avionics and automotive sectors, to provide accurate positioning and distancing, the current railway signalling systems are largely based on fixed blocks, implemented by specific trackside equipment along the railway lines. A block is a section of the track between two fixed points, which start and end at signals, with their lengths designed to allow trains to operate as frequently as necessary (i.e., ranging from many kilometres for secondary tracks to a few hundred metres for busy commuter lines). The block sizes are determined based on parameters like the line's speed limit, the train's speed, the train's braking characteristics, drivers' sighting and reaction times, etc. But the faster trains are allowed to run, the longer the braking distance and the longer the blocks need to be, thus decreasing the line's capacity. This is because the railway sector's stringent safety requirements impose the length of fixed blocks to be based on the worst-case braking distance, regardless of the actual speed of the train.

The next generation railway signalling systems no longer rely on trackside equipment for train position detection and train integrity supervision, but an onboard odometry system is responsible for monitoring the train's position and autonomously computing its current speed [32]. By exploiting knowledge of the position of the rear end of the train ahead, a safe zone around the moving train can be computed, thus considerably reducing headways between subsequent trains. The resulting moving block signalling systems allow trains in succession to close up, in principle to the braking distance (cf. Fig. 1).

Moving block signalling allows for more trains to run on existing railway tracks, in response to the ever-increasing need to boost the volume of passenger and freight rail transport and the cost and impracticability of constructing new tracks. For this to work, the precise absolute location, speed, and direction of each train needs to be known. These can be determined by a combination of sensors: active and passive markers along the track, as well as trainborne speedometers. This envisioned future switch to next generation signalling systems would not only optimise the exploitation of railway lines due to the adoption of moving block signalling, but the removal of trackside equipment would result in lower capital and maintenance costs [32]. In ASTRail, the first three authors

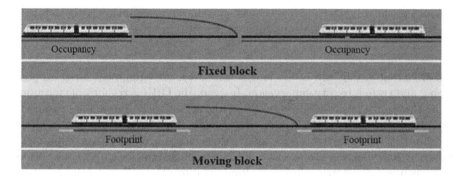

Fig. 1. Safe braking distance between trains for fixed block and moving block signalling
(Image courtesy of Israel.abad/Wikimedia Commons distributed under the CC BY-SA 3.0 license)

are involved in the formal modelling and analysis of moving block railway signalling systems by means of different formal methods and tools, and this paper
reports on one such experience (cf., e.g., [5, 28]).

ERTMS. The European Rail Traffic Management System (ERTMS) [19] is an
international standard aiming to enhance safety and efficiency and improve cross-
border interoperability of trains in Europe by the replacement of national railway signalling systems with a European standard for train control and command systems. ERTMS relies on the European Train Control System (ETCS),
an Automatic Train Protection (ATP) system continuously supervising the train
to ensure that safety speed and distances are not exceeded. The ERTMS/ETCS
standard distinguishes four levels of operation, depending on the role of trackside equipment and on the way the information is transmitted to/from trains. It
is currently deployed on several lines throughout Europe at most in its Level 2.

ERTMS Level 2. ERTMS L2 uses trackside equipment (track circuits) to detect
the occupancy of a section of a railway track by trains, determining the location
of trains with a coarse granularity. This information is sent to a trackside unit,
termed Radio Block Centre (RBC), which sends a Movement Authority (MA)
to each train. The MA is computed by summing the free track circuits ahead,
meaning L2 is based on *fixed block signalling*. The MA provides a train with the
maximum distance it is allowed to travel, the maximum speed (depending on the
track) it is allowed to travel at, and data about the track ahead (like temporary
speed restrictions and (un)conditional emergency stops). The so-called Onboard
Unit (OBU) of each train uses the MA and data stored on board (e.g., the train's
braking capability) to compute the braking curve or the dynamic speed profile
that determine the speed limit, triggering an emergency brake whenever this
limit is exceeded. In L2, so-called Eurobalise responders on the rails of a railway
are used for exact train positioning, while the required signalling information is

provided to the driver's display by continuous data transmission via GSM-R with the RBC. Further trackside equipment is needed for train integrity detection.

ERTMS Level 3. ERTMS L3 no longer uses trackside equipment for train positioning and train integrity supervision. Instead, the OBU is responsible for monitoring the train's position and computing its current speed through its odometry system. To this aim, the OBU periodically sends the train's position to the RBC and the RBC, in turn, sends back an MA to each train. The MA is computed by exploiting knowledge of the position of the rear-end of the foregoing train, meaning L3 is based on *moving block signalling*. As a result, headways between trains can be considerably reduced, in principle to the braking distance. Actually, L3 as defined in [20] does not explicitly refer to the moving block concept, but it admits any implementation able to periodically provide the RBC with the train positions and using limited trackside equipment. A few pilot implementations, referred to as Hybrid L3 [2,4,15,21,41], use virtual fixed blocks: a line is logically divided into fixed length blocks and the OBU is in charge of communicating, at specific points of the line (virtual balises), the train's position, computed using its onboard odometry system. Moving block signalling based on continuous communication and MA computation is currently implemented in some automatic metros, as part of CBTC (Communication Based Train Control) systems.

Moving Block Scenario. The components of the moving block scenario considered in this paper are depicted in Fig. 2. The train carries the Location Unit (LU) and OBU components, while the RBC is a trackside component. The LU receives the train's location from GNSS satellites, sends this location (and the train's integrity) to the OBU, which, in turn, sends the location to the RBC. Upon receiving a train's location, the RBC sends an MA to the OBU (together with speed restrictions and route configurations), indicating the space the train can safely travel based on the safety distance with preceding trains. The RBC computes the MA by communicating with neighbouring RBCs and by exploiting its knowledge of the positions of switches and other trains (head and tail position) by communicating with a Route Management System (RMS). In our scenario, we abstract from an RMS and communication among neighbouring RBCs: we consider one train to communicate with one RBC, based on a seamless handover when the train moves from one RBC supervision area to an adjacent one, as regulated by its Functional Interface Specification [48]. Next to these physical components, there are two temporal constraints for the OBU to respect: the location is continuously updated every 5 s, whereas the MA must be continuously updated within 10 s. If the OBU does not receive an MA within 10 s from the last MA, the OBU is required to force the train to brake.

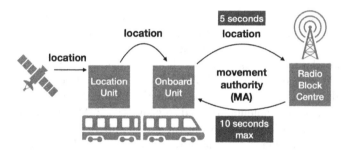

Fig. 2. Overview of ERTMS moving block railway signalling

3   Simulink Model of ERTMS L3 Moving Block

Simulink is a model-based development tool supporting graphical design, simulation, test generation, and code synthesis of dynamic systems.[3] A Simulink model's basic unit is a block, an element that acquires some input and produces some output. Simulink also includes Stateflow, a graphical language inspired by Harel's hierarchical statecharts [37]. Simulink blocks can contain Stateflow state-charts (called charts in Simulink terminology), to represent event-based systems.

In this section, we present the Simulink model of the moving block system resulting from a requirements elicitation and refinement activity performed with the industrial partners of ASTRail. It is the output of multiple iterations involving the third author and the industrial partners, carried out to consolidate an initial set of requirements for the moving block system into an executable specification. Simulink was selected as preferred tool to support this elicitation activity for two reasons. First, given its previous usage in the railway industry for similar purposes [26,27]. Second, because of the outcome of the assessment reported in [28]. As mentioned in the Introduction, we conducted a survey with railway practitioners to identify the most mature (semi-)formal methods and tools to be used in the railway context, and Simulink was one of the eight selected tools. The model, together with its documentation in HTML format, is publicly available.[4] Here, we show the model's architecture and some excerpts of its behaviour.

Model Architecture. Figure 3 reports the architecture of the model, which includes three main Simulink blocks representing the interacting subsystems, namely OBU, LU, and RBC.[5] Each block communicates with the other blocks by means of input/output messages. For example, the label named `location` is one of the outputs of the LU, and it is input to the OBU block. This indicates a

---

[3] http://www.mathworks.com/products/simulink.html.

[4] https://github.com/alessioferrari/ASTRail-simulink-models.

[5] The full model includes the train's dynamics, not reported here to ease visualisation.

virtual channel by which a message is exchanged between LU and OBU, including the current train location. Similarly, location_to_RBC is one of the outputs of the OBU block, also serving as input to the RBC block: the OBU location, received from the LU, is passed to the RBC, which, in turn, can compute the MA and send it to the OBU. The OBU is also in charge of activating the brake, and the brake's status can be visualised in the BRAKE_COMMAND scope element. Similarly, other scope elements are used to visualise a TIMER, indicating the time from the last received MA (2.4 s in Fig. 3), and SPACE_TO_EOA, which is the space from the current position to the end of the MA (996.4 m). Following the requirements, failure inputs (OBU_FAIL, RBC_FAIL, and LU_FAIL) are associated to each block to simulate external events that may trigger system failures.

Behaviour. The behaviour of each block is represented by means of a Stateflow chart. Figure 4 reports an excerpt of the chart representing the OBU behaviour. The excerpt depicts a parallel state (dashed lines indicate parallel states) named SEND_LOCATION_TO_RBC, which includes two mutually exclusive substates: one normal state (SEND_LOC_TO_RBC) and one failure state (POSITION_ERROR). When the system is in the normal state, it continuously checks whether a new location is received. This is performed through the function check_new_location(), which is graphically represented as a flowchart inside the state. Whenever a new location is received from the LU (OBU_REC_location_flg == 1), it is stored together with the current time stamp. Every five seconds, the location is sent to the RBC, if the location is not older than one second. This is enforced through the condition after(5, sec) && check_location_fresh [...].

The other parallel state named RECEIVE_MA takes care of MA reception. Specifically, when an MA is received (OBU_REC_MA_flg == 1), it is stored in the variable MA_value, and the OBU also stores the current location in the variable MA_reference. This will be used as a reference to update the variable that indicates how much space is left to the end of the MA (SPACE_TO_EOA in Fig. 3), while the train progresses its mission. Then, an ack message is sent to the RBC. The code inside the state NEW_MA_RECEIVED continuously updates the value of the variable OBU_out_timer, which represents the time that has passed since the last MA was received, and is visualised in the scope TIMER of Fig. 3.

4   UPPAAL Model of ERTMS L3 Moving Block

UPPAAL SMC [16] is a variant of UPPAAL [11], which is a well-known toolbox for the verification of real-time systems.[6] UPPAAL models are stochastic timed automata, in which non-determinism is replaced with probabilistic choices and time delays with probability distributions (uniform for bounded time and exponential for unbounded time). These automata may communicate via broadcast channels and shared variables.

---

[6] http://people.cs.aau.dk/~adavid/smc.

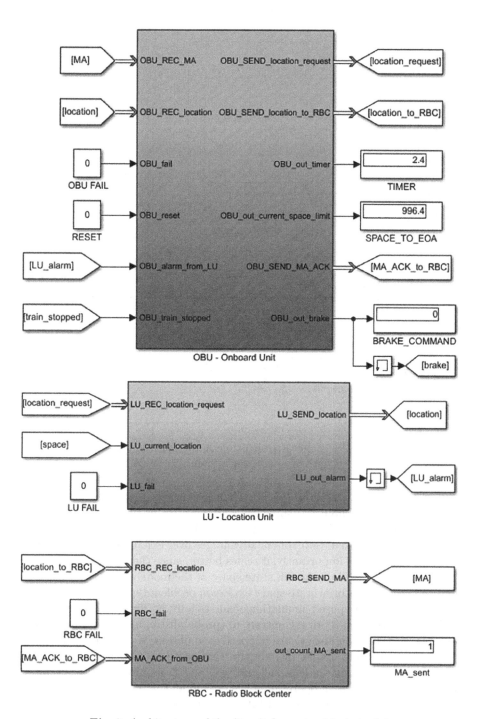

Fig. 3. Architecture of the Simulink moving block model

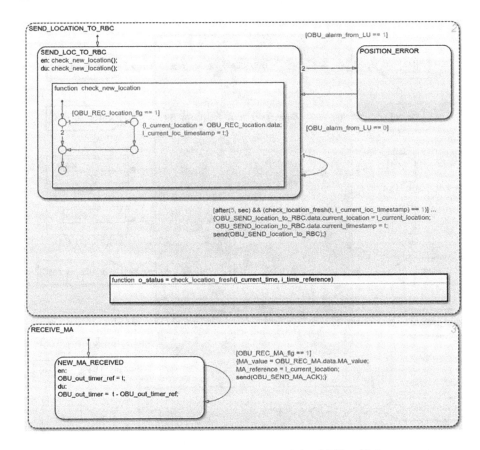

Fig. 4. Excerpt of the behaviour of the OBU model

Statistical Model Checking (SMC) [1,39] is concerned with running a sufficient number of (probabilistic) simulations of a system model to obtain statistical evidence (with a predefined level of statistical confidence) of the quantitative properties to be checked. SMC offers advantages over exhaustive (probabilistic) model checking. Most importantly, it scales better, since there is no need to generate and possibly explore the full state space of the model under scrutiny, thus avoiding the combinatorial state-space explosion problem typical of model checking. Moreover, the required simulations can trivially be distributed and run in parallel. This comes at a price. Contrary to (probabilistic) model checking, exact results (with 100% confidence) are impossible to obtain. A further advantage is related to its possible uptake in industry. Compared to model checking, SMC is simple to implement, understand and use, and it requires no specific modelling effort other than an operational system model that can be simulated and checked against (state-based) quantitative properties. In fact, SMC is becoming more and more widely accepted in industry [3,10,14,29,36,45].

In this section, we discuss the UPPAAL formalisation of the moving block system, derived from the semi-formal Simulink model presented in the previous section. The model is publicly available.[7] Here, we outline the automata constituting the model and describe the one modelling the OBU in more detail.

From Simulink/Stateflow to UPPAAL. This transformation is simplified by the fact that both formalisms use state machines. While we are aware of other efforts to map Simulink/Stateflow diagrams into UPPAAL SMC (cf., e.g., [29]), we encountered some peculiarities to be taken care of to transform the moving block model of the previous section. In particular, UPPAAL does not cater for the primitive description of machines with hierarchical states. Moreover, Simulink does not primitively provide concurrency between the processes, i.e., the scheduling is fixed a priori. This is not the case in UPPAAL, where there is an interleaving between all possible actions. Actually, the scheduling order was not part of the original ASTRail specification, so this forced scheduling was relieved in UPPAAL.

Communication between Simulink blocks is implemented through messages and input/output variables, and through shared variables inside Stateflow charts, whereas in the UPPAAL model we use communication via broadcast channels. Simulink/Stateflow diagrams and UPPAAL models use different time modelling. In the Simulink model, variables were used that memorise the time difference between events, while the UPPAAL model uses clocks that allow to memorise the time elapsed between the various events. Furthermore, the UPPAAL model was enriched with probabilities and stochastic events, which were taken from additional specifications of the moving block system by our industrial project partners. We only used rates of exponential delays, since exponential distributions are the only available distributions in UPPAAL for unbounded delays due to their memoryless property. Hence, the UPPAAL model represents a refinement of the initial semi-formal specification in Simulink. In Sect. 5, we will see that this allows subsequent verification of properties of interest with UPPAAL SMC.

The UPPAAL Model. The model consists of a number of automata composed as a synchronous product. Below, we list the various components that together form the model, followed by a more detailed description of the main automaton modelling the OBU component. As for the Simulink specification, the model consists of three main entities, namely the RBC, the LU, and the OBU, each represented by a different automaton. Each entity moreover accounts for a probabilistic failure that is modelled through three additional automata, called RBC_Failure_T, LU_Failure_T, and OBU_Failure_T, which model the failure of the respective component. The values of these probabilities are input parameters for the model, thus allowing to analyse several different scenarios, depending on, for example, the devices used. Another task within ASTRail concerns the evaluation of such numbers, input to our model. For the analysis in Sect. 5, we abstract from these automata generating failures, which is eased by their separate modelling.

---

[7] https://github.com/davidebasile/ASTRail.

The failure of these components was not foreseen in the original Simulink model, where it can be simulated by the manual intervention of the user who wants to analyse the behaviour of the system in case of failure. Note that, in the Simulink/Stateflow specification, failure transitions could be activated by shared variables whose value is assigned by the user.

All components listed next are *templates* in UPPAAL, which is a mechanism allowing to instantiate different instances of an automaton. This makes it possible to perform simulations and analyses with a certain number of RBCs, OBUs, and LUs; not fixed beforehand in the model. However, in line with the specification from our industrial partners, we assume that each component communicates with other components of the same index. For instance, RBC_0 always communicates with OBC_0 and never with OBC_1, who communicates with RBC_1. In reality, an RBC will have different threads, each one communicating with one train; each of these threads is an automaton. For simplicity, in the next section we will analyse the system considering only one OBC, one LU, and one RBC.

Furthermore, this model is parametric and highly customisable. It is possible to analyse different operational scenarios of the ASTRail moving block system by instantiating the individual parameters of the model. For instance, it is possible to customise the frequency of each of the various messages such as the frequency of requesting the location or the frequency of sending the MA. It is also possible to specify the size of the MA in terms of meters. Moreover, it is possible to model the acceleration of the train, as well as its average speed. By changing these parameters, we can perform different evaluations of the properties of interest, as we will show in the next section, so as to fine tune the setup of these parameters.

We briefly describe the model's components, followed by details of the OBU.

OBU_MAIN_GenerateLocationRequest_T: This automaton is the initial component that starts the system interactions and takes care of generating every few seconds a request for a new location to be sent to the LU.

LU_MAIN_T: This automaton models the LU. Its behaviour involves receiving a new position request from the OBU and replying with the current train location (computed via GNSS).

OBU_MAIN_SendLocationToRBC_T: This automaton, depicted in Fig. 5, is the main component of the OBU, and as such it performs a variety of operations. The first operation is the reception of the position by the LU. Subsequently, with a certain frequency, this component sends the received position to the RBC. The same component moreover receives the MA from the RBC (after sending its position). Finally, it implements one of the safety mechanisms present in the system specification. In particular, at each instant of time, the model checks that the train's position has not exceeded the MA received from the RBC; if it has, it will enter a failure state. All components listed so far provide the possibility to enter a failure state if one of the probabilistic failures foreseen by the corresponding probabilistic automata occurs.

RBC_Main_T: This automaton models the RBC. It receives the MA request from the OBU. Once this request is received, the RBC sends a certain number of times the MA message until the corresponding acknowledgement from the

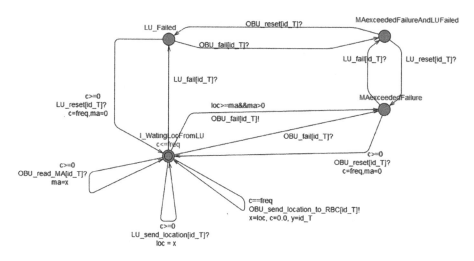

Fig. 5. The automaton OBU_MAIN_SendLocationToRBC_T

OBU is received or the number of attempts is exceeded. Also this component, like all others, enters a failure state if one of the aforementioned errors occurs.

OBU_MAIN_ReceiveMA_T: This is the last automaton modelling the logic of the OBU. It receives an MA from the RBC and sends back a corresponding acknowledgement message. This component implements an additional safety mechanism of the system specification by means of a timer that counts the time passed from the reception of the last MA. In the event that this timer is exceeded, an alarm is emitted and a failure state (TimeOutFail) is entered.

TRAIN_ATO_T: This is a special component that was introduced to model more accurately the behaviour of a train. In particular, this component models the movement of the train, its speed, and the acceleration and deceleration that are triggered by approaching the limit described by the MA. This automaton also deals with simulating braking curves when a particular failure state is reached. In particular, the position of the train is stated in an unidimensional space and identified by one coordinate. Figure 6 shows the speed of the train and its sudden braking the moment it exceeds the MA.

The OBU Model. This automaton, depicted in Fig. 5, has four states. The initial state is the nominal state I_WatingLocFromLU, drawn with two circles, while the other three states represent system failures that are due to failure of the LU (LU_Failed), failure to receive the MA (MAexceededFailure), or both failures together (MAexceededAndLUfailed). The initial state has three outgoing transitions that have the same initial state as their target state (i.e., loops). The initial state also has an invariant to guarantee that the initial state's clock c is always less than or equal to the freq parameter, which represents the frequency of sending the location to the RBC.

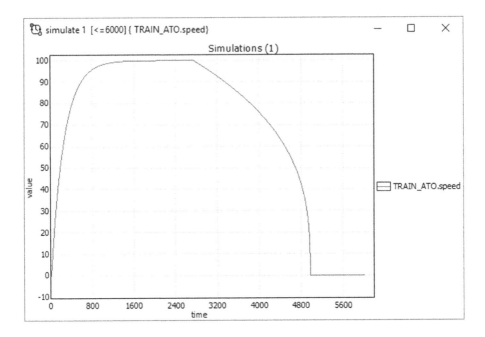

Fig. 6. A simulation showing the speed of the train in m/s

In order of execution, the first transition to be performed is the one with signal LU_send_location [id_T]?. This action represents the reception of the position from the LU; loc = x represents the assignment of the variable loc that reads from the buffer variable x used to implement value passing. The transition with guard c == freq is activated exactly when the guard is satisfied, i.e., when the clock reaches the freq parameter. This transition implements a periodic operation which is carried out every instant of time freq. The action is that of sending the position data to the RBC. The sending operation is transmitted via the signal OBU_send_location_to_RBC [id_T]!, while the assignment of variables is x = loc, c = 0.0, y = id_T; i.e., the value loc of the location and the unique train identifier id_T are stored in the buffer variables, and the clock c is reset. Similarly, OBU_read_MA [id_T]? performs the reception from the RBC of the MA stored in the variable ma.

The outgoing transition from I_WatingLocFromLU to MAexceededFailure is activated by the guard loc >= ma && ma > 0; i.e., it is activated when the train position exceeds the MA. In this case, a failure signal is sent via the OBU_fail [id_T]! channel. Transitions in other failure states likewise encode reception of failure signals arriving from the LU. Finally, note that once the system restart message is received via the reset channel, the initial MA value is set to zero.

5   Analyses of ERTMS L3 Moving Block

Next to standard model-checking queries concerning reachability and deadlock-freedom, UPPAAL SMC allows to check (quantitative) properties over simulation runs of an UPPAAL model (i.e. a network of stochastic timed automata). For instance, UPPAAL SMC supports the evaluation of the probability estimation $\mathbb{P}_M(\Diamond_{x \leq t} p)$ over a model M, where x is a clock, $t \in \mathbb{N}$, and p is a state predicate. Moreover, $\Diamond_{x \leq t} p = true\ U_{x \leq t}\ p$, in which U is a time-bounded Until operator of the form $p_1\ U_{x \leq t}\ p_2$, which is satisfied if p_1 holds on a simulation run *until* p_2 is satisfied, and this must happen before clock x exceeds time bound t. Apart from bounding over time, which may result in non-termination, we may bound runs for a number of discrete steps, which guarantees termination of the simulation. For a given model in UPPAAL SMC, the query $\Pr[<= \mathbb{N}](<> p)$, where $\mathbb{N} \in \mathbb{N}$, is satisfied if $<> p$ holds on a simulation run of at most $\mathbb{N}$ discrete steps.

We provide two temporal logic formulae to evaluate measures of interest of the moving block system. Both measure the probability of the UPPAAL model entering a failure state within 1000 steps, namely when the train's position exceeds the MA (ϕ_1) or when the timeout for the reception of a new MA is exceeded (ϕ_2):

$$\phi_1 \overset{\text{def}}{=} \Pr[<= 1000](<> \texttt{OBU\_MAIN\_SendLocationToRBC.MAexceededFailure})$$

$$\phi_2 \overset{\text{def}}{=} \Pr[<= 1000](<> \texttt{OBU\_MAIN\_ReceiveMA.TimeOutFail})$$

We now show the potential of UPPAAL SMC to analyse the modelled system for these properties of interest. The model has a myriad of possible parameters to fine tune. Here we limit ourselves to two different parameter setups, allowing to demonstrate the tool's effectiveness in confirming or rejecting parameter values.

We used academic version 4.1.19 (rev. 5649) of UPPAAL SMC, with the probabilistic deviation set to 0.01, the probability of false negatives and false positives set to 0.005 and 0.5, respectively, and the probability uncertainty set to 0.005.

As mentioned before, the experiments instantiate one OBC, one LU, and one RBC (i.e. the experiments are performed with one train communicating with an RBC). Moreover, the automata generating probabilistic failures have been deactivated.

Table 1 contains the parameter values used in the experiments. The first experiment serves to confirm the correctness of the system specification received from the domain experts, which concerns both quantitative aspects (e.g., the MA size and the communication frequencies) and qualitative aspects (i.e., failure states). Our formalisation in UPPAAL confirms that with the given parameter values the possibility to reach one of the failure states is indeed very low. More precisely, UPPAAL SMC reports with 99.5% confidence the same interval $[0, 0.00998576]$ obtained from 597 runs after just under eight minutes.

We set up a second experiment to show that UPPAAL SMC can also be used to reject parameter values that do lead to a high probability of failure and thus to hazardous scenarios. In this experiment there are less frequent updates of the train's position to the RBC and a tighter MA. Our formalisation in UPPAAL

Table 1. Parameter values used in the experiments

Component (abbreviated)	Parameter	Value		Description
		exp 1	exp 2	
RBC_Main	freq	1000 s	1000 s	Frequency of sending MA to OBU before ack
RBC_Main	ma	1000 m	500 m	Size of MA (in meters from current location)
OBU_MAIN_SendLocToRBC	freq	0.5 s	5.0 s	Frequency of sending location to RBC
OBU_MAIN_GenerateLocReq	freq	0.5 s	0.5 s	Frequency of sending location request to LU
OBU_MAIN_ReceiveMA	OBU_out_timer	10 s	10 s	Timeout for receiving MA from RBC

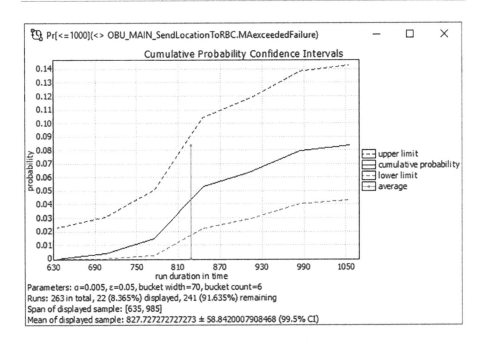

Fig. 7. The cumulative probability confidence interval of experiment 2

confirms this to be an inappropriate parameter setup, as the probability for the train to exceed the MA (as expressed by formula ϕ_1) becomes high. UPPAAL SMC reports with 99.5% confidence the interval $[0.0430205, 0.14268]$ obtained from 263 runs after approximately three minutes (cf. further details in Fig. 7).

This shows that further varying the parameters values, in principle the positive results of the first experiment could be improved. This would require more experiments and close interaction with the domain experts to understand which parameter values could theoretically be changed, without violating physical limits or fundamental requirements (e.g., an OBU cycle may take at most 500 ms).

6   Lessons Learned

In this section, we report some lessons learned from our modelling and analysis experience of a satellite-based ERTMS L3 moving block railway signalling system with Simulink and UPPAAL SMC.

Formal Evidence. The analysis of two fundamental properties of the satellite-based ERTMS L3 moving block railway signalling system with UPPAAL SMC, described in Sect. 5, provided further evidence for the applicability of UPPAAL SMC in the railway domain (cf. also, e.g., [5,6,14,29]). In particular, we showed the tool's potential for fine tuning communication parameters in satellite-based ERTMS L3 moving block railway signalling system models that are fundamental for the reliability of their operational behaviour. Given a specific parameter setup, we showed how to use UPPAAL SMC to confirm or reject parameter values. The analysis of the UPPAAL model for the parameter setup provided by our industrial partners confirmed the (desired) very low possibility to reach one of the failure states. Further analysis showed the capability of UPPAAL SMC to detect a bad parameter setup.

Complementarity of Tools. The starting point was a model in Real-Time UML [18,47] and a set of requirements, both provided by our industrial partners [5]. The requirements elicitation and refinement activity performed with the industrial partners, as briefly outlined in Sect. 3, confirmed Simulink as an appropriate tool for the initial phases of a development process. Its simulation and debugging facilities increase confidence in the initial design and facilitate interaction with the industrial partners, thus allowing to consolidate a final set of requirements. Not surprisingly, the resulting model and requirements turned out to be far more detailed than the Real-Time UML model and the initial set of requirements. In this initial phase, the focus was on the elicitation and animation of functional requirements. At the same time, the probabilistic aspects initially introduced in the Real-Time UML model [5] could not be expressed in Simulink, thus requiring the usage of UPPAAL. This confirms the need to introduce formal methods diversity [43] to properly address all the functional, quality and process-related aspects related to the development of railway signalling systems.

Transformation and Refinement. The transformation of the Simulink model into an UPPAAL model, described in Sect. 4, required us to revisit in particular the communication among the different processes, removing the fixed scheduling through shared variables in favour of action interleaving via broadcast channels. Moreover, in the UPPAAL model time is no longer modelled by memorising the time difference between events in variables, but by explicit clocks. Most notably, UPPAAL allows to model events to occur with certain probabilities and to consider stochastic timed behaviour, which we used to enrich the initial model according to additional specifications of the moving block system provided by our industrial partners. As such, the UPPAAL model represents a refinement of the initial semi-formal Simulink specification into a more formal specification amenable to quantitative analyses.

Challenges. We presented only some preliminary analyses in Sect. 5. Further properties of interest would require a more complex model with more than one train and more than one RBC, next to running more systematic experiments. Moreover, it remains to further vary the parameter values to investigate whether the parameter setup provided by our industrial partners can be improved. However, while it is not too difficult to use UPPAAL SMC to either confirm or reject a parameter setup, it is much more difficult to use it to find an optimal parameter setup. We believe this requires profound knowledge of the statistical model-checking algorithms underlying the tool as well as of the tool's functionality, combined with expert knowledge from the railway domain concerning the physical limits of certain parameter values as well as best practices from the field.

7   Conclusion

In this paper, we have presented an experience in modelling a satellite-based ERTMS L3 moving block signalling system from the railway industry with Simulink (upon close interaction with the domain experts) and UPPAAL and in performing preliminary analyses of the UPPAAL model with UPPAAL SMC (to be continued in close interaction with the domain experts). In the previous section, we have reported some lessons learned from this experience.

Future Work. We plan to extend the model with more actors. This would allow us to consider properties like deadlocks (e.g., following [14], we could model several trains and use SMC to verify deadlock avoidance under intra communications). The work could also be extended by using UPPAAL Stratego [17], an SMC and learning-based tool, to synthesise best routes to avoid deadlocking and match performance objectives (e.g., arrival delays). This would require a drastic modification of the model to introduce measure of performances. We could also see if UPPAAL Stratego can be used for the optimisation of the model's parameters.

Finally, it would be worth to consider cyber attacks, e.g., by modelling the attacker and attacks with attack trees and combine the new model with that of the train. The result could be analysed via the UPPAAL extension for cyber security [33]. Note, however, that this would be a major challenge as it would require a model of potential attacks (and thus know attacks typically kept secret).

Acknowledgments. This work was partially funded by the Tuscany Region project SISTER (SIgnalling & Sensing TEchnologies in Railway application) and by the EU project ASTRail (SAtellite-based Signalling and Automation SysTems on Railways along with Formal Method and Moving Block validation), which received funding from the Shift2Rail Joint Undertaking under the EU's H2020 Research and Innovation programme under Grant Agreement No. 777561. The content of this paper reflects only the authors' view, and the Shift2Rail JU is not responsible for any use that may be made of the included information.

We thank our colleagues in the Formal Methods and Tools lab at ISTI-CNR and our project partners for discussions on the models analysed in the paper. We thank the four anonymous reviewers for their suggestions to improve the paper.

References

1. Agha, G., Palmskog, K.: A survey of statistical model checking. ACM Trans. Model. Comput. Simul. **28**(1), 6:1–6:39 (2018)
2. Arcaini, P., Ježek, P., Kofroň, J.: Modelling the hybrid ERTMS/ETCS level 3 case study in spin. In: Butler, M., Raschke, A., Hoang, T.S., Reichl, K. (eds.) ABZ 2018. LNCS, vol. 10817, pp. 277–291. Springer, Cham (2018). https://doi.org/10.1007/978-3-319-91271-4_19
3. Arnold, A., et al.: An application of SMC to continuous validation of heterogeneous systems. EAI Endorsed Trans. Ind. Netw. Intell. Syst. **4**(10), 1–19 (2017). https://doi.org/10.4108/eai.1-2-2017.152154
4. Bartholomeus, M., Luttik, B., Willemse, T.: Modelling and analysing ERTMS hybrid level 3 with the mCRL2 toolset. In: Howar, F., Barnat, J. (eds.) FMICS 2018. LNCS, vol. 11119, pp. 98–114. Springer, Cham (2018). https://doi.org/10.1007/978-3-030-00244-2_7
5. Basile, D., ter Beek, M.H., Ciancia, V.: Statistical model checking of a moving block railway signalling scenario with UPPAAL SMC. In: Margaria, T., Steffen, B. (eds.) ISoLA 2018. LNCS, vol. 11245, pp. 372–391. Springer, Cham (2018). https://doi.org/10.1007/978-3-030-03421-4_24
6. Basile, D., Di Giandomenico, F., Gnesi, S.: Statistical model checking of an energy-saving cyber-physical system in the railway domain. In: SAC, pp. 1356–1363. ACM (2017)
7. Basile, D., et al.: On the industrial uptake of formal methods in the railway domain. In: Furia, C.A., Winter, K. (eds.) IFM 2018. LNCS, vol. 11023, pp. 20–29. Springer, Cham (2018). https://doi.org/10.1007/978-3-319-98938-9_2
8. ter Beek, M.H., Fantechi, A., Ferrari, A., Gnesi, S., Scopigno, R.: Formal methods for the railway sector. ERCIM News **112**, 44–45 (2018)
9. ter Beek, M.H., Gnesi, S., Knapp, A.: Formal methods for transport systems. Int. J. Softw. Tools Technol. Transf. **20**(3), 355–358 (2018)
10. ter Beek, M.H., Legay, A., Lluch Lafuente, A., Vandin, A.: Statistical model checking for product lines. In: Margaria, T., Steffen, B. (eds.) ISoLA 2016. LNCS, vol. 9952, pp. 114–133. Springer, Cham (2016). https://doi.org/10.1007/978-3-319-47166-2_8
11. Behrmann, G., et al.: UPPAAL 4.0. In: QEST, pp. 125–126. IEEE (2006)
12. Beugin, J., Marais, J.: Simulation-based evaluation of dependability and safety properties of satellite technologies for railway localization. Transp. Res. C-Emer. **22**, 42–57 (2012)

13. Boulanger, J.L. (ed.): Formal Methods Applied to Industrial Complex Systems - Implementation of the B Method. Wiley, Hoboken (2014)
14. Cappart, Q., et al.: Verification of interlocking systems using statistical model checking. In: HASE, pp. 61–68. IEEE (2017)
15. Cunha, A., Macedo, N.: Validating the hybrid ERTMS/ETCS level 3 concept with electrum. In: Butler, M., Raschke, A., Hoang, T.S., Reichl, K. (eds.) ABZ 2018. LNCS, vol. 10817, pp. 307–321. Springer, Cham (2018). https://doi.org/10.1007/978-3-319-91271-4_21
16. David, A., Larsen, K.G., Legay, A., Mikučionis, M., Poulsen, D.B.: UPPAAL SMC tutorial. Int. J. Softw. Tools Technol. Transf. **17**(4), 397–415 (2015)
17. David, A., et al.: On time with minimal expected cost!. In: Cassez, F., Raskin, J.-F. (eds.) ATVA 2014. LNCS, vol. 8837, pp. 129–145. Springer, Cham (2014). https://doi.org/10.1007/978-3-319-11936-6_10
18. Douglass, B.P.: Real-time UML. In: Damm, W., Olderog, E.-R. (eds.) FTRTFT 2002. LNCS, vol. 2469, pp. 53–70. Springer, Heidelberg (2002). https://doi.org/10.1007/3-540-45739-9_4
19. EEIG ERTMS Users Group: ERTMS/ETCS RAMS Requirements Specification – Chapter 2 - RAM, 30 September 1998
20. EEIG ERTMS Users Group: System Requirements Specification v3.6.0 - SUBSET-026, 15 June 2016
21. EEIG ERTMS Users Group: Hybrid ERTMS/ETCS Level 3: Principles, 14 July 2017
22. European Committee for Electrotechnical Standardization: CENELEC EN 50128 – Railway applications - Communication, signalling and processing systems - Software for railway control and protection systems, 01 June 2011
23. Fantechi, A.: Twenty-five years of formal methods and railways: what next? In: Counsell, S., Núñez, M. (eds.) SEFM 2013. LNCS, vol. 8368, pp. 167–183. Springer, Cham (2014). https://doi.org/10.1007/978-3-319-05032-4_13
24. Fantechi, A., Ferrari, A., Gnesi, S.: Formal methods and safety certification: challenges in the railways domain. In: Margaria, T., Steffen, B. (eds.) ISoLA 2016. LNCS, vol. 9953, pp. 261–265. Springer, Cham (2016). https://doi.org/10.1007/978-3-319-47169-3_18
25. Fantechi, A., Fokkink, W., Morzenti, A.: Some trends in formal methods applications to railway signaling. In: Formal Methods for Industrial Critical Systems: A Survey of Applications, pp. 61–84. Wiley (2013). (chap. 4)
26. Ferrari, A., Fantechi, A., Gnesi, S., Magnani, G.: Model-based development and formal methods in the railway industry. IEEE Softw. **30**(3), 28–34 (2013)
27. Ferrari, A., Fantechi, A., Magnani, G., Grasso, D., Tempestini, M.: The Metrô Rio case study. Sci. Comput. Program. **78**(7), 828–842 (2013)
28. Ferrari, A., et al.: Survey on formal methods and tools in railways: the ASTRail approach. In: Collart-Dutilleul, S., Lecomte, T., Romanovsky, A. (eds.) RSSRail 2019. LNCS, vol. 11495, pp. 226–241. Springer, Cham (2019). https://doi.org/10.1007/978-3-030-18744-6_15
29. Filipovikj, P., Mahmud, N., Marinescu, R., Seceleanu, C., Ljungkrantz, O., Lönn, H.: Simulink to UPPAAL statistical model checker: analyzing automotive industrial systems. In: Fitzgerald, J., Heitmeyer, C., Gnesi, S., Philippou, A. (eds.) FM 2016. LNCS, vol. 9995, pp. 748–756. Springer, Cham (2016). https://doi.org/10.1007/978-3-319-48989-6_46
30. Flammini, F. (ed.): Railway Safety, Reliability, and Security: Technologies and Systems Engineering. IGI Global, Hershey (2012)

31. Fränzle, M., Hahn, E., Hermanns, H., Wolovick, N., Zhang, L.: Measurability and safety verification for stochastic hybrid systems. In: HSCC, pp. 43–52. ACM (2011)
32. Furness, N., van Houten, H., Arenas, L., Bartholomeus, M.: ERTMS level 3: the game-changer. IRSE News **232**, 2–9 (2017)
33. Gadyatskaya, O., Hansen, R.R., Larsen, K.G., Legay, A., Olesen, M.C., Poulsen, D.B.: Modelling attack-defense trees using timed automata. In: Fränzle, M., Markey, N. (eds.) FORMATS 2016. LNCS, vol. 9884, pp. 35–50. Springer, Cham (2016). https://doi.org/10.1007/978-3-319-44878-7_3
34. Ghazel, M.: Formalizing a subset of ERTMS/ETCS specifications for verification purposes. Transp. Res. C-Emer. **42**, 60–75 (2014)
35. Ghazel, M.: A control scheme for automatic level crossings under the ERTMS/ETCS level 2/3 operation. IEEE Trans. Intell. Transp. Syst. **18**, 2667–2680 (2017)
36. Gilmore, S., Tribastone, M., Vandin, A.: An analysis pathway for the quantitative evaluation of public transport systems. In: Albert, E., Sekerinski, E. (eds.) IFM 2014. LNCS, vol. 8739, pp. 71–86. Springer, Cham (2014). https://doi.org/10.1007/978-3-319-10181-1_5
37. Harel, D.: Statecharts: a visual formalism for complex systems. Sci. Comput. Program. **8**(3), 231–274 (1987)
38. Herde, C., Eggers, A., Fränzle, M., Teige, T.: Analysis of hybrid systems using HySAT. In: ICONS, pp. 196–201. IEEE (2008)
39. Larsen, K.G., Legay, A.: Statistical model checking – past, present, and future. In: Margaria, T., Steffen, B. (eds.) ISoLA 2014. LNCS, vol. 8803, pp. 135–142. Springer, Heidelberg (2014). https://doi.org/10.1007/978-3-662-45231-8_10
40. Littlewood, B., Popov, P., Strigini, L.: Modeling software design diversity: a review. ACM Comput. Surv. **33**(2), 177–208 (2001)
41. Mammar, A., Frappier, M., Tueno Fotso, S.J., Laleau, R.: An EVENT-B model of the hybrid ERTMS/ETCS level 3 standard. In: Butler, M., Raschke, A., Hoang, T.S., Reichl, K. (eds.) ABZ 2018. LNCS, vol. 10817, pp. 353–366. Springer, Cham (2018). https://doi.org/10.1007/978-3-319-91271-4_24
42. Mazzanti, F., Ferrari, A.: Ten diverse formal models for a CBTC automatic train supervision system. In: MARS. EPTCS, vol. 268, pp. 104–149 (2018)
43. Mazzanti, F., Ferrari, A., Spagnolo, G.O.: Towards formal methods diversity in railways: an experience report with seven frameworks. Int. J. Softw. Tools Technol. Transf. **20**(3), 263–288 (2018)
44. Nardone, R., et al.: Modeling railway control systems in Promela. In: Artho, C., Ölveczky, P.C. (eds.) FTSCS 2015. CCIS, vol. 596, pp. 121–136. Springer, Cham (2016). https://doi.org/10.1007/978-3-319-29510-7_7
45. Puch, S., Fränzle, M., Gerwinn, S.: Quantitative risk assessment of safety-critical systems via guided simulation for rare events. In: Margaria, T., Steffen, B. (eds.) ISoLA 2018. LNCS, vol. 11245, pp. 305–321. Springer, Cham (2018). https://doi.org/10.1007/978-3-030-03421-4_20
46. Rispoli, F., et al.: Recent progress in application of GNSS and advanced communications for railway signaling. In: RADIOELEKTRONIKA, pp. 13–22. IEEE (2013)
47. Selic, B.: The real-time UML standard: definition and application. In: DATE, pp. 770–772 (2002)
48. UNISIG: FIS for the RBC/RBC handover, version 3.1.0, 15 June 2016

Formal Modelling and Verification of an Interlocking Using mCRL2

Mark Bouwman[1($\boxtimes$)], Bob Janssen[2], and Bas Luttik[1]

[1] Eindhoven University of Technology, Eindhoven, The Netherlands
{m.s.bouwman,s.p.luttik}@tue.nl
[2] Siemens Mobility NL, Zoetermeer, The Netherlands

Abstract. This paper presents an application of the formal modelling and model checking toolkit mCRL2 and the model-based testing tool JTorX in the signalling domain. The mCRL2 toolkit is used to formally model the behaviour of a system at the core of signalling solutions: the interlocking. The model of the interlocking is validated through model-based testing. We use the mCRL2 toolkit to verify high-level safety properties of the interlocking software. The suitability of mCRL2, JTorX and our modelling approach is evaluated and suggestions are given for future research to improve the applicability of mCRL2 in the signalling domain.

1 Introduction

Developing railway signalling systems is a tough engineering challenge. From the design of higher level protocols to their electrical/mechanical implementation and to guidelines for train drivers: scrutiny is essential, a single flaw could potentially lead to an unacceptable hazard. As the higher level protocols of railway signalling become more and more complex it also becomes increasingly difficult and costly to verify the correctness of these protocols. Formal methods have proven useful to improve the quality of (software) systems [22], including within the railway domain [10].

The system at the core of signalling solutions is the interlocking, which controls the trackside equipment and contains most of the logic to prevent unsafe train movements. We were given access to a simulator of the software of an interlocking developed by Siemens with the challenge to verify the safety of the interlocking software. The relevant safety properties we investigated in this paper are the absence of collisions and the absence of derailments caused by moving an occupied point. We were given the simulator as a black-box. To construct a formal model of the interlocking we combined input from signalling experts and validated the model through model-based testing. We chose to model the behaviour using the mCRL2 toolkit [9], which features state-of-the-art verification technology as well as a connection to the model-based testing tool JTorX [3].

The model we obtained revealed potential collisions. By consulting signalling experts we were able to conclude that the dangerous scenario is excluded through assumptions on how fast a train can move through the network, giving the

© Springer Nature Switzerland AG 2019
K. G. Larsen and T. Willemse (Eds.): FMICS 2019, LNCS 11687, pp. 22–39, 2019.
https://doi.org/10.1007/978-3-030-27008-7_2

interlocking time to process inputs. By building these assumptions into the model we were able to obtain a collision-free model. Interestingly, the new model could be validated using model-based testing, while we were also able to replay collision scenarios found in the initial model on the simulator. This revealed that model-based testing with JTorX could not test for certain behaviour that relies on a quick succession of stimuli.

Formal methods have been used extensively within the railway domain [2,10]. Several recent applications use bounded model checking [6,7,14,15,17,18]. A recent survey [2] shows that a number of other techniques and tools are used in academia and industry, most notably the B method (and variants of it). mCRL2 and its predecessor μCRL have been used in the signalling domain before [1,12]. Traditionally, an authoritative model is used to put the interlocking software to the test, such as in [14]. Model-learning techniques can also be applied to obtain a model from an implementation [16,21]. In our work we combine the two approaches by creating an approximate model and improving the model using model-based testing.

2   Railway Signalling Systems

In this section we will touch on some of the core interlocking concepts before presenting the formal model in the next section. We do not cover all aspects of the behaviour, for example, behaviour regarding level crossings is not considered. Signalling system behaviour is specified in national rules and regulations that have grown over the years as a corpus of texts in natural language. As the interlocking software of the simulator is designed for the Netherlands, our model captures the Dutch signalling rules (*seinreglement 1955*). The necessary information to construct the model was provided mainly by Siemens, complemented by infrastructure manager ProRail. An example of a track layout with various field elements is depicted in Fig. 1.

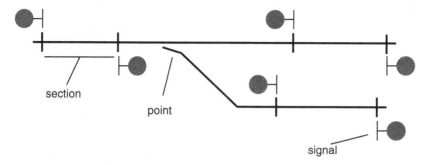

Fig. 1. Example track layout

Railway systems consist of a number of layers. On the top level is the traffic management layer in which the logistics and timetables are planned out. In the layer beneath, signalmen or automated systems request routes to move the right train to the right place. These route requests are passed to the interlocking which handles the requests and controls the field elements to move the points along the route in the correct position and to guide the train through the route by controlling the signals along the route. The interlocking plays an important role in ensuring safety, for example by excluding conflicting routes. Signals and trainside safety systems ensure that when the interlocking disallows a train movement, the train is automatically stopped.

An interlocking controls various elements in its yard, with which it can exchange the messages listed in Table 1. It controls the points in the yard, which it can place in the left or right position. Sections of track are equipped with train detection systems to notify the interlocking whether the section is occupied. Signals are present at the borders of sections to control train movements. An interlocking also has a communication channel with a signalman from which it receives route requests. A signalman requests a route with an entry signal and an exit signal. Note that the interlocking does not have a connection with the train, it can only indirectly observe the train via occupancy detection. Trains interact with sections by occupying them, with signals by obeying them and with points by being guided by their position. The signalling setup used in our simulator features sequential release (in the event that, due to loss of shunt or timing issues, occupations occur non-sequentially in the view of the interlocking, a section is marked as logically occupied and is thus not released for future routes). A section that is occupied can only be marked as free if at the moment the interlocking sees that the section has become unoccupied, the next section along the route is marked as occupied.

Table 1. Overview of messages exchanged between the interlocking and its environment.

From	To	Communication	Data passed
Signalman	Interlocking	Request route	IDs of entry signal and exit signal
Interlocking	Signalman	Route decision	Decision: accepted or rejected
Interlocking	Point	Set position	The desired position (left or right)
Interlocking	Signal	Set aspect	Signal aspect: red, yellow or green
Section	Interlocking	Inform occupancy	Boolean to indicate occupancy

There are two major interlocking-families distinguished by the way they implement signalling rules; the control table family lays down in a table the logical conditions for allowing a route. The geographical family regards signals, sections and points as networked objects. These objects communicate and allow a route only when the neighbouring objects reports a safe state. We model an interlocking of the geographical family, in accordance with the simulator.

Siemens designs and manufactures both the interlocking and field elements. To test the software of their interlocking they have developed a testing/simulation platform called TeSys (short for Test Systemen). TeSys is a PC platform that emulates the Simis W vital hardware and operating system. This allows TeSys to run the real interlocking software and test various signalling scenarios. As a user it is possible to request routes and to simulate train movements by making sections occupied. Output from the interlocking software is displayed visually and in text.

The aim is to construct a formal model that describes the behaviour of the Siemens interlocking software. The properties we would like to prove for this model are the two classical safety properties for interlockings: absence of train collisions (which we interpret as two trains being allowed to move to the same section) and derailments (for which we only consider derailments due to train movements while occupied).

3   mCRL2 Model of an Interlocking

The mCRL2 process algebra is a formal language in the lineage of the Algebra of Communication Processes (ACP) [4]. The associated toolkit offers state-of-the-art verification technology. The supported language for specifying properties is a first order extension of the modal μ-calculus. For a more elaborate description of the mCRL2 language and the extension of the modal μ-calculus we refer to [11] and for recent advances of the toolkit we refer to [9]. The toolkit itself can be downloaded from www.mcrl2.org.

In Sect. 3.1 we describe how we used the data language of mCRL2 to capture both the static and dynamic data aspects such as the track layout and the conditions to change the status of a route. In Sect. 3.2 we describe how we have modelled the behaviour of the interlocking, trains and field elements. The complete model can be found in the appendix of [8] or in plain text[1].

3.1   Modelling Data and Predicates

As the interlocking's behaviour depends on its internal data state (section occupations, routes, etc.) a specification of the internal memory of the interlocking needs to be included in the formal model. The mCRL2 language includes a rich data language in which users can construct data types, and define functions on them. Common data types such as natural numbers and Booleans are built-in, as well as a few container types such as lists, sets and bags. Data structures can be created using structured types and function types and they can be manipulated through mappings and equations that act as rewrite rules.

Enumerations such as the status of a section, the position of a point and the status of a route are modelled using structured types. Various attributes of an element can also be grouped together in a structured type, as shown below.

---

[1] https://www.win.tue.nl/~luttik/Models/IxL/original.mcrl2.

```
sort
  signal_colour = struct RD | GL | GR;
  driving_direction = struct L | R;

  section_id = Nat;
  signal_id = Nat;

  signal_info =
    struct signal_info(
      colour: signal_colour,
      direction: driving_direction,
      virtual: Bool,
      section_before: section_id,
      section_after: section_id
);
```

The constructed sort `signal_info` contains information about its position in the track topology as well as its current colour aspect, as recorded by the interlocking. Virtual signals do not correspond to physical signals but can be used to specify a route to a particular location. In order to let the interlocking distinguish different signals, identifiers are needed. A function type is used to create a mapping of a signal identifier to `signal_info` objects, as shown below. This way, `signals` is a data structure similar to a key value mapping, mapping the ID to the associated object.

```
sort
  signals = signal_id -> signal_info;
```

Sections and points are modelled in a similar fashion. The benefit of using these function types is that structured types referencing sections, signals and/or points can store the IDs, instead of duplicating the entire type.

Based on the data structure, operations can be defined to update data, evaluate some condition based on the current state, or do some other computation. Mappings and equations, which are interpreted as rewrite rules, can be defined to specify how these computations are to be performed. The data types are used to specify the processes. The following mapping and equation give an example of an operation on the topology:

```
map
  legal_signal: signal_id -> Bool;
  signal_between_sections: section_id#section_id#signals -> Bool;
var
  se,se2: section_id;
  si: signal_id;
  sic: signals;
eqn
  legal_signal(si) = si >= first_signal && si <= last_signal;
  signal_between_sections(se,se2,sic) =
```

```
exists signal:signal_id. legal_signal(signal)
&& section_before(sic(signal)) == se
&& section_after(sic(signal)) == se2
&& !virtual(sic(signal));
```

The mapping `signal_between_sections` maps two section IDs and the mapping `signals` to a Boolean. In natural language the predicate is true if and only if there exists a non-virtual signal between the given sections, facing the first given section. The `legal_signal` predicate checks whether the given ID is a valid ID for which a `signal_info` object is defined. This is necessary as the ID is a natural number and thus part of an infinite set. The mCRL2 toolkit recognizes that the existential quantification is bounded by the `legal_signal` predicate, and as there are finitely many legal signals it is not necessary to consider all natural numbers when evaluating the existential quantification.

3.2 Modelling the Behaviour of the Interlocking and the Field Elements

We have defined a process for each section, signal, point and train as well as for the interlocking itself. The processes for the field elements act as a kind of variables; their only behaviour is that they keep track of the state of the element. The processes of the field elements always allow their states to be changed, which is achieved by specifying the processes in such a way that in every state they accept communications that change their state; a section always allows communication with a train to make the section occupied and points and signals always allow communication with the interlocking to change the aspect of a signal or the position of a point, respectively. The train processes interact with the field elements by making sections occupied, obeying signal aspects and moving across the track in accordance with the positions of points.

The process representing the behaviour of the interlocking is more complex: it reads the status of the sections, moves points, sets signals and processes route requests. To avoid implementation decisions we use non-determinism to specify that any action for which the condition in the guard is satisfied may happen, without assuming a particular order of processing inputs or outputs. The mCRL2 fragment below shows the main process of the interlocking as well as one of its subprocesses, which can result in the update of a signal aspect. Based on the data state, as maintained by the interlocking, `compute_signal` determines what the colour aspect of a signal should be. In the case that the signal currently has a different aspect, the signal aspect is updated. In mCRL2 . denotes sequential composition, -> denotes a conditional, + denotes non-deterministic choice and sum expresses a non-deterministic choice over a quantified domain.

```
proc
  Interlocking(sec: sections, sic: signals,
      roc:List(route_info), poc: points,
      pro:Set(route_info), rro: List(route_info)) =
```

```
InterlockingUpdatingSignal()
+ InterlockingReadingSection()
+ InterlockingMovingPoint()
+ InterlockingReceivingRouteRequest()
+ InterlockingProcessingRoute()
+ InterlockingReadyRoute()
+ InterlockingNotReadyRoute()
+ InterlockingPermitTrainEntry();

InterlockingUpdatingSignal(sec: sections, sic: signals,
    roc: List(route_info), poc: points, pro:Set(route_info),
    rro: List(route_info)) =
  sum result: signal_colour. sum si: signal_id.
    (legal_signal(si)
  && result == compute_signal(si,sec,sic,roc,poc)
  && !signal_get_virtual(si,sic))
    -> ((!(result == signal_get_colour(si,sic)))
    -> setSignalSend(si, result)
    .Interlocking(sic = signal_update_colour(si, result, sic),
      roc = routes_handle_update_signal(si,result,sec,sic,roc)));
```

The processes are specified independently of a particular track layout. The processes are parametrized on the track layout (`sections`, `signals` and `points`), as can be seen in the example above. At initialization, the processes are given a particular track layout. We added a configuration mechanism to specify a configuration that is used in the initialization. It allows us to specify different configurations in one file of which one can be selected. By example, the fragment below specifies a mapping `signals_config` from a configuration number to `signals`. The equations specify that configuration number 3 consists of 3 signals and the location of these signals. The constructed `signals` object can then be used to initialize the interlocking process, as well as the signal processes.

```
map
    signals_config : Nat -> signals
eqn
    signals_config(3)(1) = signal_info(RD, R, false, 1,2);
    signals_config(3)(2) = signal_info(RD, L, false, 3,2);
    signals_config(3)(3) = signal_info(RD, L, false, 4,2);
```

This approach allows us to quickly switch between configurations. The configuration also specifies the number of trains and which section they will enter on.

4   Formal Verification of the mCRL2 Model

4.1   Requirements

The safety requirements on which we focus are collisions and derailments. As we only consider collisions within the yard and disallow shunting movements, the requirement for collisions reduces to: a section may never be occupied by two trains. If we formulate this in terms of actions in the model we would like to verify that it can never happen that setStatusSection(section_id, true) occurs twice without setStatusSection(section_id, false) in between, for every section ID. This is captured by the modal μ-formula $\phi_{no\_collision}$:

$$\forall s : \text{section\_id. legal\_section}(s) \implies [\text{true}^* . \text{setStatusSection}(s, \text{true})$$
$$. \,!\text{setStatusSection}(s, \text{false})^* . \text{setStatusSection}(s, \text{true})] \text{ false}.$$

Regarding derailments, as in the model points instantaneously change position, it suffices to verify that a point is not moved while the section in which it is located, is occupied. To make verification easier, the model is adapted such that the section ID is included in the communication between a point and the interlocking. Formulated in terms of actions in the model we would like to verify that it can never happen that an occurrence of setStatusSection(section_id, true) is followed by setPositionPoint(point_id,left,section_id) or setPositionPoint(point_id,right,section_id) without setStatusSection(section_id, false) in between, captured by the modal μ-calculus formula $\phi_{no\_derailment}$:

$$\forall s:\text{section\_id, } p:\text{point\_id.}(s \leq \text{last\_section} \wedge p \leq \text{last\_point})$$
$$\implies [\text{true}^* . \text{setStatusSection}(s, \text{true}) . \,!\text{setStatusSection}(s, \text{false})^*]$$
$$([\text{setPositionPoint}(p,\text{left},s)]\text{false} \wedge [\text{setPositionPoint}(p,\text{right},s)]\text{false}).$$

We also like to verify that the interlocking satisfies certain liveness properties. We might want to verify that the interlocking does not prevent trains from reaching the other side of the yard. In some cases, for example when two trains are facing each other without options to pass each other, we can not expect that all trains can reach the other side of the yard. For some track layouts, however, it is to be expected that all trains can cross the yard. Suppose that we have a configuration where all trains enter the yard on the right side and there is a single section on the left side denoted by Z connected to the open track. Also suppose that for each entry section on the right side the section on the left side is reachable. In this case it is expected that eventually all trains are able to cross the yard. The property is captured by the modal μ-calculus formula $\phi_{inv\_possibly\_cross}$:

$$\nu X(c:\text{Nat} = 0, t:\text{Nat} = \text{last\_train}). ([!\text{setStatusSection}(Z,\text{false})]X(c,t) \wedge$$
$$[\text{setStatusSection}(Z,\text{false})]X(c + 1,t) \wedge \phi_{possibly\_cross}(c,t)),$$

$$\phi_{possibly\_cross}(x,y) = \mu Y(c: \text{Nat} = x, t:\text{Nat} = y).$$
$$(\langle !\text{setStatusSection}(Z,\text{false})\rangle \, Y(c,t) \vee \langle \text{setStatusSection}(Z,\text{false})\rangle \, Y(c+1,t) \vee c = t).$$

The formula $\phi_{possibly\_cross}$ keeps track of the current number of trains that have crossed the yard c and the total number of trains that should eventually cross the yard t. Using a smallest fixed point operator it specifies that within finitely many steps c should be equal to t. The formula holds in states from which there is a path on which there are $t - c$ occurrences of SetStatusSection(Z,false), i.e., in all states from which a state is reachable in which all trains have crossed the yard. In $\phi_{inv\_possibly\_cross}$ a largest fixed point operator is used to specify that invariantly, the remaining trains can cross the yard. Note that, purposely, this formula does not specify that all trains always cross the yard within finitely many steps. Such a formula would not hold as the behaviour of the interlocking contains loops of routes being requested and rejected.

4.2 Verification Toolchain

The model needs to be configured with a track layout to verify a property. This track layout should contain a wide variety of possible scenarios as the safety properties will only be proven for this yard. On the other hand, the state space of the model should be small enough to perform the verification, restricting the number of sections, signals and trains we can put in the configuration. To achieve both a variety of scenarios and a limited amount of field elements it is also possible to verify several differently configured models. We picked the yard depicted in Fig. 2, as it contains a point, routes that may conflict head on or on flanks, and it contains trains following each other on the same route. To verify the safety properties we constructed two scenarios: one where one train may enter via Sect. 1 and one train may enter via Sect. 4, and a scenario where two trains may enter via Sect. 4. To verify the liveness properties the latter configuration is used with the restriction that only routes from signal 3 to signal 6 may be requested.

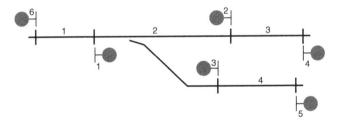

Fig. 2. Track layout used for model checking.

The mCRL2 toolkit provides a collection of tools to verify properties of mCRL2 models. The first step of the analysis of a model is to linearise it to a Linear Process Specification (LPS). To prove a property, a Parameterized Boolean Equation System (PBES) is generated and solved. The PBES can be generated directly from the LPS, but, for our model and properties, solving such a PBES is relatively slow compared to another strategy: first generating the LTS. The LTS can be minimised modulo divergence-preserving branching bisimilarity. From the LTS the PBES can be obtained, which can subsequently be solved, answering whether the given formula holds for the mode, providing a counterexample if does not.

4.3   Results

Property $\phi_{no\_derailment}$ holds for the model configured with the track layout shown in Fig. 2. Liveness property $\phi_{inv\_possibly\_cross}$ does not hold. If a train leaves behind a logical occupation (see Sect. 2) this might prevent other trains from being able to cross the yard. We would still require that the model contains at least a trace where all trains cross the yard, expressed in the formula $\phi_{possibly\_cross}$. This weaker property was proven to hold for the model.

   We found that $\phi_{no\_collision}$ does not hold for the model, as it contains collision scenarios. The scenario depicted in Fig. 3 shows how a dangerous situation can be reached. The scenario begins with a train on the entry section (Sect. 2) of the yard with a route set from signal 2 to some signal further ahead. The train passes the signal and Sect. 2 is seen by the interlocking to be free but the section after the signal is not yet seen as occupied. This causes the entry signal to be set to show stop again in step 3. Signal 1, facing the chasing train on the open track, is set to show yellow and the chasing train enters the entry section of the interlocking area. As the section before the entry signal of the route is now occupied signal 2 is set to show green, creating a dangerous situation.

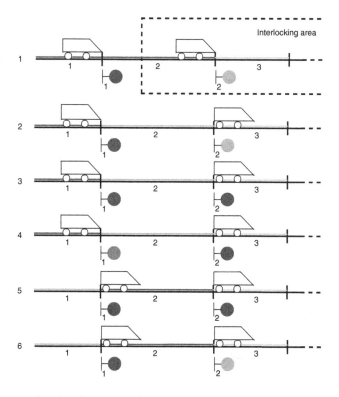

Fig. 3. Scenario showing dangerous situation, colour depicts occupancy as seen by the interlocking (green = free, red = occupied). (Color figure online)

According to signalling experts, this scenario is not likely as the time between step 2 and 5 should be sufficient to detect the train on Sect. 3. The scenario would be possible in the event that Sect. 3 would never detect a train due to detection problems, called loss of shunt. We were able to replay the scenario on the TeSys simulator by not marking Sect. 3 as occupied, simulating the loss of shunt.

By making sections long enough and adding delays in some situations such timing issues are excluded by infrastructure managers. As such a loss of shunt is not likely to occur in reality we would like to exclude this scenario from the model. We were able to find three ways to remove the observed type of collision from the model and prove the safety property concerning collisions. The first is to exclude that the interlocking observes an entry section to be free before it observes that the next section is occupied, yielding model variant **Fix read order**. The dangerous situation is possible because the entry section is not part of the route and can therefore not become logically occupied. Another way to exclude collisions is then to make the entry section part of the route, guarded by sequential release (see Sect. 2), model variant **Guard entry section**. Note that guarding the entry section deviates from the behaviour of the Siemens interlocking simulated in TeSys. It is unclear why it was chosen to not include the entry section in routes. A model in which the interlocking is always perfectly up to date regarding section occupations, variant **Instant update**, also satisfies $\phi_{no\_collision}$. For this last variant $\phi_{inv\_possibly\_cross}$ also holds as logical occupations can not occur in this model. An overview of the results is presented in Table 2 and statistics on the model variants can be found in Table 3. The different variants are accessible online[2]

Table 2. Statistics of state spaces of the model variants. Total running time is up to 30 min with 30 GB of memory usage on a MacBook pro 2018.

	Original	Fix read order	Guard entry section	Instant update
#states	110229	7170	9837	1713
#transitions	483428	26015	38929	4925
#states (minimized)	4621	577	598	190
#transitions (minimized)	23131	2322	2421	640

5   Model-Based Testing to Validate Model

In order to increase confidence that the formal model, based on the description of signalling experts, accurately describes the behaviour of the interlocking software. To this end, we have used the model-based test tool JTorX [3] to fully automatically test whether our model accurately describes the behaviour of the interlocking software.

---

[2] https://www.win.tue.nl/~luttik/Models/IxL/.

Table 3. Overview of what properties hold for which variant of the model.

	Original	Fix read order	Guard entry section	Instant update
$\phi_{no\_collision}$	False	True	True	True
$\phi_{no\_derailment}$	True	True	True	True
$\phi_{inv\_possibly\_cross}$	False	False	False	True

A testing theory defined for Labelled Transition Systems (LTS) is the input output conformance testing theory (**ioco**) [20]. The theory considers both the specification and the implementation as an LTS (while in practice the System Under Test (SUT) is of course not an LTS). From the specification, test cases can be generated, which can be executed on the implementation, resulting in a pass (the implementation conforms to the specification) or a fail (the implementation deviates from the specification). The test derivation algorithm and when an implementation passes a test case are formally defined using LTSs.

We use JTorX as testing tool. Like its predecessor TorX [19] it implements the **ioco** testing theory. JTorX derives from a given specification which stimuli it can send to the SUT and which observations it should expect. JTorX accepts Labelled Transition Systems as input, as well as linearised mCRL2 models that represent a possibly infinite transition system via lps2torx (included in the mCRL2 toolkit but considered deprecated). We used the random stimulus selection and automated testing features of JTorX to perform online automated tests (Fig. 4).

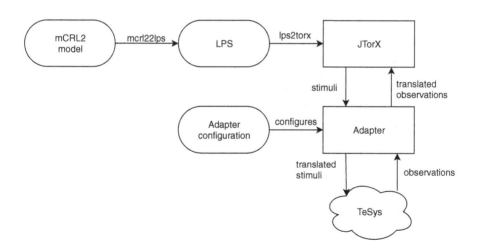

Fig. 4. Toolchain to perform model-based testing using JTorX.

We connected the Siemens simulator TeSys to JTorX via an adapter that translates transition labels from the model to stimuli in TeSys and translates events generated by the interlocking to transition labels. The adapter is configured with a two-way mapping between identifiers used in the model and in TeSys. We chose to validate the instant update variant as it is the most restrictive variant. For testing we used the track layout depicted in Fig. 5, with trains being allowed to enter on all border sections. Note that for this yard it is no longer feasible to generate the state space, mainly due to the large number of trains that may be present on the yard.

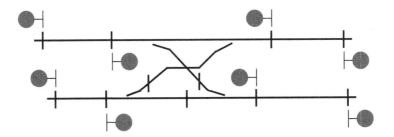

Fig. 5. Track layout used for testing on the simulator.

Results of Testing. Testing with JTorX revealed several inconsistencies between the model and the interlocking software. An example of an inconsistency was that the original model specified that after requesting a route, the next action of the interlocking is to accept or reject the route, no other action could come in between. It turns out that when a route is requested and some section occupation is changed shortly after, the interlocking might respond to the section occupation (by updating a signal aspect) before it accepts/rejects the requested route. These inconsistencies were fixed in the model, resulting in a model to which the behaviour of the interlocking conforms according to JTorX. Twenty test runs consisting of, on average, 50 stimuli/observations have been performed with the adjusted model. Note that due to the size of the state space test coverage is low. Moreover, as the connection between the adapter and the simulator was not completely stable it can not be guaranteed that all messages arrive at the other end, still model-based testing has allowed us to construct a better model. We have verified that the revised model (all variants) still satisfy the same properties listed in Table 3.

6   Discussion and Conclusions

6.1   Lessons Learned

Importance of Modelling the Environment. Safety properties can be specified in terms of conflicting routes or other proxies for collisions without needing to model the environment explicitly. However, we were able to find a type of collision that is hard to express directly in terms of behaviour of the interlocking as no conflicting routes need to be approved or opposing signals need to be set to show proceed. This was possible because we included the behaviour of trains in the model. This allowed us to specify the absence of collisions more directly, independently of how trains might collide.

This approach shifts work from the modeller to the model checking toolkit, allowing the modeller to be more naive in *how* unsafe behaviour might emerge. In some cases the size of the state space might increase by including the environment into the model, though in this case study, modelling the behaviour of trains helped to restrict what orders of section occupations are realistic.

Shortcomings of Model-Based Testing. The initial model (and some of the variants) contain behaviour where a section becomes logically occupied when section occupations occur non-sequentially in the view of the interlocking. This behaviour did not occur during testing. The issue is that it only occurs when section occupations follow each other quickly. JTorX is not able to compute stimuli quickly enough to test this aspect of the behaviour. JTorX can therefore not differentiate between a model where the interlocking is notified instantly of a section occupation and a model that allows a delay.

At some point during the initial modelling phase we had to make a decision on how to model the environment and more specifically section occupations. We decided to allow as much behaviour as possible by making the interaction between a train and a section, and the interaction between a section and the interlocking distinct actions in the model. This allowed us to find collision scenarios that we would not have found otherwise. It can thus be helpful to initially allow too much behaviour and restrict unrealistic behaviour later, especially in a setting where model-based testing cannot test all time related behaviour. An additional benefit is that you learn more about which assumptions are necessary to ensure safety.

6.2 Research Challenges for mCRL2 and JTorX

An issue that is prevalent in the signalling domain is how to deal with different configurations. Track layout configurations are different for each interlocking but also the behaviour of the interlocking is dependent on several factors. For example, the behaviour depends on the country and the Automatic Train Protection system used in that area. The mCRL2 toolkit currently has limited features to handle these configuration issues as an mCRL2 model is a closed model. In this case study we used the data language of the mCRL2 language to construct a function that maps a natural number to a configuration, allowing us to select a configuration by changing a single line in the model. The different variants of the model that we created to exclude specific collision scenarios could not so easily be incorporated into the model, forcing us to create separate models, duplicating most of the mCRL2 code.

Another challenge is that it is currently very hard to troubleshoot performance issues. The mCRL2 toolkit rewrites data terms, a predicate in the data

is, for example, rewritten to true or false. The sum operator in process defini-
tions and forall/exists statements in data equations, may cause the rewriter to
evaluate an infinite domain, such as all natural numbers. If the rewriter does not
evaluate an infinite domain but nevertheless does need a large number of rewrite
steps to rewrite certain terms it can have a significant impact on the performance
of the toolkit. The issue is that it is hard to figure out which term slows down
the rewriter. It would be helpful if the toolkit would provide some feedback to
the user. A possibility would be to provide the user with the option to display a
log of the rewriter. In some cases the toolkit might be improved to recognise that
an infinite domain will be evaluated, though, in general, termination of rewriting
is undecidable.

6.3   Further Research for Development of Signalling Systems

Other modelling languages than mCRL2 are already in use in the signalling
domain. Siemens currently uses GRACE, a graphical modelling language, to
design the interlocking logic. From GRACE the interlocking software is generated. The EULYNX initiative[3] uses SysML models to standardize interfaces and
certain aspects of the behaviour of field elements. It would be beneficial for them
if they could profit from the advantages of formal methods without needing to
develop formal models from scratch or radically changing their current workflow.

  If it would be possible to generate a formal model from the models already
being used, the flow depicted in Fig. 6 could be achieved. In the setting where an
authoritative model is created from the requirements, model-based testing could

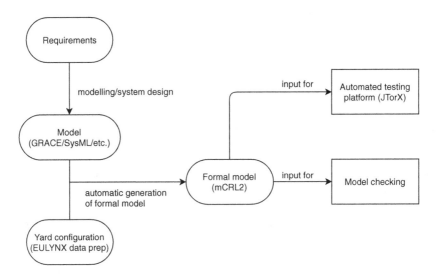

Fig. 6. Further integration formal methods in signalling system/standard development.

---

[3] https://www.eulynx.eu/.

be used to (automatically) check the software. Some research has been done on generating mCRL2 code from other modelling languages [5,13].

Signalling engineers generally do not have the expertise to use formal modelling languages and toolkits. Getting the expertise in formal methods requires a significant time investment. Using an intermediate modelling language would allow signalling experts to use more intuitive modelling languages while formal methods experts could manage the analysis of the formal models.

6.4 Concluding Remarks on Formal Methods in Railway Signalling

Traditionally, the level of experience and rigour of the people who design and test signalling systems determined the quality of the systems, and consequently the safety of systems. This is not by definition an undesirable situation, considering the high level of safety that is achieved in this way.

That is not to say that formal methods could not play a valuable role in the development of signalling systems. By also employing formal methods to find flaws, one can reduce the sole dependency on human experience. Moreover, the development of formal models promotes the discussion about why signalling systems are safe and the models themselves provide a more detailed account of the design than plain text. Finally, finding flaws in early design phases and automation of testing could offer significant cost reductions.

Acknowledgements. We would like to thank Daan van der Meij from ProRail for his contributions to this work by sharing his expertise on signalling systems.

References

1. Bartholomeus, M., Luttik, B., Willemse, T.: Modelling and analysing ERTMS hybrid level 3 with the mCRL2 toolset. In: Howar, F., Barnat, J. (eds.) FMICS 2018. LNCS, vol. 11119, pp. 98–114. Springer, Cham (2018). https://doi.org/10.1007/978-3-030-00244-2_7

2. Basile, D., et al.: On the industrial uptake of formal methods in the railway domain - a survey with stakeholders. In: Furia, C.A., Winter, K. (eds.) IFM 2018. LNCS, vol. 11023, pp. 20–29. Springer, Heidelberg (2018). https://doi.org/10.1007/978-3-319-98938-9_2

3. Belinfante, A.: JTorX: a tool for on-line model-driven test derivation and execution. In: Esparza, J., Majumdar, R. (eds.) Proceedings of TACAS 2010. LNCS, vol. 6015, pp. 266–270. Springer, Heidelberg (2010). https://doi.org/10.1007/978-3-642-12002-2_21

4. Bergstra, J., Klop, J.: Algebra of communicating processes with abstraction. Theor. Comput. Sci. **37**, 77–121 (1985). https://doi.org/10.1016/0304-3975(85)90088-X

5. van Beusekom, R., et al.: Formalising the Dezyne modelling language in mCRL2. In: Petrucci, L., Seceleanu, C., Cavalcanti, A. (eds.) FMICS-AVoCS 2017. LNCS, vol. 10471, pp. 217–233. Springer, Heidelberg (2017). https://doi.org/10.1007/978-3-319-67113-0_14

6. Bonacchi, A., Fantechi, A., Bacherini, S., Tempestini, M.: Validation process for railway interlocking systems. Sci. Comput. Program. **128**, 2–21 (2016)

7. Bonacchi, A., Fantechi, A., Bacherini, S., Tempestini, M., Cipriani, L.: Validation of railway interlocking systems by formal verification, a case study. In: Counsell, S., Núñez, M. (eds.) SEFM 2013. LNCS, vol. 8368, pp. 237–252. Springer, Cham (2014). https://doi.org/10.1007/978-3-319-05032-4_18

8. Bouwman, M.S.: A model-based test platform for rail signalling systems. Master's thesis, Eindhoven University of Technology (2018)

9. Bunte, O., et al.: The mCRL2 toolset for analysing concurrent systems - improvements in expressivity and usability. In: Vojnar, T., Zhang, L. (eds.) TACAS 2019. LNCS, vol. 11428, pp. 21–39. Springer, Heidelberg (2019). https://doi.org/10.1007/978-3-030-17465-1_2

10. Fantechi, A.: Twenty-five years of formal methods and railways: what next? In: Counsell, S., Núñez, M. (eds.) SEFM 2013. LNCS, vol. 8368, pp. 167–183. Springer, Cham (2014). https://doi.org/10.1007/978-3-319-05032-4_13

11. Groote, J.F., Mousavi, M.R.: Modeling and Analysis of Communicating Systems. MIT Press, Cambridge (2014)

12. Groote, J., van Vlijmen, S., Koorn, J.: The safety guaranteeing system at station Hoorn-Kersenboogerd. In: COMPASS 1995, pp. 57–68. IEEE (1995). https://doi.org/10.1109/CMPASS.1995.521887

13. Hansen, H.H., Ketema, J., Luttik, B., Mousavi, M.R., van de Pol, J., dos Santos, O.M.: Automated verification of executable UML models. In: Aichernig, B.K., de Boer, F.S., Bonsangue, M.M. (eds.) FMCO 2010. LNCS, vol. 6957, pp. 225–250. Springer, Heidelberg (2010). https://doi.org/10.1007/978-3-642-25271-6_12

14. Haxthausen, A.E., Peleska, J.: Model checking and model-based testing in the railway domain. In: Drechsler, R., Kühne, U. (eds.) Formal Modeling and Verification of Cyber-Physical Systems, pp. 82–121. Springer, Wiesbaden (2015). https://doi.org/10.1007/978-3-658-09994-7_4

15. Haxthausen, A.E., Peleska, J., Pinger, R.: Applied bounded model checking for interlocking system designs. In: Counsell, S., Núñez, M. (eds.) SEFM 2013. LNCS, vol. 8368, pp. 205–220. Springer, Cham (2014). https://doi.org/10.1007/978-3-319-05032-4_16

16. Huistra, D., Meijer, J., van de Pol, J.: Adaptive learning for learn-based regression testing. In: Howar, F., Barnat, J. (eds.) FMICS 2018. LNCS, vol. 11119, pp. 162–177. Springer, Cham (2018). https://doi.org/10.1007/978-3-030-00244-2_11

17. James, P., Moller, F., Nga, N.H., Roggenbach, M., Schneider, S.A., Treharne, H.: Techniques for modelling and verifying railway interlockings. STTT 16(6), 685–711 (2014). https://doi.org/10.1007/s10009-014-0304-7

18. James, P., Roggenbach, M.: Automatically verifying railway interlockings using SAT-based model checking. ECEASST 35 (2010). https://doi.org/10.14279/tuj.eceasst.35.547

19. Tretmans, G., Brinksma, H.: Torx: automated model-based testing. In: Hartman, A., Dussa-Ziegler, K. (eds.) First European Conference on Model-Driven Software Engineering, pp. 31–43, December 2003

20. Tretmans, J.: Model based testing with labelled transition systems. In: Hierons, R.M., Bowen, J.P., Harman, M. (eds.) Formal Methods and Testing. LNCS, vol. 4949, pp. 1–38. Springer, Heidelberg (2008). https://doi.org/10.1007/978-3-540-78917-8_1

21. Willemse, T.A.C.: Heuristics for ioco-based test-based modelling. In: Brim, L., Haverkort, B.R., Leucker, M., van de Pol, J. (eds.) FMICS/PDMC 2006. LNCS, vol. 4346, pp. 132–147. Springer, Heidelberg (2006). https://doi.org/10.1007/978-3-540-70952-7_9

22. Woodcock, J., Larsen, P.G., Bicarregui, J., Fitzgerald, J.S.: Formal methods: practice and experience. ACM Comput. Surv. 41(4), 19:1–19:36 (2009). https://doi.org/10.1145/1592434.1592436

A DFT Modeling Approach for Infrastructure Reliability Analysis of Railway Station Areas

Matthias Volk[1]([envelope]), Norman Weik[2], Joost-Pieter Katoen[1], and Nils Nießen[2]

[1] Chair of Software Modeling and Verification, RWTH Aachen University, Aachen, Germany
{matthias.volk,katoen}@cs.rwth-aachen.de
[2] Institute of Transport Science, RWTH Aachen University, Aachen, Germany
{weik,niessen}@via.rwth-aachen.de
https://moves.rwth-aachen.de/, http://www.via.rwth-aachen.de/

Abstract. Infrastructure failures—in particular in station and junction areas—are one of the most important causes for train delays in railway systems. Individually, subsystems, such as track circuits or radio communication, are well understood and have been analyzed using formal methods. However, verification of the capability of station areas to fulfill operational design specifications as a whole remains widely open.

In this paper, we present a fully automatic translation from station area infrastructure to dynamic fault trees (DFT) with special emphasis on field elements including switches, signals and track occupation detection systems. Reliability is assessed in terms of train routability, where feasible train routes consist of the set of train paths projected in the interlocking system including their requirements w.r.t. the state of field elements. Analysing the DFTs by probabilistic model checking techniques allows for new performance metrics based on, e.g., conditional events or the sequence of failures, which can serve to provide additional insights into the criticality of field elements.

We demonstrate the feasibility of the DFT-based analysis based on data for railway stations in Germany where the generated DFTs consist of hundreds of elements.

Keywords: Railway infrastructure · Dynamic fault trees · Reliability

1 Introduction

Strategic decisions in infrastructure design and asset management of railway networks are extremely critical as renewal cycles can easily span several decades

---

Supported by German Research Foundation (DFG) with Research Training Group 2236 "UnRAVeL" and Research Grant 283085490 "Integral capacity and reliability analysis of guided transport systems based on analytical models".

© Springer Nature Switzerland AG 2019
K. G. Larsen and T. Willemse (Eds.): FMICS 2019, LNCS 11687, pp. 40–58, 2019.
https://doi.org/10.1007/978-3-030-27008-7_3

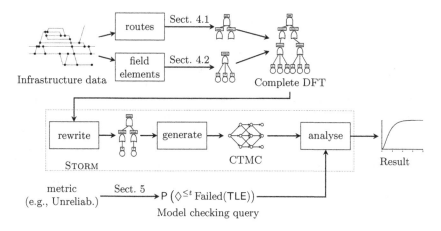

Fig. 1. Overview of the DFT-based analysis approach for railway stations

and decisions tend to shape the network layout for decades. This is why a quantitative a-priori analysis of infrastructure reliability and performance is highly important.

Formal methods have found widespread application in verification of hard- and software standards in safety-critical applications such as interlockings [10,11,18,19,26] or train communications [3,5,24,37]. The need for formal system analysis in a broader RAMS setting has recently been emphasized in the rail-specific CENELEC norms EN 50126-1, 50128, 50129, 50159 [12,13]. To date, formal method applications in this context are mostly delimited to the verification of specifications of individual components by original equipment manufacturers (OEMs), whereas – on the network level – heuristic or manual approaches continue to dominate [32].

This paper presents an infrastructure reliability model based on dynamic fault trees (DFTs) [17,40] for the performance analysis and verification of railway station areas. The system description is based on train paths projected in the interlocking system, which are the fundamental element for train routing and operation in railway systems. Train path functionality is conditioned on the operability of tracks as well as field elements such as switches or signals, which are typically specified in interlocking tables (cf. e.g., [19]). Quality parameters of these systems or subsystems thereof are reported to the infrastructure manager by OEMs and can also often be deduced from network records.

An overview of our approach is depicted in Fig. 1. The fully automatic approach translates station infrastructure data to DFTs by combining DFTs for train paths and dedicated DFTs for field elements into one complete DFT (top row). We place special emphasis on field elements including switches, signals and track occupation detection systems, which are known to be responsible for the majority of infrastructure failures in station and junction areas [4]. We develop new performance metrics for asset management (bottom row) and apply probabilistic model checking (middle row) for analysis. The results can be used to gain a deeper understanding on the long term effects of strategic decisions in infrastructure design and maintenance planning.

The paper is structured as follows: In Sect. 2 we review the current status of reliability analysis for railway networks and previous applications of formal methods in this context. Section 3 discusses the principles of railway operation procedures and briefly introduces DFTs. Section 4 presents our DFT-based modeling approach for railway networks on the system level. In Sect. 5 we discuss new performance metrics for quantitative analysis of the state of the infrastructure. The metrics become accessible through the state-based DFT model. We demonstrate the functionality and the capabilities of our approach in application scenarios for three German railway stations in Sect. 6.

2   Related Work

Train operations in railway networks are based on interlocking systems, a combination of technical systems that prohibit conflicting movements of trains. In order to set a train route and to grant movement authority to a train, preconditions on the state of tracks and field elements have to be met, which are typically stored in interlocking control tables [19,43]. Due to the safety-criticality of train control, formal methods are widely used for hard- and software verification in this area.

For a broad methodological overview on formal methods for railway software development, see [7]. The suitability of formal methods and tools for railway signaling and control applications with respect to the safety integrity level (SIL)— 4 being the highest, 0 the lowest—has been reviewed in [18]. In station areas, solid state interlocking programs (e.g., [26]) and railway signalling data (e.g., [25]) have been formally verified. In view of the migration of "old" signal-based train control systems to new radio-based infrastructure such as ERTMS/ETCS (European Rail Traffic Management System/European Train Control System), verification of train control specifications has received new attention recently, especially with respect to train radio communications: [15] verifies consistency of ETCS requirements in a hybrid system setting including train dynamics using a combination of temporal logic with regular expressions. In [37], ETCS is viewed as a hybrid system controller and controllability, safety, liveness and reactivity of ETCS in view of perturbations in train dynamics are investigated using deductive verification. [24] presents a statechart extension and its transformation to discrete event simulation-based analysis of reliability in this context to verify compliance with QoS standards for train radio communication. [5] focuses on failure modeling of ERTMS/ETCS Level 3, an entirely radio-based control system standard. Stochastic Petri nets are used to provide a quantitative assessment of the effects of communication losses. In [3], a Level 3 moving block signalling scenario is modelled and analysed with UPPAAL SMC.

Quality and safety requirements for electrotechnical systems in railway signaling applications have been specified in the CENELEC standards EN 50128,

EN 50129 and EN 50159 [12]. EN 50128 recommends the use of formal methods even for software applications at SIL 1 and 2. The related EN 50126-1 standard [13] provides guidelines for risk and asset management, also emphasizing the qualities of formal modeling approaches in this context.

To date, the use of formal methods in railway asset management remains limited and often focuses on specific elements or subsystems only. [22] and [31] discuss failure modes of tracks and switches and develop Failure Mode and Effect Analysis (FMEA) schemes for asset management based on application scenarios from the British and Swedish railway networks. Markovian models for degradation modeling of rails and track foundations have been discussed in [38] and extended to a Petri net-based approach in [1].

Another class of models mentioned in EN 50126 are fault trees. Henry [23] uses fault trees to model train protection systems in a metro transit system. The railway power supply system and the effects of different maintenance strategies have been analyzed using (static) fault trees in [14]. The model is solved using binary decision diagrams. [21] discusses a DFT model for the investigation of general railway failure scenarios and maintenance strategies. By integrating new "dynamic" gates, functional dependencies and spare parts typical for repair processes can be modeled. Probabilistic model checking based on a Markov chain representation of the fault tree is applied to solve the model. An extension is provided in [39], where DFTs are used to optimize maintenance strategies for insulating joints, which are essential for train detection based on track circuits. A first step to transfer the use of fault trees to performability analysis of entire stations have been recently undertaken in [43], where the main focus has been on the modeling of fallback levels in case of infrastructure disruptions.

3 Preliminaries

3.1 Fundamentals of Railway Operations

In the following we recap infrastructure reliability in railway station areas. Apart from the permanent way including tracks, switches and crossings, the wayside infrastructure also includes field elements required by the signaling and train control system such as signals and axle counters or track circuits to detect train movements. For radio-based train control systems track-bound balises transmitting position indication and movement authority are required, as well. In this paper we focus on elements in *signal-based fixed-block train control*, which remains the standard for train operations in stations (see Fig. 2 for an example).

Similar to [43] and the verification of interlocking systems (cf. [18]), our analysis is based on train routes. *Train routes* denote paths on the infrastructure which are delimited by signals governing station entry and exit. As no additional driving indication is given to train drivers en route in standard operations, the entire route has to be cleared and set for the train before the movement authority (by means of signals) is given. As a result, train routes can be seen as the fundamental routing elements in station areas and will be the base of our model.

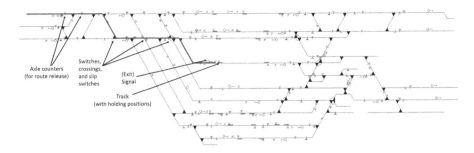

Fig. 2. Railway station with exit route. The central station area in the middle of the figure is connected to three adjacent railway lines: Two double-track lines to the right and a 3-track line segment to the left. Field elements including signals, axle counters and switches included in the interlocking system are marked.

3.2 Fault Trees

Fault trees [40,41] (FTs) are directed acyclic graphs (DAG) with typed nodes (AND, OR, etc.). We refer to nodes of type T as "a T".

Successors of a node v in the DAG are called *children* of v. Nodes without children are *basic events* (BEs), nodes with children are *gates*. We say a BE "*fails*", if the event occurs. Similarly, a gate fails if the failure condition over the children holds. The *top-level event* ($\mathsf{TLE}(F)$) is a specifically marked node of FT F. We write TLE if F is clear from the context. The FT F fails iff $\mathsf{TLE}(F)$ fails.

In the following, we recapitulate the different node types in a fault tree as presented in [20]. A detailed account of the semantics is given in [29].

Static Fault Trees. *Static fault trees* (SFTs) have node types BE and VOT.

Basic events. BEs (Fig. 3(a)) represent system components which can fail according to an exponential failure distribution defined by the *failure rate*. A special case of BEs are *constant fail-safe* BEs ($\mathsf{CONST}(\bot)$, Fig. 3(b)) which never fail.

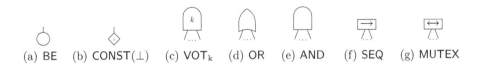

(a) BE   (b) CONST($\bot$)   (c) VOT$_k$ (d) OR   (e) AND   (f) SEQ   (g) MUTEX

Fig. 3. Node types in ((a)–(e)) static and (all) dynamic fault trees

Voting Gate. The *voting gate* with threshold k (VOT$_k$, Fig. 3(c)) is the key gate for static fault trees. A VOT$_k$-gate fails, if k of its children have failed. The OR-gate (Fig. 3(d)) fails if at least one child has failed and can be represented by a VOT$_1$-gate. The AND-gate (Fig. 3(e)) with n children fails if all children have failed and can be represented by a VOT$_n$-gate.

Dynamic Fault Trees. For complex systems, SFTs lack expressive power to faithfully model many required aspects such as spare components, order-dependent failures, functional dependencies or failure restrictions. *Dynamic fault trees* (DFTs) [17] are an extension of SFTs including these aspects. In the following, we only describe the gate types required for our modelling purposes.

Restrictors. Restrictors limit the possible failures of events. The *sequence enforcer* (SEQ, Fig. 3(f)) only allows failures of its children from left to right. A special case of the SEQ is the *mutual exclusion restriction* (MUTEX, Fig. 3(g)). A MUTEX prevents the failure of more than one of its children. As an example, consider the DFT in Fig. 4(a).

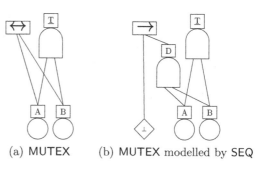

(a) MUTEX   (b) MUTEX modelled by SEQ

Fig. 4. A Mutex

If A has failed, the MUTEX prevents the failure of B, and vice versa. MUTEX are syntactic sugar [28] and can be modelled with a SEQ and a fail-safe BE as shown in Fig. 4(b).

3.3   Markov Chains

For analysis purposes, the DFTs are translated into *continuous-time Markov Chains (CTMCs)* [2].

Definition 1 *(CTMC). A CTMC is a tuple $\mathcal{C} = (S, P, R, L)$ with*

- *S a finite set of states,*
- *$P : S \times S \to [0, 1]$ a stochastic matrix i.e., $\sum_{s' \in S} P(s, s') = 1$ for all $s \in S$,*
- *$R : S \to \mathbb{R}_{>0}$ a function assigning an exit rate $R(s)$ to each state $s \in S$,*
- *$L : S \to 2^{AP}$ a labeling function assigning a set of atomic propositions $L(s)$ to each state $s \in S$.*

The residence time in each state s is defined by the negative exponential distribution parameterised by exit rate $R(s)$. The *transition rate* between states s and s' is defined as $R(s, s') = R(s) \cdot P(s, s')$. *State labels* identify states in the DFT fulfilling specific conditions, e.g., states where a specific DFT event has occurred. For example, an atomic proposition A_{fail} could be added to all states where DFT element A has failed.

4   DFT Model for Railway Station Reliability Analysis

4.1   DFT Model for Railway Station

The fault tree model for the railway station area focuses on the possible train routing options. Different train types are associated with *route sets*, sets of possible train routes within the station area. The train routes in a route set are prioritised and the train route with the highest priority is the *standard route*. A *train route* consists of up to two train paths: a train path leading from the station entry to a halt in the station area, and similarly a train path leading to the station exit. For trains starting or ending in the station, only one train path is present. A *train path* is specified in the interlocking system and determines, for example, the required state of switches and signals along the path.

Figure 5 depicts the DFT model for a railway station. A station is considered failed if at least for one train type no routing is possible anymore. The routing for a train type is impossible if all train routes in the corresponding route set are unavailable. A train route is unavailable if at least one of the train paths (tp1, tp2) is unavailable. Note that a train path can be used in different train routes. Lastly, a train path tp is unavailable if at least one element (e.g., signal, crossing, etc.) along the path has failed. For switches and slip switches the correct track of the component has to be unavailable. If, for instance, a train path requires the main track of a switch and only the branch track is unavailable, the train path is still available. Field elements can be used in multiple train paths as well.

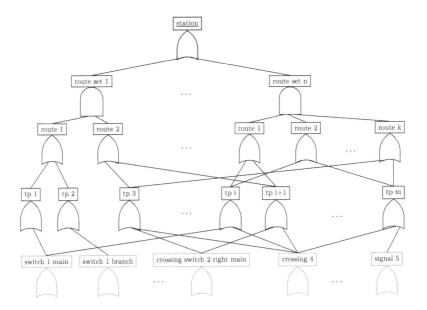

Fig. 5. Railway station fault tree

4.2   DFT Models for Infrastructure Components

In the following, we present DFT models for all relevant wayside infrastructure elements in the station area. A special focus lies on switches which are most important for routing, and are modelled with the greatest detail.

Switches. Switches allow routing on either the *main track* or the *branching track* depending on the current state of the blades. When changing the routing, the actuation and the control of the motor have to work in order to move the blades. Moreover, the locking mechanism has to work as well, to ensure that the blades are safely locked in their final position and do not move underneath a train. One important aspect of the switch is that a failure in one of the tracks might still allow routing on the other track. For example, if the actuation fails to move the blades, but they are still safely lockable in their present position, the current route can still be used.

The DFT modelling the different failure types of a switch is depicted in Fig. 6. We separately consider the status of the main track and the branch track. Both of the corresponding OR-gates (switch main and switch branch) might have connections to other parts of the DFT.

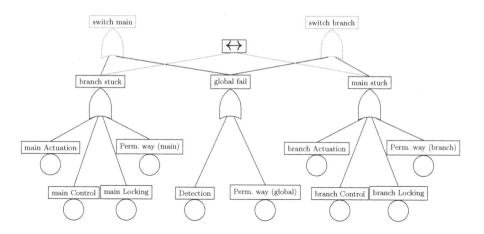

Fig. 6. Switch fault tree

For the modeling of the failure modes we rely on the detailed categorisation of switch failures provided in [4] (for the UK network), where 5 technical categories have been identified:

- Actuation (A) – failures in the track switching process (blade movement, lock actuation),
- Control/Power (C) – failures in control or power supply of switch subsystems,
- Detection (D) – failure to detect/transmit the position of switch rails/locks,
- Locking (L) – failure to lock the switch blades,

– Permanent Way (P) – mech. failures of rails, stretcher bars, slide chairs, etc.

Whereas failures to detect the current switch position/locking (D) will render the entire switch unusable, failures of the permanent way (P) can be both position specific (blade rail, guiding rail failures) or global (ballast, crossing failures). Locking (L), Control (C) and Actuation (A) failures originate in the context of blade movements and typically only affect one of the two switch routing options. For example, switch main is unavailable if branch stuck occurred, i.e. if the blades cannot be moved from their current position "branch" and locked to the "main" position any more. The MUTEX ensures that the switch can only be stuck in one position and not in both positions at the same time.

Slip Switches. Slip switches allow up to four different routing options from two ingoing to two outgoing tracks. Intuitively, they can be seen as a combination of two switches that each move the blades in two tracks. One motor sets the position of the blades on the two ingoing tracks—the *right track* and the *left track*. The other motor sets the position of the blades in the two outgoing tracks. Depending on the joint position of the blades, a train arriving on any ingoing track can be routed to the corresponding outgoing *main* or *branch track*. Note that not all routing options need be technically realised in a slip switch.

The DFT model for a slip switch is depicted in Fig. 7. It has four top events (right/left × main/branch) which all might have connections to other DFT parts. Again, we distinguish between stuck branches and total failures. As the slip switch consists of two switches, if one has failed completely (switch 1 fail or switch 2 fail), all four routing options become unavailable and the slip switch has failed. However, if the blades for one switch are stuck, only two tracks become unavailable. These cases are represented by the four OR-gates with stuck. As before, two MUTEX ensure that the blades can only be stuck in one position.

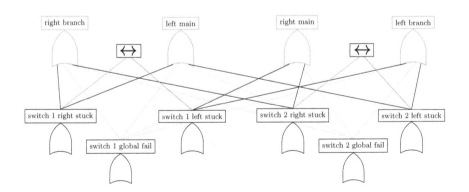

Fig. 7. Slip switch fault tree (without BEs)

For better visualisation, we omitted the BEs in the slip switch DFT, but they are similar as for the single switch DFT. For example, the OR-gate switch 1 right stuck has four BEs for actuation, control, locking and permanent way failures.

Crossings. Crossings allow overlapping of two tracks without switching the tracks as in a slip switch. Without the presence of electromechanical components such as the motor or switch blades, the failure causes reduce to permanent way failures. The corresponding fault tree is depicted in Fig. 8(a).

Further Components. As we focus on train routability in our DFT model, sub fault trees for switches have the richest topology. Further components such as signals or track clearance detection can be modelled as atomic components without detailed failure behaviour for routability. If desired, these components can of course be modelled in greater detail using all available gate types in DFTs. An overview of the fault trees for further components is given in Fig. 8.

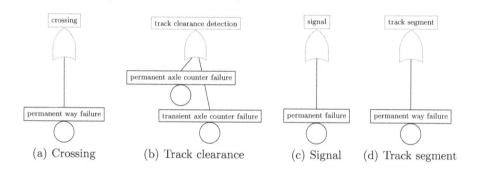

(a) Crossing   (b) Track clearance   (c) Signal   (d) Track segment

Fig. 8. Fault trees for further components

Track Clearance Detection. Track clearance detection reports whether the current track segment is occupied by a train. In Germany, axle counters are predominantly used for track clearance detection. Failures for axle counters (Fig. 8(b)) can be subdivided into permanent failures of the component and transient failures, where a train axle was not detected and functionality is quickly restored by a reset [30].

Signals. Signals failures (Fig. 8(c)) are often confused with other system malfunctions connected with the interlocking system that prohibit the signal being switched to green. We here consider intrinsic failures of the signal as a field element. With the establishment of highly reliable LED technology they are typically not caused by the lamps, but by wayside electronics of the signal [30].

Track Segments. Track segments (Fig. 8(d)) only experience failures due to wear from the trains running on the tracks. Failure rates for short track segments in stations, which are travelled at low speed, are typically small (cf. Sect. 4.3).

4.3 Failure Rates

Switches and Crossings. For the switch and crossing failure rates we rely on the extensive data from the UK Railway Network provided in [4], assuming electromechanical actuation systems (Type HW/W63) for switches, which are the most widespread designs both in the UK and in the German railway network. Failure rates for the different failure causes are based on the MTTFRI data (mean time to failure requiring intervention) in [4, Table 4].

Type (L), (C) and (A) failures originate in the context of blade movements, only. As [22] shows, almost 80% of switch failure causes are due to blade obstruction (snow/ice, ballast) and insufficient lubrication of slide chairs. As these failures are more likely to occur when moving the switch blades to the position used less frequently it could be argued for load dependent failure rates at this point. However, as no consistent information on the effects of load could be found in the literature, an even spread over the two branches has been assumed.

Permanent way (P) failures can yield both a complete failure of the switch (T) in case elements used by all tracks are affected (crossings, ballast) or depend on the branch (guiding rails, blades). The share of permanent way failures that renders the entire switch unusable, regardless of the blade position, is denoted by $\eta_{T,P}$ and is estimated based on the share of ballast, crossing, fishplate and sleeper failures in UK failure cause data for switches provided in [22, Table 1]. The parameters are summarised in Table 1.

Table 1. Failure parameters for switches based on HW/W63 switch data in [4, Table 4]. Failure rates $\lambda_A, \lambda_C, \lambda_D, \lambda_L, \lambda_P$ correspond to failure causes (A), (C), (D), (L) and (P), $\eta_{T,P}$ denotes the share of permanent way failures rendering the switch totally failed.

λ_P [1/d]	λ_A [1/d]	λ_C [1/d]	λ_D [1/d]	λ_L [1/d]	$\eta_{P,G}$
$1.46 \cdot 10^{-4}$	$4.98 \cdot 10^{-4}$	$2.26 \cdot 10^{-4}$	$2.32 \cdot 10^{-4}$	$1.28 \cdot 10^{-4}$	0.11

Data for crossings and slip switches rely on the same parameters. For crossings only Type (P) failures have to be considered. For slip switches Type (A), (C), (D) and (L) failures apply to both switching motors, independently.

Further Components. Track segments, track clearance detection and signals do not have degraded modes bearing on train routability, such that aggregated values can be used. For track segments and signals, failure rates consistent to the switch failure rates for the UK network can be estimated based on the number of reported failures and the approximate number of elements in the UK network in [35]. The number of track circuits and axle counters in the UK could not be found, such that failure data from [39] and [30] was chosen in Table 2.

Table 2. Failure rates [1/d] for track segments, signals, axle counters and track circuits.

Track Segments	Signals	Track Circuits	Axle Counters	
Failure	Failure	Failure	Reset request	Failure
$4.4 \cdot 10^{-4}$ (per km)	$2.9 \cdot 10^{-4}$	$5.5 \cdot 10^{-4}$	$2.8 \cdot 10^{-4}$	$1.1 \cdot 10^{-4}$

5   Quality Metrics for Railway Station Areas

Fault tree analysis can be performed by translating the DFT into a CTMC [8,17,42]. The analysis is performed on the CTMC by applying the standard model checking algorithms for a set of relevant properties. The properties to analyse are specified in *continuous stochastic logic (CSL)* with reward extensions [2].

We use atomic label Failed(v) to indicate the failure of DFT node v. The label Failed(TLE(F)) represents a failure of FT F. The labeling function of the CTMC assigns atomic labels to those states where the corresponding DFT node has failed. A set of states indicating certain failures is specified by a Boolean combination over the corresponding labels.

Table 3. Model-checking queries

Measure	Model-checking queries
Unreliability	$\mathsf{P}^{s_0}\left(\lozenge^{\leq t} \text{Failed}(\text{TLE}(F))\right)$
MTTF	$\mathsf{ET}^{s_0}\left(\lozenge \text{Failed}(\text{TLE}(F))\right)$
Unrel. for route i	$\mathsf{P}^{s_0}\left(\lozenge^{\leq t} \text{Failed}(\text{route i})\right)$
Unrel. for train path i	$\mathsf{P}^{s_0}\left(\lozenge^{\leq t} \text{Failed}(\text{tp i})\right)$
Criticality of element v	$\widetilde{I}_v(t)$
Unrel. after comp. v failed	$\displaystyle\sum_{s \in S, \text{Failed}(v) \in L(s)} \mathsf{P}^{s_0}\left(\neg\text{Failed}(v) \, \mathsf{U} \, s\right) \cdot \mathsf{P}^s\left(\lozenge^{\leq t} \text{Failed}(\text{TLE}(F))\right)$
MTTF after comp. v failed	$\displaystyle\sum_{s \in S, \text{Failed}(v) \in L(s)} \mathsf{P}^{s_0}\left(\neg\text{Failed}(v) \, \mathsf{U} \, s\right) \cdot \mathsf{ET}^s\left(\lozenge \text{Failed}(\text{TLE}(F))\right)$

Most metrics are reduced to the *reachability probability* $\mathsf{P}^s(\lozenge^{\leq t} event)$ of reaching a state e satisfying the labeling *event* from state s within time bound t. In the following, we present the metrics we computed in the context of railway station areas. The corresponding model-checking queries are formalised in Table 3.

General Metrics. As for static fault trees, the standard metrics such as *unreliability* and *mean-time-to-failure (MTTF)* can be checked on the CTMC. The *unreliability* is given by the reachability probability of a state where TLE(F) has failed from initial state s_0. The MTTF is computed as the expected time ET of the failure of TLE(F) from the initial state. Analysing the unreliability of the routing options is performed by computing the reachability probability for a route or a train path.

Re-routing Probability. The TLE represents the complete failure of at least one route set. To assess the probability that at least one train must be re-routed, we change the DFT model. The DFT is changed by only considering the standard route for each route set and removing all alternative train routes. The unreliability in the changed DFT corresponds to the re-routing probability.

Criticality of Infrastructure Elements. We denote the unreliability of a set of states e from initial state s_0 at time t by the transient probability $\mathsf{Unr}^t(e) = \mathsf{P}^{s_0}(\lozenge^{=t} e)$. One important metric in the station area model is the criticality of infrastructure elements, i.e., the influence of failures of a specific field element on the overall unreliability. A common way to measure the sensitivity of the system to an element is the *Birnbaum importance index* [6] defined as $I_v(t) = \frac{\partial \mathsf{Unr}^t(\mathsf{TLE})}{\partial \mathsf{Unr}^t(v)}$.

Following [36], we can approximate the importance index $I_v(t)$ by

$$\widetilde{I}_v(t) = x \cdot \left(\frac{\mathsf{Unr}^t(\mathsf{Failed}(\mathsf{TLE}) \wedge \mathsf{Failed}(v)))}{\mathsf{Unr}^t(\mathsf{Failed}(v)))} - \frac{\mathsf{Unr}^t(\mathsf{Failed}(\mathsf{TLE}) \wedge \neg\mathsf{Failed}(v))}{\mathsf{Unr}^t(\neg\mathsf{Failed}(v))} \right)$$

with $x = \frac{\mathsf{Unr}^t_F(\mathsf{Failed}(v))}{\mathsf{Unr}^t_{F_{iso}}(\mathsf{Failed}(v))}$. The factor x computes the fraction of the unreliability of the element *in the system* F and *in isolation* F_{iso}. The FT F_{iso} for element v is obtained from F by setting $\mathsf{TLE}(F_{iso}) = v$ and removing all restrictions on v. Computing $\widetilde{I}_v(t)$ for each element v gives insight into which element failures have the most impact on the routing in the station area.

Reliability Until Next Maintenance. If an element has failed, it is important to know how fast the element should be repaired or replaced. We can compute the *unreliability after component failure* for a component v by looking at all states where v has already failed. Each state s should be the first instance where v has failed, i.e., v is operational in all predecessors of s. We compute the unreliability in each state s and multiply it with the probability to reach s in the first place. The time bound for the unreliability is chosen as a typical maintenance interval. In a similar fashion, the *MTTF after component failure* can be computed. Both computations use the improved algorithm from [20] which avoids performing the model checking query for each state and uses only two checks instead.

6   Application Scenarios

6.1   Test Cases

As application scenarios for our fault-tree based station reliability model we consider three railway stations in the German state North Rhine Westphalia:

Aachen Hbf, Mönchengladbach Hbf and Herzogenrath Bf. Aachen Hbf and Mönchengladbach Hbf are major stations with multiple starting and ending train lines, and 9 and 10 tracks, respectively (7/9 platform tracks). Herzogenrath is a considerably smaller medium size station with 4 platform tracks (3 in use) and a small freight yard.

In the following analysis we focus on switches; track segments, axle counters and signals are not considered. While including the other elements is perfectly viable from a computational point of view we focus on switches for three reasons:

- First, switches possess the most interesting routability properties as they exhibit various degraded modes which still allow the use in some train routes, depending on whether the branching or the main track of the switch is used.
- Second, switch failures have been shown to be one of the most important factors in delay build-up [4]. As a result, more reliable switch designs have been discussed both by research [16] and OEMs (e.g. [33]). There now exist multiple switch layouts to choose from, such that switches are interesting from an asset management and investment point of view, as well. Failure rates of track segments, by contrast, can only be optimized to some extent by shortening inspection intervals, for instance.
- Finally, signal and axle counter failures tend to yield milder disruptions as fallback levels such as *visual driving mode* exist [43]. In addition, about 70% of axle counter failures are detection errors only requiring a reset once track clearance has been confirmed [30, Table 6]. Hence, the majority of axle counter failures are transient failures that can be resolved by train dispatchers.

6.2   Input Data

For the input data we rely on infrastructure and train data for the German railway network, as specified in the XML-ISS and XML-KSS standards [9], data exchange formats for railway infrastructure and train data currently used by German infrastructure manager DB Netz AG. The format is related to the railML standard [34], to which our method could be adapted with minor modifications. As discussed before, the requirements of train routes with respect to the state of field elements are typically specified in control tables, to which access is highly restrictive. We therefore follow a similar approach as the one recently discussed in [32] and construct control tables from the infrastructure data. While this approach can only provide an approximation to the actual situation specified in the interlocking control tables – which tend to vary between countries and even locally as a result of the exact track topology – it provides comparable data input, such that the approach is transferable to actual interlocking data.

6.3   Results and Discussion

We run Storm [42] on a HP BL685C G7 restricted to 16 GB RAM and use a single 2.0-GHz core. We generate the DFT models from the input railway infrastructure and simplify the resulting DFT models with the rewrite framework from [27]. The complete workflow as presented in Fig. 1 is fully automatized.

We evaluate our approach on the three stations for two different route sets: either a route set consists of only the standard route (*std*) or a route set contains the 5 most feasible routes according to priorities in the input data (*alt 5*).

Results. The model characteristics are given in Table 4. The first three columns specify the scenario by a unique id, the station and the variant. The fourth column indicates the maximal length of explored subsequent failures. The next four columns give the number of route sets, routes, train paths and components in the station. The next three columns characterise the resulting DFTs in terms of number of BEs, static gates and dynamic gates. The last two columns give the number of states and transitions in the resulting CTMCs. Note, that the maximal failure sequence length is required to mitigate the state space growth for larger models. It is reasonable to only consider a fixed number of subsequent failures as repairs or replacements would be performed after multiple failures.

Table 4. Model characteristics

Scenario				Railway				DFT			CTMC	
id	Station	Variant	Max	Rset	Rou	Tp	Com.	BE	Stat.	Dyn.	States	Trans.
1	Aachen	std	∞	61	61	62	53	544	459	54	2,049	13,313
2		alt 5	4	23	115	41	54	536	451	53	11,371,990	45,946,651
3	Herzog.	std	∞	11	11	15	22	194	137	19	257	1,281
4		alt 5	4	9	19	15	24	214	153	21	275,073	1,109,037
5		alt 5	6	9	19	15	24	214	153	21	17,592,280	106,375,167
6	M'gladb.	std	∞	26	26	32	40	480	325	48	8,193	61,441
7		alt 5	4	11	43	25	41	490	325	49	6,224,521	24,798,158

We analyse the resulting CTMCs according to the model checking queries specified in Sect. 5. The time bound is 90 days (a typical maintenance interval). The results are presented in Table 5. The id in the first column references the scenario. The second column gives the time (in seconds) for building the CTMC. The next three columns give results for unreliability and MTTF, and the time needed to compute both metrics. The remainder presents the results for more intricate metrics: the unreliability of each route, the criticality of each switch and the MTTF after a switch failed. For all three metrics we give an exemplary result and the average analysis time. Note that we gain upper and lower bounds for all results on the partially explored models and present the worst-case results here.

Analysis results for all switches in Mönchengladbach Hbf (scenario 7) are depicted in Fig. 9. The criticality results $\widetilde{I}_v(t)$ are given in Fig. 9(a) and the MTTF after the switch failures are given in Fig. 9(b). Each coloured dot represents a switch and its analysis result where red indicates a higher and yellow

Table 5. Analysis results (MTTF in [days], comp. times in [seconds])

id	Build Time	General metrics			Unrel. route		Criticality		MTTF aft. fail	
		Unrel.	MTTF	Time	Result	avg. Time	Result	avg. Time	Result	avg. Time
1	0.11	0.996	16.39	0.01	0.246	0.05	0.025	7.86	0.00	0.58
2	2006.16	0.895	46.71	10.75	0.758	1.31	0.569	63.86	1.31	75.84
3	0.04	0.826	51.54	0.00	0.172	1.41	0.196	1.78	0.00	0.95
4	12.33	0.715	70.09	0.39	0.273	0.03	0.312	0.36	1.89	0.28
5	1110.48	0.711	72.41	17.78	0.274	0.43	0.214	4.40	2.24	2.43
6	27.79	0.991	19.02	0.02	0.203	0.20	0.037	5.95	0.00	0.33
7	645.51	0.842	55.77	6.09	0.650	0.90	0.673	73.54	1.22	41.39

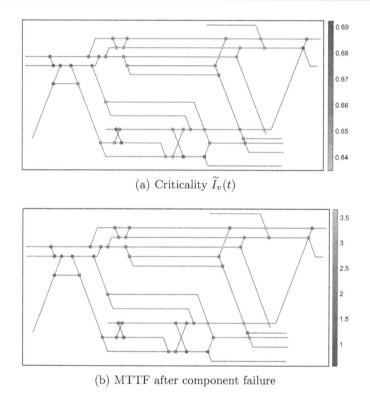

(a) Criticality $\widetilde{I}_v(t)$

(b) MTTF after component failure

Fig. 9. Analysis of switches in Mönchengladbach Hbf for the considered route sets (scenario 7) (Color figure online)

a lower value. Grey dots indicate switches which are not amongst the 5 train routes with highest priority for any train type.

Discussion. All models experience high unreliability within a 3-months period. Allowing multiple alternative paths instead of a standard path increases the reliability of the stations and the MTTF nearly triples for Aachen and Mönchengladbach.

When considering alternative paths, the state space growth and therefore the building times become the main limiting factor. The time needed for model checking remains negligible even for the largest models. For Herzogenrath we increased the maximal failure sequence from 4 to 6. While the state space greatly increases, the results only slightly change. Thus, it is reasonable to limit the number of considered subsequent failures and still get insightful results.

The criticality results in Fig. 9(a) show that the switches on the ingoing and outgoing tracks are the most critical. Unavailable switches in these positions render large parts of the station area unavailable. It is also possible to see that the two yellow switches to the top right are not critical. This might indicate that most routes we considered are not using those tracks. The MTTF after switch failures in Fig. 9(b) yield a similar result with subtle differences such as more distinct differences between the switches in the bottom right corner.

7   Conclusion

We presented a DFT-based model for the infrastructure in railway station areas focussing on field elements, e.g., switches. Probabilistic models allow computing new metrics and offer insights into routing options based on the reliability of field elements. Future work includes extending the existing DFTs, for example dynamical adaptions of component failures rates according to the current load.

References

1. Andrews, J., Prescott, D., Rozières, F.D.: A stochastic model for railway track asset management. Reliab. Eng. Syst. Saf. **130**, 76–84 (2014)
2. Baier, C., Hahn, E.M., Haverkort, B.R., Hermanns, H., Katoen, J.P.: Model checking for performability. Math. Struct. Comput. Sci. **23**(4), 751–795 (2013)
3. Basile, D., ter Beek, M.H., Ciancia, V.: Statistical model checking of a moving block railway signalling scenario with UPPAAL SMC. In: Margaria, T., Steffen, B. (eds.) ISoLA 2018. LNCS, vol. 11245, pp. 372–391. Springer, Cham (2018). https://doi.org/10.1007/978-3-030-03421-4_24
4. Bemment, S.D., Goodall, R.M., Dixon, R., Ward, C.P.: Improving the reliability and availability of railway track switching by analysing historical failure data and introducing functionally redundant subsystems. Proc. Inst. Mech. Eng. Part F: J. Rail Rapid Transit **232**(5), 1407–1424 (2017)
5. Biagi, M., Carnevali, L., Paolieri, M., Vicario, E.: Performability evaluation of the ERTMS/ETCS – level 3. Transp. Res. Part C **82**, 314–336 (2017)
6. Birnbaum, Z.: On the importance of different components in a multicomponent system. In: Multivariate Analysis-II, pp. 581–592 (1969)
7. Bjørner, D.: New results and trends in formal techniques for the development of software for transportation systems. In: FORMS. L'Harmattan Hongrie (2003)
8. Boudali, H., Crouzen, P., Stoelinga, M.: Dynamic fault tree analysis using input/output interactive Markov chains. In: Proceedings of DSN, pp. 708–717. IEEE (2007)

9. Brünger, O., Gröger, T.: Fahrplantrassen managen und Fahrplanerstellung simulieren. In: 19. Verkehrswissenschaftliche Tage (VWT), Dresden, Germany (2003)
10. Busard, S., Cappart, Q., Limbrée, C., Pecheur, C., Schaus, P.: Verification of railway interlocking systems. Electron. Proc. Theor. Comput. Sci. **184**, 19–31 (2015)
11. Cappart, Q., Limbrée, C., Schaus, P., Quilbeuf, J., Traonouez, L., Legay, A.: Verification of interlocking systems using statistical model checking. In: HASE, pp. 61–68. IEEE Computer Society (2017)
12. CENELEC: EN 50128: Railway applications - Communication, signalling and processing systems - Software for railway control and protection systems (2012), EN 50129: Railway applications - Communication, signalling and processing systems - Safety related electronic systems for signalling (2017), EN 50159: Railway applications - Communication, signalling and processing systems - Safety-related communication in transmission systems (2011)
13. CENELEC: EN 50126–1/50126-2: Railway applications - The specification and demonstration of reliability, availability, maintainability and safety (rams) (2018)
14. Chen, S., Ho, T., Mao, B.: Reliability evaluations of railway power supplies by fault-tree analysis. IET Electric Power Appl. **1**(2), 161–172 (2007)
15. Cimatti, A., Roveri, M., Tonetta, S.: Requirements validation for hybrid systems. In: Bouajjani, A., Maler, O. (eds.) CAV 2009. LNCS, vol. 5643, pp. 188–203. Springer, Heidelberg (2009). https://doi.org/10.1007/978-3-642-02658-4_17
16. Coleman, I.: In2Rail Project Innovative Intelligent Rail, Deliverable D2.1 - Development of Novel S&C Motion/Locking Mechanisms: Design Concept Report. Technical report, Network Rail (NWR) (2015)
17. Dugan, J.B., Bavuso, S.J., Boyd, M.A.: Fault trees and sequence dependencies. In: Proceedings of RAMS, pp. 286–293 (1990)
18. Fantechi, A.: Twenty-five years of formal methods and railways: what next? In: Counsell, S., Núñez, M. (eds.) SEFM 2013. LNCS, vol. 8368, pp. 167–183. Springer, Cham (2014). https://doi.org/10.1007/978-3-319-05032-4_13
19. Ferrari, A., Magnani, G., Grasso, D., Fantechi, A.: Model checking interlocking control tables. In: Schnieder, E., Tarnai, G. (eds.) FORMS/FORMAT 2010, pp. 107–115. Springer, Heidelberg (2011). https://doi.org/10.1007/978-3-642-14261-1_11
20. Ghadhab, M., Junges, S., Katoen, J.P., Kuntz, M., Volk, M.: Safety analysis for vehicle guidance systems with dynamic fault trees. Reliab. Eng. Syst. Saf. **186**, 37–50 (2019)
21. Guck, D., Katoen, J.P., Stoelinga, M., Luiten, T., Romijn, J.: Smart railroad maintenance engineering with stochastic model checking. In: Proceedings of RAILWAYS. Civil-Comp Press (2014)
22. Hassankiadeh, S.J.: Failure analysis of railway switches and crossings for the purpose of preventive maintenance. MA thesis, KTH Stockholm (2011)
23. Henry, J.: Automatic fault tree construction for railway safety systems. Ph.D. thesis, Loughborough University (1996)
24. Hermanns, H., Jansen, D.N., Usenko, Y.S.: From StoCharts to MoDeST. In: Proceedings of WOSP. ACM Press (2005)
25. Iliasov, A., Romanovsky, A.B.: Formal analysis of railway signalling data. In: HASE, pp. 70–77. IEEE Computer Society (2016)
26. Iliasov, A., Taylor, D., Laibinis, L., Romanovsky, A.: Formal verification of signalling programs with SafeCap. In: Gallina, B., Skavhaug, A., Bitsch, F. (eds.) SAFECOMP 2018. LNCS, vol. 11093, pp. 91–106. Springer, Cham (2018). https://doi.org/10.1007/978-3-319-99130-6_7

27. Junges, S., Guck, D., Katoen, J.P., Rensink, A., Stoelinga, M.: Fault trees on a diet: automated reduction by graph rewriting. Formal Asp. Comput. **29**, 1–53 (2017)
28. Junges, S., Guck, D., Katoen, J.P., Stoelinga, M.: Uncovering dynamic fault trees. In: Proceedings of DSN, pp. 299–310. IEEE (2016)
29. Junges, S., Katoen, J.-P., Stoelinga, M., Volk, M.: One net fits all. In: Khomenko, V., Roux, O.H. (eds.) PETRI NETS 2018. LNCS, vol. 10877, pp. 272–293. Springer, Cham (2018). https://doi.org/10.1007/978-3-319-91268-4_14
30. Kalvakunta, R.G.: Reliability modelling of ERTMS/ETCS. MA thesis, NTNU (2017)
31. Kassa, E.: Analysis of failures within switches and crossings using failure modes and effects analysis methodology. In: Proceedings of Intelliswitch Symposium (2017)
32. Luteberget, B., Johansen, C.: Efficient verification of railway infrastructure designs against standard regulations. Formal Methods Syst. Des. **52**(1), 1–32 (2018)
33. Morant, S.: New generation of turnouts promises to improve reliability and reduce costs. IRJ Int. Rail. J. **56**(12) (2016)
34. Nash, A., Huerlimann, D., Schütte, J., Krauss, V.: RailML - a standard data interface for railroad applications, pp. 3–10. WIT Press, Southampton (2004)
35. ORR - Office of Road and Rail: Online data portal, Rail infrastructure, assets and environmental (2013). https://dataportal.orr.gov.uk/. Accessed 01 May 2019
36. Ou, Y., Dugan, J.B.: Approximate sensitivity analysis for acyclic Markov reliability models. IEEE Trans. Rel. **52**(2), 220–230 (2003)
37. Platzer, A., Quesel, J.-D.: European train control system: a case study in formal verification. In: Breitman, K., Cavalcanti, A. (eds.) ICFEM 2009. LNCS, vol. 5885, pp. 246–265. Springer, Heidelberg (2009). https://doi.org/10.1007/978-3-642-10373-5_13
38. Prescott, D., Andrews, J.: Modelling maintenance in railway infrastructure management. In: Proceedings of RAMS, pp. 1–6. IEEE (2013)
39. Ruijters, E., Guck, D., van Noort, M., Stoelinga, M.: Reliability-centered maintenance of the electrically insulated railway joint via fault tree analysis: a practical experience report. In: Proceedings of DSN. IEEE (2016)
40. Ruijters, E., Stoelinga, M.: Fault tree analysis: a survey of the state-of-the-art in modeling, analysis and tools. Comput. Sci. Rev. **15–16**, 29–62 (2015)
41. Stamatelatos, M., Vesely, W., Dugan, J.B., Fragola, J., Minarick, J., Railsback, J.: Fault Tree Handbook with Aerospace Applications. NASA Headquarters (2002)
42. Volk, M., Junges, S., Katoen, J.P.: Fast dynamic fault tree analysis by model checking techniques. IEEE Trans. Ind. Inform. **14**(1), 370–379 (2018)
43. Weik, N., Nießen, N.: Performability analysis of railway systems. In: 2018 International Conference on Intelligent Rail Transportation (ICIRT). IEEE (2018)

Multiple Analyses, Requirements Once:
Simplifying Testing and Verification in Automotive Model-Based Development

Philipp Berger[1(✉)], Johanna Nellen[1], Joost-Pieter Katoen[1], Erika Ábrahám[1], Md Tawhid Bin Waez[2], and Thomas Rambow[3]

[1] RWTH Aachen University, Aachen, Germany
{berger,johanna.nellen,katoen,abraham}@cs.rwth-aachen.de
[2] Ford Motor Company, Dearborn, USA
mwaez@ford.com
[3] Ford Research and Innovation Center Aachen, Aachen, Germany
trambow@ford.com

Abstract. In industrial model-based development (MBD) frameworks, requirements are typically specified informally using textual descriptions. To enable the application of formal methods, these specifications need to be formalized in the input languages of all formal tools that should be applied to analyse the models at different development levels. In this paper we propose a unified approach for the computer-assisted formal specification of requirements and their fully automated translation into the specification languages of different verification tools. We consider a two-stage MBD scenario where first Simulink models are developed from which executable code is generated automatically. We (i) propose a specification language and a prototypical tool for the formal but still textual specification of requirements, (ii) show how these requirements can be translated automatically into the input languages of Simulink Design Verifier for verification of Simulink models and BTC EmbeddedValidator for source code verification, and (iii) show how our unified framework enables besides automated formal verification also the automated generation of test cases.

1 Introduction

In the automotive industry, software units for controllers are often implemented using *model-based development* (*MBD*). The industry standard ISO26262 recommends *formal verification* to ensure that such safety-critical software is implemented in accordance with the functional requirements. The work of our previous two papers [2,20] and this paper not only applies to safety critical automotive software but also to quality management (QM) or non-safety critical automotive software. In fact, we worked only on Ford QM software features in our papers. To optimally exploit recent academic developments as well as the capabilities of state-of-the-art verification tools, Ford Motor Company and RWTH Aachen University initiated an alliance research project to analyze how

© Springer Nature Switzerland AG 2019
K. G. Larsen and T. Willemse (Eds.): FMICS 2019, LNCS 11687, pp. 59–75, 2019.
https://doi.org/10.1007/978-3-030-27008-7_4

formal verification techniques for discrete-time systems can be embedded into Ford's model-based controller development framework, and to experimentally test their feasibility for industrial-scale C code controllers for mass production.

In our previous works [2, 20], we considered an MBD process starting with the development of Simulink controller models and using Simulink's code generation functionality to derive C code for software units. For formal verification, we analyzed the feasibility of both *Simulink Design Verifier (SLDV)* for Simulink models as well as *BTC EmbeddedPlatform* verification tool for the generated C code. Our papers [2, 20] present our observations and give recommendations for requirement engineers, model developers and tool vendors how they can contribute to a formal verification process that can be smoothly integrated into MBD.

The most serious pragmatic obstacles that we identified for the integration of formal methods are related to the *requirement specifications*. The requirement specifications were given informally in natural language. All the considered natural language requirements described time-bounded linear temporal logic (LTL) properties, which we manually formalized for both the SLDV and the BTC verification tools. During the formalization we detected ambiguity, incompleteness or inconsistency for roughly half of the textual requirements.

The manual formalizations needed discussions with requirement engineers to clarify and correct these flaws. However, a high degree of automation is a prerequisite for mass production and the integration of formal methods into the established MBD process at Ford. Automation allows the usage of formal verification within a development team of engineers with little knowledge of formal verification. Ideally, verification is automatically triggered whenever changes have been made to either the requirements, the Simulink model, or the used verification tools. Verification results can then be stored and compared with previous runs, making deviations from previous results easily detectable. All deviations can then be reported to a person with a strong background in formal methods for thorough investigation.

We also encountered problems rooted in the fact that the formalizations for the two different formal tools were done independently due to syntactic differences: in Simulink, requirements are themselves Simulink models that need to be embedded into the models that should satisfy them, whereas in BTC the requirements can be specified either using a graphical interface for pattern-based specification or directly in an XML-based file input format.

The independence of multiple requirement formalizations has several disadvantages. First and foremost, basically the same work is done multiple times, using different input languages. In addition, the formalizations have the risk to be slightly different. This may result in potentially incompatible analysis results requiring a deep and time-consuming analysis. *When the formalizations are done independently, they cost additional resources in time and expert knowledge, raising development cost.*

In addition, typically several programming and modeling languages are used within a company such as Ford. The preference of these languages changes over time and each language has its own analyses tools. Different teams within a company like Ford may use different tools for the same purpose. The fact that almost every formal verification tool has its unique input language is a big obstacle to introduce formal methods into versatile companies like Ford. *A common requirement language for all formal verification tools may help to take advantage of the strengths of different tools.*

To diminish these problems, this paper presents a *common formal requirement specification framework*. We focus on Simulink and C code verification in the automotive domain, but our framework is naturally extensible to further languages and tools. Concretely, the paper makes the following main contributions:

1. We identify *a small fragment of LTL* as a formal specification language that is expressive enough *for the formalization of typical requirements in the context of MBD in the automotive sector*.
2. We describe our *tool* that was designed as a prototype for use inside this research project as a proof of concept. Similar to BTC EmbeddedSpecifier it assists users who are not experts in formal methods to specify unambiguous and complete formal requirements using textual descriptions according to a pattern-based syntax.
3. We propose an approach for the *fully automated translation of the above-specified formal requirements into Simulink models* that can be embedded in SLDV verification processes.
4. We describe how to *automatically generate BTC models* from those formal requirements for source code verification.
5. We show how to *automatically generate test objectives* from formal requirements that can be used for automated test-case generation.

Our framework is illustrated in Fig. 1. While computer-assisted approaches for formal requirement specification have been proposed (see Sect. 2), we believe that our approach supporting direct analysis using multiple tools at different development levels is novel, especially the automated specification export to Simulink and the generation of test-cases.

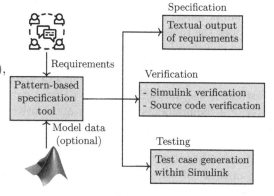

Fig. 1. The structure of our unified specification and analysis framework.

2   Related Work

Patterns for specifying properties in formal verification were introduced by Dwyer et al. [7]. Cheng et al. has extended this work to real-time properties [14] and Grunske introduced a pattern system for probabilistic properties [10].

Autili et al. [1] recently presented a unified pattern catalog that combines known patterns for qualitative, real-time and probabilistic properties. Then the work has been extended by some new patterns. Our works relies on the pattern catalogs from [1,7]. Inspired by our experience with Ford [2,20], we selected a set of patterns that covers more than 90% of our investigated automotive requirements.

Several tools are available for pattern-based specifications. The PSPWizard [17] and the SESAMM Specifier [8] provide for a given pattern library export functionalities to a formal logic or to a textual representation. The SESAMM specifier has been integrated into an industrial toolchain in the automotive domain. The tool PASS (**P**roperty **ASS**istant) [21] guides the user by a set of questions towards a suitable pattern from which a μ-calculus formula and a UML sequence diagram can be generated. The tool PROPEL [22] represents patterns in natural language and by finite-state automata. The COMPASS toolset [6] supports the original patterns by Dwyer, real-time- and probabilistic patterns. While the previous mentioned tools use the pattern catalog from [1,6,7], the work [16] presents different patterns and a tool for the requirement specification and automated translation to a formal language. The tool DDPSL [11] goes a step further by allowing the user to fill the templates in a pattern with assumptions on the variables using a defined set of logical and temporal operators. The ReSA tool [18] allows an automated consistency check of requirements on multiple abstraction levels using SAT checking. The commercial tool BTC EmbeddedPlatform[1] also offers the possibility to formalize textual requirements in a pattern-based language. Former versions of the tool support a pattern catalog but the latest release uses the *universal pattern* [23] that offers a graphical specification for trigger-action based requirements. Our tool focuses on the key patterns but allows for automated generation of test cases, as well as properties for Simulink model and source code verification.

Besides the tools for pattern-based specifications, several experience reports on using specification patterns have been published. In [4], a case study in the field of service-based applications is presented. [24] reports on an approach using pattern-based specifications in the area of work flow modeling. Bosch company investigated the suitability of the pattern catalog from [14] for 289 informal behavioral requirements from their automotive projects. A report on the integration of a pattern-based specification tool in an industrial (automotive) tool chain is given in [8,9]. A restricted set of patterns was used for the formal specifications within the PICASSOS project [5]. A system for modeling and testing flight critical software was presented in [19], but their focus lies on test-case generation and modeling structural aspects of the software system, whereas our focus is on the automated translation of requirements.

3   Pattern-Based Requirement Specification Language

Requirement documents are commonplace in the automotive industry and are usually written in natural language by a large number of stakeholders. These

---

[1] https://www.btc-es.de/en/products/btc-embeddedplatform/.

Table 1. Pattern distributions for three different controller models.

Pattern	LSC		DSR		ECC	
Invariant	35	85.4%	50	92.6%	80	97.6%
Time-bounded response (exact bound)	5	12.2%	4	7.4%	2	2.4%
Event-bounded response	1	2.4%	0	0.0%	0	0.0%

can include engineers and other people without a strong background in formal methods, which may lead to ambiguous requirements. Specification patterns may assist engineers in writing complete and unambiguous textual requirements. A pattern defines the behavior that is described by a requirement and uses templates for additional information like the specification of events and durations. In contrast to most existing approaches, events are specified by a constrained grammar, and higher-order operators, e.g. hysteresis[2], are supported to enable specifying new operations on events.

Goals. The pattern-based specification language should produce human readable specifications. A formal semantics avoids ambiguities and allows the automated generation of tool-specific requirement specifications. Our aim is to keep the pattern language simple such that no expert knowledge is needed and the learning curve for requirement engineers is low. We believe that a limited number of simple patterns reduces incorrect choices of patterns or scopes when writing requirements while still covering a high percentage of requirements.

Why Yet Another Specification Language? Tools like BTC EmbeddedPlatform come with their own, existing, pattern-based specification language and there are existing tools for pattern-based specification. Nonetheless we decided that creating our own language and tool was the better choice. A key difference from many established pattern-based specification languages is that we also require the events to be specified using a constrained grammar, enforcing the events to be formalizable properties. This, in turn, allows us to immediately export the entire property to a supported format without the need for any further user interaction.

Adding new features or constructs like higher-order operators (e.g. hysteresis) is easy to achieve, requiring only very modular changes to the grammar and the back-end exporter classes. We want to be able to create our own pool of higher-order operators for event specification that can be used to ease the burden of formalization for the engineers. Our own language allowed us to do rapid prototyping while coming up with new ideas, without the burden of getting all stakeholders of an established language on board beforehand.

Syntax. We used [1,7,14] as a starting point to design our *pattern-based requirement specification language* $\mathcal{L}$, whose grammar is shown in Fig. 2; for more details see also Appendix A.

---

[2] Hysteresis is a functionality often used to prevent rapid toggling when observing an input signal against some threshold by introducing an upper and a lower delta.

```
specification: scope pattern;
scope:          initially | globally;
pattern:        invariant | response;
initially:      'At system start,';
globally:       'At each time step,';
invariant:      '[' event '] holds.';
response:       'if [' event '] has been valid for [' duration '],'
                'then in response, after a delay of [' duration '],'
                '[' event '] is valid for [' duration '].';
event:          identifier | event AND event | ...| term ≤ term | ...
term:           identifier | term + term |...
duration:       uint unit;
uint:           [1..9] [0..9]*;
unit:           'simulation steps' | 'milliseconds' | 'seconds'
                | 'minutes' | 'hours';
```

Fig. 2. Syntax of our pattern-based requirement specification language.

Requirement *specifications* consist of a scope followed by a pattern. We start with a limited set of scopes and patterns that can be extended later to cover further specification types. However, these limited sets were sufficient to formalize more than 90% of the requirements in all three case studies (Low Speed Control for Parking (LSC), Driveline State Request (DSR) and E-Clutch Control (ECC)) we considered in [2,20] (see Table 1). Other internal case studies from Ford show similar results.

Currently two *scopes* are supported: the `initially` scope is used to express that a property should hold at system start, i.e. at time step 0 of a simulation before any operations have been performed, while the `globally` scope expresses that a property should hold at each time step of an execution, but starting after the first execution. In [1,7,14] there are further scopes like `before R`, `after Q`, `between Q and R` and `after Q until R` that can be considered for future inclusion.

We support two *patterns* for defining which property is required to hold for a given scope. The `invariant` pattern allows to state that a certain event holds (at each time step within the specified scope), and covers both the `absence` and the `universality` patterns from [7] if the negation of events is supported. The `response` pattern specifies causalities between two events: the continuous validity of a trigger event for a given trigger duration implies that after a fixed separative duration the response event holds continuously for a given response duration.

The *events* in the above patterns are built from identifiers (`signals`, constants and (calibration) `parameters`) using a set of `functions` and `operators`. We support those operators and functions that were used in our case studies, including the Boolean operators AND, OR, NOT and IMPLIES, the relational operators $<$, $\leq$, $>$, $\geq$ and $=$, the arithmetic operators $+$, $-$, $\cdot$ and $/$, absolute value, minimum, maximum, functions for bit extraction (bit x of variable y) and

scopes: $\llbracket \texttt{initially pattern} \rrbracket = \llbracket \texttt{pattern} \rrbracket$
          $\llbracket \texttt{globally pattern} \rrbracket \ = \bigcirc \, \square \, \llbracket \texttt{pattern} \rrbracket$

patterns: $\llbracket [e] \ holds. \rrbracket \qquad = \llbracket e \rrbracket$
          $\llbracket if \ [e_P] \ has \ been \ valid \ for \ [d_P], \ then \ in \ response, \ after \ a \ delay \ of \ [d],$
          $[e_Q] \ is \ valid \ for \ [d_Q]. \rrbracket$

$$= \left(\square^{[\le \llbracket d_P \rrbracket]} \ \llbracket e_P \rrbracket \right) \to \left(\lozenge^{[= \llbracket d_P \rrbracket + \llbracket d \rrbracket]} \ \square^{[\le \llbracket d_Q \rrbracket]} \ \llbracket e_Q \rrbracket \right)$$

events: $\llbracket \texttt{identifier} \rrbracket \quad = \texttt{identifier} \quad \dots$
           $\llbracket e_1 \ \texttt{AND} \ e_2 \rrbracket \quad = \llbracket e_1 \rrbracket \wedge \llbracket e_2 \rrbracket \quad \dots$
           $\llbracket t_1 \le t_2 \rrbracket \qquad = \llbracket t_1 \rrbracket \le \llbracket t_2 \rrbracket \quad \dots$
durations: $\llbracket n \ seconds \rrbracket \qquad = \frac{1000 \cdot n}{D_{\text{Step}}} \quad \dots$

Fig. 3. Semantics of our pattern-based requirement specification language.

time delays (value of x n steps ago). The complete ANTLR grammar for events is presented in Appendix A. We plan in future work to incorporate more advanced operators like *state change* ("the value of [param] transitions from [const1] to [const2]"), different variants of *hysteresis* functions, *saturation, rate limiter* and *ramping up* functions and *lookup tables*. Note that though custom operators and functions allow users a more efficient specification, special operators (e.g. lookup tables) might not be realizable in all specification languages for which export is provided.

Semantics. We define the semantics of requirement specifications using linear temporal logic with quantitative temporal operators to express time durations, that is MTL [15]. The main semantical components are shown in Fig. 3 using only future temporal modalities (straightforward and therefore not listed in Fig. 3 are the semantics for events and durations, see Appendix A for a complete definition). We use D_{Step} to denote the step-size, here in milliseconds. We support durations that are multiples of D_{Step}. An equivalent semantics using past temporal modalities is given in Appendix A. The difference in terms of a time-shift between the formulations using past (resp. future) operators is illustrated in Fig. 4. The two equivalent semantics support the export of a pattern-based specification into different specification languages. For example the specification language of the analysis tool SLDV only supports past temporal operators.

4   Pattern-Based Requirement Specification Tool

We have implemented a pattern-based specification tool as a prototype for use inside this research project to support requirement engineers in writing unambiguous and complete textual requirements. Our focus was to create a modular tool that is easy to learn and extendible, if in the future a larger set of scopes, patterns or operators needs to be supported.

A user can either import signals, calibratables and constants from a file, or create, change and delete them manually. Calibratable parameters remain constant during software execution but can be adjusted before the execution for

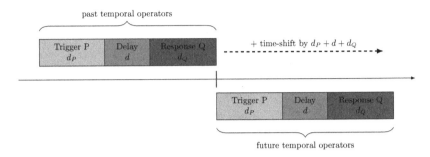

past temporal operators

| Trigger P d_P | Delay d | Response Q d_Q |

+ time-shift by $d_P + d + d_Q$

| Trigger P d_P | Delay d | Response Q d_Q |

future temporal operators

Fig. 4. Evaluation of a response pattern with past or future operators. The present is represented by the red tick on the timeline. (Color figure online)

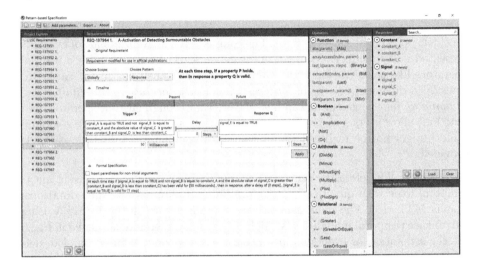

Fig. 5. User interface of our pattern-based specification tool.

tuning or selecting the possible functionalities. Captured data includes a name, description, minimum and maximum values, dimensions, a value, the data type and the variable type (signal, calibratable or constant). With the information of available variables readily available, the tool checks specified events for whether all referenced variables actually exist.

The current version of the tool provides export functionality for a selected requirement or for all of them. Export formats are textual (.txt), SLDV (.m), BTC (.spec) and C (.c) specifications. The last one is compatible with the SV-COMP standard [3] and can be used for formal verification with e.g. the *Ultimate Automizer* [12].

The requirement specification panel in Fig. 5 is the main panel of our tool. A scope and a pattern must be selected for the requirement. A textual translation of the scope and pattern is given as well as a visualization that shows the time steps where the chosen pattern is evaluated, see Fig. 5. Events are built using operators, functions, signals, constants and calibration parameters. For each event, a duration and a time unit can be specified. Additionally, for patterns with more than one event, a time delay between events can be specified, again together with a time unit.

If the pattern-based specification is incomplete or if it contains specification errors, the lower part of the specification panel provides the list of errors and warnings. When all issues are resolved, a textual formal specification is generated from the specification. The modular set-up of the tool allows to add further exporters, e.g. to generate specification in a logic like MTL in a straightforward manner.

Our prototypical implementation supports the functions `abs(param)`, `min(param1, param2)`, `max(param1, param2)`, `last(param)`, `last(param, steps)` and `extractBit(index, param)`. For an explanation see Appendix A. Parenthesis expressions can be built using `(param)` and the basic boolean operators `not`, `and`, `or` and `implication` are provided.

5   Requirement Specification Export to Verification Tools

5.1   Export to SLDV

A formal pattern specification is exported to Simulink in the form of a Matlab script. This script generates a specification block inside a model on the currently selected hierarchy level. For verification on model-level, the topmost level of a model should be selected, whereas for verification on subsystem-level the topmost level of the subsystem should be selected. To implement the semantics of $\mathcal{L}$ in Simulink, we use a custom-build, modular and interchangeable block library and existing Simulink logic blocks.

The following requirement is used as a running example to illustrate the various steps:

Example 1. At each time step if [(((signal_A is equal to TRUE) and ((not signal_B) is equal to constant_A)) and ((the absolute value of signal_C) is greater than constant_B)) and (signal_D is less than constant_C)] has been valid for [50 ms], then in response, after a delay of [0 steps], [signal_E is equal to TRUE] is valid for [1 step].

To support the requirement specification for SLDV, we implemented a Simulink library with building blocks for all elements of our requirement specification language. The library provides sub-libraries for the specification of scopes, patterns and events.

Verification Subsystem. Figure 6 shows the topmost generated block, a verification subsystem. Its input are all input and output signals of the Simulink model that are used by the generated requirement specification. The content of verification subsystems is considered during formal verification but ignored during code generation and is not part of the generated code. The top-level verification subsystem contains a separate verification subsystem for each requirement.

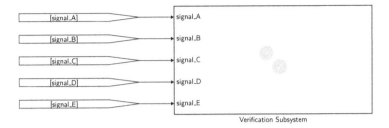

Fig. 6. A sample verification subsystem block.

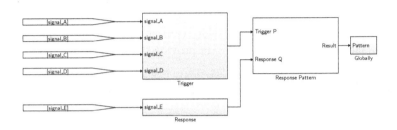

Fig. 7. The `responseTbEb` pattern of the verification subsystem in Fig. 6.

The verification subsystem subsumes the implementation of the actual requirements, i.e. encoding the expected functional behavior, by separating it into parts: Transformations on inputs, and implementing timed behavioral aspects. A requirement specification consists of three parts: a set of events, a pattern and a scope; each is represented by distinct blocks in the library. Figure 7 shows an example requirement specification that consists of a `globally` scope, a `response` pattern and two events.

Scopes. A scope block defines the time steps during which a pattern needs to be evaluated. The pattern result is a Boolean input parameter. At each simulation step, either the pattern result or `true` (if the pattern result needs not to be evaluated at the current time step) is the input of a proof objective. During formal verification, `SLDV` analyzes this proof objective. A requirement is violated if the input of a proof objective can be `false` at any simulation step.

The `initially` scope evaluates the pattern result only at system start, while the `globally` scope evaluates the pattern result at each time step. Figure 8(a) and (b) show the implementations of scopes `globally` and `initially`, respectively. The delay block is initialized with the value 1, while all subsequent output values will be 0. The time shift (see Sect. 3) is realized by the `Detector` block.

Patterns. A pattern receives the Boolean signals from the events as inputs along with the time duration and delays between events specified as mask parameters of the pattern. A pattern block ensures the correct order of events and handles timing aspects like event durations and delays between events. Simulink blocks

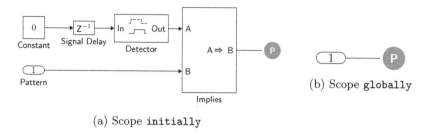

(a) Scope `initially`

(b) Scope `globally`

Fig. 8. Proof objectives for the scopes `initially` and `globally`.

for time durations and delays are provided by our Simulink specification library. The output of a pattern block is again a Boolean signal. In Fig. 7, the blocks Trigger and Response contain the part of signal transformation, whereas the block labeled Response Pattern represents the details of the duration- and delay checks, as shown in Fig. 9. Inside this subsystem block, the event order (trigger before response) is established together with the specified time delay between the two events.

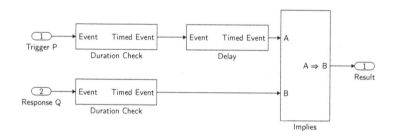

Fig. 9. The implementation of the Trigger/Response pattern.

In our example, the trigger has to be true for 50 ms. This duration is checked by the Duration Check block which returns a Boolean true iff its input evaluated to true for a given number of time steps. A delay block is then used to account for the response duration and a possible fixed delay between trigger and response.

Events. Each event is specified in its subsystem. The event subsystems are connected with the input signals of the verification subsystem using From blocks. An event is built using the blocks provided by our Simulink specification library. These building blocks must be connected in accordance with the rules of our event grammar. The output of an event specification is a Boolean signal. Figure 10 shows the necessary signal transformations for the trigger of the example requirement.

Connection to the Simulink Model. After the automated insertion of the verification subsystem at a user-chosen level in the model, the inputs of the

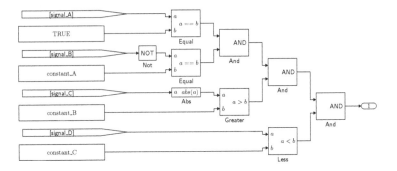

Fig. 10. The logic of the trigger condition of the example requirement.

verification system need to be connected to the corresponding signals in the model. Because of possible data dependency issues, we use global data store blocks for accessing the signals. For selecting the source signal, we traverse the model in a hierarchical approach and try to find the first match of a named signal matching the one being looked for. A data store write is then inserted into the model at the matched location, allowing us to generate the corresponding global data store read block next to our verification subsystem.

5.2   Export to BTC EmbeddedPlatform

We support the export of formalized requirements to BTC's input format, so-called SPEC files. They contain an XML-based structured representation of the requirements and their patterns. Small transformations are applied during export to match BTC's pattern semantics. We consider the time step 0 to be the first time step in the initially scope. This means that we start to evaluate the pattern directly after initialization, i.e. before the first computation step. In contrast, BTC starts the evaluation after the first computation step. It is not possible to check initial variable valuations in BTC, therefore, an error is presented when exporting a requirement with scope initially to BTC. The generated SPEC files can then be imported into BTC EmbeddedPlatform and used for verification.

5.3   Export to Textual Requirements

Formally specified requirements can easily be exported to textual form. As many engineers and stakeholders without a solid background in formal methods are involved in the design, testing and implementation of the defined software components, it is vital to present the agreed-upon requirements in a textual representation, which is easy to understand, distribute and review. Our export feature for textual requirements additionally supports automatically introducing parenthesis around all non-trivial arguments used in the specification to prohibit misinterpretations or misunderstandings of the written specification—a problem we encountered several times in [2, 20].

5.4   Export to SV-Comp-style C Code

To enable the use of state-of-the-art academic C code model checkers, we explicitly encode our pattern semantics in C code. This enables to embed all assumptions and behavior directly in the code, instead of going around it with LTL specifications or similar, as supported by some tools. We built a boiler-plate framework for initializing parameters and calibratables (enabling verifying with varying calibrations) and updating input variables after every step. We decided to use the established __VERIFIER_error(); functionality for encoding violations of the behavior allowed by the patterns as supported by many code verifiers such as more than 20 tools participating in the SV-comp.

6   Requirement-Based Test Vector Generation

The automated generation of an SLDV specification can be reused for automated requirement-based test vector generation. The Automotive Functional Safety standard ISO26262 [13] recommends to identify missing test vectors and unintended behavior of the implemented model by: "For each requirement, a set of test vectors should be generated. Afterwards, the structural coverage of the requirement-based test vectors shall be measured according to a suitable coverage metrics. The industry norm recommends different coverage metrics depending on the ASIL-level of the model. In case the coverage metrics reveals uncovered parts of the model, a further analysis is needed: either test vectors are missing or unintended functionality in the model has been detected".

If requirements are verified using formal verification and the implemented requirement is shown to be valid, additional, manual creation of test vectors should not be necessary. Manual creation of test vectors is a tedious work and should be limited to those requirements that are not tested using formal verification. We propose to reuse the automated generation of SLDV requirement specification for generating test vectors for these same requirements. For this purpose, we annotate the generated specification with so-called *test objectives* (see Fig. 11) automatically. The test objectives specify the signal valuations that must be considered during test-vector generation.

The set of requirement-based test vectors depends on the chosen coverage metric. For *condition coverage*, a set of test vectors is required such that each condition takes every possible value, while for *decision coverage* a set of test vectors must generate every possible outcome for each decision. Decision coverage is closely related to *branch coverage*, where conditional and unconditional branches are considered. According to ISO26262, branch coverage is suitable for requirement coverage at software unit-level for ASIL A to C. However, for ASIL D, *modified condition/decision coverage* (MC/DC) is highly recommended. Additionally, it is required that all conditions contributing to a decision must independently affect the outcome of the decision.

To achieve condition coverage, test objectives must be added to all Boolean input signals. For decision coverage, test objectives are needed for all Boolean output signals. If test objectives are added to all Boolean output signals and to all Boolean input signals of blocks with more than one input parameter, *condition/decision coverage* is achieved, which guarantees both condition and decision coverage. For MC/DC coverage, test objectives are hard to generate and currently out of scope of our project. One way to at least partly cover MC/DC would be to generate test objectives for all Boolean combinations of possible input signals. For an OR block, we currently generate vectors for both outcomes, but "true" could be generated by inputs 01, 10 or 11—by adding additional logic we can enforce all combinations to be generated.

Alternatively, we propose to use the built-in function of SLDV to compute a set of test vectors for MC/DC coverage. Unfortunately, this functionality is currently only available on model-level. To get requirement-based test vectors for the model, MC/DC must be checked at requirement (i.e. subsystem) level while test vectors must be generated for the complete model.

To automate the requirement-based test vector generation, we added test objectives for *condition/decision coverage* to all blocks in our Simulink formal specification library. The relational operators compute Boolean output signals that also must be annotated with test objectives. Additional test objectives are necessary for all temporal operators to assure the correct length of generated test cases. Since we handle Boolean signals only, all test objectives can take the values true and false. Figure 11 presents the implementation of the annotated Boolean *Or* operator from our specification library.

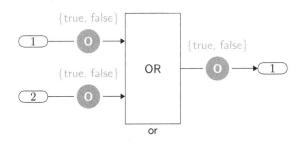

Fig. 11. A logic OR block with test objectives attached.

Annotating the specification library allows the flexibility of adding/removing test objectives without adapting the source code of the specification tool. This enables the user to maintain a set of specification libraries for different coverage metrics or to create a library without any test objective annotations.

7   Conclusion and Future Work

In this paper we presented a prototypical pattern-based specification tool together with automated translations to SLDV and BTC EmbeddedPlatform together with an adaption of the SLDV input for automated test-case generation. This corresponds to the vision of enabling engineers to specify requirements with formal semantics *once* and then applying the requirements in *multiple analyses*. The tool was designed as a prototype for use inside this research project as a proof of concept.

Although a big step towards a highly automated automotive verification process has been made within this project and investigations by Ford have been producing encouraging results, this is only a proof-of-concept and many open problems still need to be resolved.

As future work we plan the extension of our pattern set with a few further relevant elements like time- and event-bounded response patterns. We plan to tackle the automated translation of textual legacy requirements into formal notation. Scripts are needed to further automate verification at different development levels with suitable configuration parameters, and to trigger the verification process if changes are applied to the model or the requirements. Another module should monitor the verification results and automatically report conspicuous behavior if the comparison with previous results reveals deviations. In case of invalid verification results, counterexamples should be analyzed.

We plan to use the export of formalized requirements to SV-COMP like C-code patterns in order to benchmark academic C-code model checkers on industrial examples against commercial tools.

A   Appendix

A version of this paper containing the full appendix can be found at http://arxiv.org/abs/1906.07083.

References

1. Autili, M., Grunske, L., Lumpe, M., Pelliccione, P., Tang, A.: Aligning qualitative, real-time, and probabilistic property specification patterns using a structured English grammar. IEEE Trans. Softw. Eng. **41**(7), 620–638 (2015). https://doi.org/10.1109/TSE.2015.2398877
2. Berger, P., Katoen, J.-P., Ábrahám, E., Waez, M.T.B., Rambow, T.: Verifying auto-generated C code from simulink. In: Havelund, K., Peleska, J., Roscoe, B., de Vink, E. (eds.) FM 2018. LNCS, vol. 10951, pp. 312–328. Springer, Cham (2018). https://doi.org/10.1007/978-3-319-95582-7_18
3. Beyer, D.: Software verification with validation of results. In: Legay, A., Margaria, T. (eds.) TACAS 2017. LNCS, vol. 10206, pp. 331–349. Springer, Heidelberg (2017). https://doi.org/10.1007/978-3-662-54580-5_20
4. Bianculli, D., Ghezzi, C., Pautasso, C., Senti, P.: Specification patterns from research to industry: a case study in service-based applications. In: Proceedings of ICSE, pp. 968–976. IEEE (2012). https://doi.org/10.1109/ICSE.2012.6227125
5. Botham, J., et al.: PICASSOS - Practical applications of automated formal methods to safety related automotive systems. In: SAE Technical Paper. SAE International (2017). https://doi.org/10.4271/2017-01-0063
6. Bozzano, M., Cimatti, A., Katoen, J., Nguyen, V.Y., Noll, T., Roveri, M.: Safety, dependability and performance analysis of extended AADL models. Comput. J. **54**(5), 754–775 (2011). https://doi.org/10.1093/comjnl/bxq024

7. Dwyer, M.B., Avrunin, G.S., Corbett, J.C.: Patterns in property specifications for finite-state verification. In: Proceedings of ICSE, pp. 411–420. ACM (1999). https://doi.org/10.1145/302405.302672

8. Filipovikj, P., Jagerfield, T., Nyberg, M., Rodriguez-Navas, G., Seceleanu, C.: Integrating pattern-based formal requirements specification in an industrial toolchain. In: Proceedings of COMPSAC, pp. 167–173. IEEE (2016). https://doi.org/10.1109/COMPSAC.2016.140

9. Filipovikj, P., Nyberg, M., Rodriguez-Navas, G.: Reassessing the pattern-based approach for formalizing requirements in the automotive domain. In: Proceedings of RE, pp. 444–450. IEEE (2014). https://doi.org/10.1109/RE.2014.6912296

10. Grunske, L.: Specification patterns for probabilistic quality properties. In: Proceedings of ICSE, pp. 31–40. ACM (2008). https://doi.org/10.1145/1368088.1368094

11. Guglielmo, L.D., Fummi, F., Orlandi, N., Pravadelli, G.: DDPSL: an easy way of defining properties. In: Proceedings of ICCD, pp. 468–473. IEEE (2010). https://doi.org/10.1109/ICCD.2010.5647654

12. Heizmann, M., Hoenicke, J., Podelski, A.: Software model checking for people who love automata. In: Sharygina, N., Veith, H. (eds.) CAV 2013. LNCS, vol. 8044, pp. 36–52. Springer, Heidelberg (2013). https://doi.org/10.1007/978-3-642-39799-8_2

13. ISO Central Secretary: Road vehicles - Functional safety. Standard ISO 26262-1:2011. International Organization for Standardization, Geneva, CH (2011). https://www.iso.org/standard/62711.html

14. Konrad, S., Cheng, B.H.C.: Real-time specification patterns. In: Proceedings of ICSE, pp. 372–381. ACM (2005). https://doi.org/10.1145/1062455.1062526

15. Koymans, R.: Specifying real-time properties with metric temporal logic. Real-Time Syst. **2**(4), 255–299 (1990). https://doi.org/10.1007/BF01995674

16. Liu, S., Wang, X., Miao, W.: Supporting requirements analysis using pattern-based formal specification construction. In: Butler, M., Conchon, S., Zaïdi, F. (eds.) ICFEM 2015. LNCS, vol. 9407, pp. 100–115. Springer, Cham (2015). https://doi.org/10.1007/978-3-319-25423-4_7

17. Lumpe, M., Meedeniya, I., Grunske, L.: PSPWizard: machine-assisted definition of temporal logical properties with specification patterns. In: Proceedings of SIGSOFT/FSE, pp. 468–471. ACM (2011). https://doi.org/10.1145/2025113.2025193

18. Mahmud, N., Seceleanu, C., Ljungkrantz, O.: Resa tool: structured requirements specification and sat-based consistency-checking. In: FedCSIS, pp. 1737–1746 (2016)

19. Moitra, A., et al.: Towards development of complete and conflict-free requirements. In: RE, pp. 286–296. IEEE Computer Society (2018)

20. Nellen, J., Rambow, T., Waez, M.T.B., Ábrahám, E., Katoen, J.-P.: Formal verification of automotive simulink controller models: empirical technical challenges, evaluation and recommendations. In: Havelund, K., Peleska, J., Roscoe, B., de Vink, E. (eds.) FM 2018. LNCS, vol. 10951, pp. 382–398. Springer, Cham (2018). https://doi.org/10.1007/978-3-319-95582-7_23

21. Remenska, D., Willemse, T.A.C., Templon, J., Verstoep, K., Bal, H.: Property specification made easy: harnessing the power of model checking in UML designs. In: Ábrahám, E., Palamidessi, C. (eds.) FORTE 2014. LNCS, vol. 8461, pp. 17–32. Springer, Heidelberg (2014). https://doi.org/10.1007/978-3-662-43613-4_2

22. Smith, R.L., Avrunin, G.S., Clarke, L.A., Osterweil, L.J.: PROPEL: an approach supporting property elucidation. In: Proceedings of ICSE, pp. 11–21. IEEE (2002). https://doi.org/10.1109/ICSE.2002.1007952

23. Teige, T., Bienmüller, T., Holberg, H.J.: Universal pattern - Formalization, testing, coverage, verification, and test case generation for safety-critical requirements. In: Proceedings of MBMV (2016)

24. Wong, P.Y.H., Gibbons, J.: Property specifications for workflow modelling. In: Leuschel, M., Wehrheim, H. (eds.) IFM 2009. LNCS, vol. 5423, pp. 56–71. Springer, Heidelberg (2009). https://doi.org/10.1007/978-3-642-00255-7_5

The Impact of Requirement Splitting on the Efficiency of Supervisory Control Synthesis

Martijn Goorden[1]($\boxtimes$) (ID), Joanna van de Mortel-Fronczak[1](ID), Michel Reniers[1](ID),
Wan Fokkink[2](ID), and Jacobus Rooda[1]

[1] Eindhoven University of Technology, Eindhoven, The Netherlands
{m.a.goorden,j.m.v.d.mortel,m.a.reniers,j.e.rooda}@tue.nl
[2] Vrije Universiteit, Amsterdam, The Netherlands
w.j.fokkink@vu.nl

Abstract. Supervisory control theory provides means to synthesize supervisors for a cyber-physical system based on models of the uncontrolled system components and models of the control requirements. Although several synthesis procedures have been proposed and automated, obtaining correct and useful models of industrial-size applications that are needed as their input remains a challenge. We show that the efficiency of supervisor synthesis techniques tends to increase significantly if a single large requirement is split into a set of smaller requirements. A theoretical underpinning is provided for showing the strength of this modeling guideline. Moreover, several examples from the literature as well as some real-life case studies are included for illustration.

Keywords: Supervisory control synthesis · Automata · Requirements engineering

1 Introduction

The design of supervisors for cyber-physical systems has become a challenge as they include more and more components to control and functions to fulfill, while at the same time market demands require verified safety, decreasing costs, and decreasing time-to-market for these systems. Model-based systems engineering methods can help in overcoming these difficulties, see [23].

For the design of supervisors, the supervisory control theory of Ramadge-Wonham [21,22] provides means to synthesize supervisors from a model of the uncontrolled plant (describing what the system *could* do) and a model of the control requirements (describing what the system *should* do). Such a supervisor interacts with the plant by dynamically disabling some controllable events. Then

Supported by Rijkswaterstaat, part of the Dutch Ministry of Infrastructure and Water Management.

K. G. Larsen and T. Willemse (Eds.): FMICS 2019, LNCS 11687, pp. 76–92, 2019.
https://doi.org/10.1007/978-3-030-27008-7_5

synthesis guarantees by construction that the closed-loop behavior of the supervisor and the plant adheres to all requirements and furthermore is nonblocking, controllable, and maximally permissive.

A major drawback of synthesizing monolithic supervisors is its computational complexity, both in the time and memory domain. Although the time complexity of this step is polynomial in the number of states that represent the system, this number increases exponentially with the number of constituent models of the different components in the system, as already observed in [22]. For industrial systems, the number of states can easily reach an order of 10^{100} states. Different supervisor architectures are exploited in an attempt to overcome these computational difficulties: modular [20], hierarchical [34], decentralized [28], distributed [3], multilevel [12], and compositional supervisory control synthesis [18]. Modular, decentralized, and multilevel synthesis are closely related and in this paper we refer to them as module-based supervisor architectures.

While these architectures claim to gain computational efficiency, in practice the observed gain depends on the models provided as input for these synthesis algorithms. Moreover, as systems can be modeled in several ways, i.e., there is not a single correct model formulation for a certain plant and its requirements, an engineer might model an industrial system in a disadvantageous way and might (wrongly) conclude that supervisory control synthesis is not possible for his system.

To the best of our knowledge, not much attention has been paid in the literature to the fact that the way in which models are defined can be of a significant influence on the efficiency of the synthesis procedure. A notable exception is [11], where symmetry in the model is exploited to efficiently synthesize a supervisor. Others [6,7,10] have indicated that modeling the system and its requirements is difficult, and introduced concepts like, e.g., templates to assist the engineer in modeling correctly, i.e., the obtained models exhibit the behavior the engineer intended to model.

The purpose of this paper is to provide a modeling guideline to (re)formulate the models such that the applicability of supervisory control synthesis techniques increases. This modeling guideline concerns the modeling of the requirements and expresses that they should be split into smaller ones when possible. We show theoretically why this modeling guideline increases the applicability of supervisory control synthesis. Essentially, smaller requirements allow module-based synthesis techniques to solve numerous but computationally easier problems instead of those obtained with large requirements, because each new requirement relates to fewer plant models than the original large requirement. For multilevel synthesis, this effect is visualized by displaying the dependencies with a Dependency Structure Matrix, see [5]. Experimental results of several case studies show that this efficiency gain can indeed be obtained in practice. By proposing this guideline and by providing examples, our aim is to assist practitioners in applying supervisory control synthesis.

Requirement specifications in practice often violate the aforementioned guideline, which turns out to be detrimental for supervisory control synthesis.

Although the guideline may sound somewhat obvious, it required several real-life case studies with supervisory control synthesis to grasp its importance [25–27]. These case studies were performed in the context of a research project with Rijkswaterstaat, the national organisation responsible for the main infrastructure like roads and bridges in the Netherlands. Notably, the so-called Oisterwijksebaan revolving bridge in the Dutch city of Tilburg was recently operated by PLC code automatically generated from the requirements, by means of the CIF supervisory control toolset [2]. These case studies have inspired us to formulate several modeling guidelines. The aim of this paper is to describe one of them in detail.

The paper is structured as follows. Section 2 provides the preliminaries of this paper. Section 3 continues by discussing the guideline concerning the model of the requirement in detail including a theoretical substantiation. In Sect. 4, the guideline is demonstrated with an example of supervisory control for an infrastructural system. Section 5 provides experimental results with cases also from other application domains where applying the guideline benefits supervisory control synthesis. The paper concludes with Sect. 6.

2   Preliminaries

This section provides a brief summary of concepts related to automata and supervisory control theory relevant for this paper. These concepts are taken from [4,33].

2.1   Automata

An automaton is a five-tuple $G = (Q, \Sigma, \delta, q_0, Q_m)$, where Q is the (finite) state set, Σ is the alphabet of events, $\delta : Q \times \Sigma \to Q$ the partial function called the transition function, $q_0 \in Q$ the initial state, and $Q_m \subseteq Q$ the set of marked states. The alphabet $\Sigma = \Sigma_c \cup \Sigma_u$ is partitioned into sets containing the controllable events (Σ_c) and the uncontrollable events (Σ_u), and Σ^* is the set of all finite strings of events in Σ, including empty string ε.

We denote with $\delta(q, \sigma)!$ that there exists a transition from state $q \in Q$ labeled with event σ, i.e., $\delta(q, \sigma)$ is defined. The transition function can be extended in the natural way to strings as $\delta(q, s\sigma) = \delta(\delta(q, s), \sigma)$ where $s \in \Sigma^*$, $\sigma \in \Sigma$, and $\delta(q, s\sigma)!$ if $\delta(q, s)! \wedge \delta(\delta(q, s), \sigma)!$. We define $\delta(q, \varepsilon) = q$ for the empty string. The language generated by the automaton G is $\mathcal{L}(G) = \{s \in \Sigma^* \mid \delta(q_0, s)!\}$ and the language marked by the automaton is $\mathcal{L}_m(G) = \{s \in \Sigma^* \mid \delta(q_0, s) \in Q_m\}$.

A state q of an automaton is called reachable if there is a string $s \in \Sigma^*$ with $\delta(q_0, s)!$ and $\delta(q_0, s) = q$. A state q is coreachable if there is a string $s \in \Sigma^*$ with $\delta(q, s)!$ and $\delta(q, s) \in Q_m$. An automaton is called nonblocking if every reachable state is coreachable.

Two automata can be combined by synchronous composition.

Definition 1. *Let $G_1 = (Q_1, \Sigma_1, \delta_1, q_{0,1}, Q_{m,1})$, $G_2 = (Q_2, \Sigma_2, \delta_2, q_{0,2}, Q_{m,2})$ be two automata. The synchronous composition of G_1 and G_2 is defined as*

$$G_1 \parallel G_2 = (Q_1 \times Q_2, \Sigma_1 \cup \Sigma_2, \delta_{1\parallel 2}, (q_{0,1}, q_{0,2}), Q_{m,1} \times Q_{m,2})$$

where

$$\delta_{1\|2}((x_1,x_2),\sigma) = \begin{cases} (\delta_1(x_1,\sigma),\delta_2(x_2,\sigma)) & \textit{if } \sigma \in \Sigma_1 \cap \Sigma_2, \delta_1(x_1,\sigma)!, \\ & \textit{and } \delta_2(x_2,\sigma)! \\ (\delta_1(x_1,\sigma),x_2) & \textit{if } \sigma \in \Sigma_1 \setminus \Sigma_2 \textit{ and } \delta_1(x_1,\sigma)! \\ (x_1,\delta_2(x_2,\sigma)) & \textit{if } \sigma \in \Sigma_2 \setminus \Sigma_1 \textit{ and } \delta_2(x_2,\sigma)! \\ \textit{undefined} & \textit{otherwise.} \end{cases}$$

Synchronous composition is associative and commutative up to reordering of the state components in the composed state set. Two automata are called asynchronous if no events are shared, i.e., they do not synchronize over any event.

A composed system $\mathcal{G}$ is a collection of automata, i.e., $\mathcal{G} = \{G_1,\ldots,G_m\}$. The synchronous composition of a composed system $\mathcal{G}$, denoted by $\| \, \mathcal{G}$, is defined as $\| \, \mathcal{G} = G_1 \| \ldots \| G_m$, and the synchronous composition of two composed systems $\mathcal{G}_1 \| \mathcal{G}_2$ is defined as $(\| \, \mathcal{G}_1) \| (\| \, \mathcal{G}_2)$. A composed system $\mathcal{G} = \{G_1,\ldots,G_m\}$ is called a product system if the alphabets of the automata are pairwise disjoint, i.e., $\Sigma_i \cap \Sigma_j = \emptyset$ for all $i,j \in [1,m], i \neq j$ [22].

Finally, let G and K be two automata with the same alphabet Σ. K is said to be controllable with respect to G if, for every string $s \in \Sigma^*$ and $u \in \Sigma_u$ such that $\delta_K(q_{0,K},s)!$ and $\delta_G(q_{0,G},su)!$, it holds that $\delta_K(q_{0,K},su)!$.

2.2 Supervisory Control Theory

The objective of supervisory control theory is to design an automaton called a supervisor which function is to dynamically disable controllable events so that the closed-loop system of the plant and the supervisor obeys some specified behavior, see [4,21,22,33]. More formally, given a plant model P and requirement model R, the goal is to synthesize supervisor S that adheres to the following control objectives.

- *Safety*: all possible behavior of the closed-loop system $P \| S$ should always satisfy the imposed requirements, i.e., $\mathcal{L}(P \| S) \subseteq \mathcal{L}(P \| R)$.
- *Controllability*: uncontrollable events may never be disabled by the supervisor, i.e., S is controllable with respect to P.
- *Nonblockingness*: the closed-loop system should be able to reach a marked state from every reachable state, i.e., $P \| S$ is nonblocking.
- *Maximal permissiveness*: the supervisor does not restrict more behavior than strictly necessary to enforce safety, controllability, and nonblockingness, i.e., for all other supervisors S' satisfying safety, controllability, and nonblockingness it holds that $\mathcal{L}(P \| S') \subseteq \mathcal{L}(P \| S)$.

For the purpose of supervisor synthesis, requirements can be modeled with automata and state-based expressions, as introduced in [15,16]. The latter is useful in practice, as engineers tend to formulate requirements based on states of the plant. To refer to states of the plant, we introduce the notation $P.q$ which refers to state q of plant P. State references can be combined with the Boolean literals $\mathbf{T}$ and $\mathbf{F}$ and logic connectives to create predicates.

A state-event invariant expression formulates conditions on the enablement of an event based on states of the plant, i.e., the condition should evaluate to true for the event to be enabled. A state-event invariant expression is of the form σ **needs** C where σ is an event and C a predicate stating the condition. Let R be a state-event invariant expression, then $event(R)$ returns the event used in R and $cond(R)$ returns the condition predicate. An example of a state-event invariant expression is a **needs** $P_1.q_1 \wedge P_2.q_2$ formulating that event a is only allowed when automaton P_1 is in state q_1 and automaton P_2 is in state q_2.

Given a composed system representation of the plant $P_s = \{P_1, \ldots, P_m\}$ and a collection of requirements $R_s = \{R_1, \ldots, R_n\}$, we define the tuple (P_s, R_s) as the *control problem* for which we want to synthesize a supervisor.

Monolithic supervisory control synthesis results in a single supervisor S from a single plant model and a single requirement model [21]. There may exist multiple automata representations of the maximally permissive, safe, controllable, and nonblocking supervisor. When the plant model and the requirement model are given as a composed system P_s and R_s, respectively, the monolithic plant model P and requirement model R are obtained by performing the synchronous composition of the models in the respective composed system.

Modular supervisory control synthesis uses the fact that the desired behavior is often specified with a collection of requirements R_s [32]. Instead of first transforming the collection of requirements into a single requirement, as monolithic synthesis does, modular synthesis calculates for each requirement a supervisor based on the plant model. In other words, given a control problem (P_s, R_s) with $R_s = \{R_1, \ldots, R_n\}$, modular synthesis solves n control problems $(P_s, \{R_1\}), \ldots, (P_s, \{R_n\})$. Each control problem $(P_s, \{R_i\})$ for $i \in [1, n]$ results in a safe, controllable, nonblocking, and maximally permissive supervisor S_i. Unfortunately, the collection of supervisors $S_s = \{S_1, \ldots, S_n\}$ can be conflicting, i.e., $S_1 \parallel \ldots \parallel S_n$ can be blocking. A nonconflicting check can verify whether S_s is nonconflicting, see [19,30]. In the case that S_s is nonconflicting, S_s is also safe, controllable, nonblocking, and maximally permissive for the original control problem (P_s, R_s) [32]. In the case that S_s is conflicting, an additional coordinator C can be synthesized such that $S_s \cup \{C\}$ is safe, controllable, nonblocking, and maximally permissive for the original control problem (P_s, R_s) [29]. An extension to this approach, as proposed by [20], states that instead of synthesizing each time with the complete plant P_s, it suffices to only consider those automata that relate to the requirement that is considered. This extension is used in the remainder of this paper.

Decentralized supervisory control synthesis has a similar setting as modular supervisory control synthesis, except that each supervisor is only allowed to observe certain events, called local events, instead of all events [14]. This results in the notion of observability, which is not further discussed in this paper. Nevertheless, also for decentralized supervisory control synthesis with multiple requirements, the obtained supervisors may be conflicting.

Multilevel supervisory control synthesis is inspired by decompositions of systems by engineers [12]. For each subsystem, a supervisor is synthesized based on requirements for only those subsystems. For synthesis, this resembles modular supervisory control in the sense that for multilevel synthesis requirements related to the same subsystem are grouped together before synthesis is performed using those requirements and the plant model representing the subsystem. Again, the collection of synthesized supervisors may be conflicting.

3   Modeling Guideline and Theoretical Substantiation

When formulating the requirements, engineers often tend to think in desired control logic and formulate this logic as requirements. The benefit of supervisory control synthesis is that an engineer is able to focus on *what* the system should do, not *how* it should do it. By shifting from specifying how to specifying what, requirements do not always become smaller. In this section, we show that module-based supervisor architectures benefit from having small requirement models.

We specifically focus on requirements formulated with state-event invariant expressions. This form matches well with requirements formulated in a natural language like, e.g., English, see [16]. Furthermore, requirements for industrial-size applications often originate from failure-mode analysis [17]. States are identified in which some actuator actions would result in unsafe behavior. Therefore, this form is frequently used in real-life case studies of infrastructural systems, see [25–27].

The modeling guideline is formulated as follows:

Split requirements formulated with state-event invariant expressions into a set of smaller ones.

Splitting a state-event invariant expression can be done as follows. Consider requirement σ **needs** C expressing that event σ is only allowed when condition C holds. When this condition is denoted in conjunctive normal form, i.e., $C = C_1 \wedge \ldots \wedge C_l$, the single requirement can be split into multiple requirements σ **needs** $C_1, \ldots, \sigma$ **needs** C_l. Due to the safety property of synthesized supervisors, mentioned in Sect. 2.2, the set of requirements is equivalent to the single requirement. In the rest of this section, we show the benefit of having small requirements theoretically.

Splitting requirements in the form of propositional formula to benefit controller synthesis is a well-known strategy for software product lines, see for example [1,9]. Here, a requirement, called a feature constraint, is split into several configurations (or products) each describing a specific feature combination. For each configuration a controller is synthesized. There are two main differences between that work and the work in this paper. First, a feature constraint limits the possible configurations, while requirements in this paper limit the behavior of one configuration. Second, only one of the synthesized supervisors for a software product line is active (the one for that specific configuration), while in this work all modular supervisors work in conjunction.

3.1   Theoretical Substantiation

Consider the plant being modeled with a product system $P_s = \{P_1, \ldots, P_n\}$, and assume that a requirement R may also be modeled with a set of requirements $R_s = \{R_1, \ldots, R_m\}$ such that $R = \parallel R_s$.[1] Any module-based supervisor architecture ensures that for each (set of) requirement(s) synthesis is performed with only those plant models that are related to the (set of) requirement(s). Reformulating a larger requirement into smaller requirements ensures that module-based supervisor architectures can identify smaller control problems to solve. Hence, a reduction in computational effort is gained.

For modular supervisory control synthesis, the analysis above can be even further detailed as follows. Assume for simplicity that requirement R relates to *all* plant models in P_s, while each smaller requirement $R_j \in R_s$ only refers to a subset $P_{s,j} \subseteq P_s$. In the case of a single requirement R, modular supervisory control synthesis obtains a supervisor for control problem $(P_s, \{R\})$. In the case of multiple smaller requirements, m supervisors are obtained for each control problem $(P_{s,j}, \{R_j\}), 1 \le j \le m$. As $|P_{s,j}| \le |P_s|$ holds, the state-space size of $P_{s,j}$ is smaller or equal than P_s. The computational effort for each synthesis problem is therefore at most equal to that of monolithic synthesis. Yet, m supervisors are synthesized instead of just one, so there is a tradeoff between more control problems to solve and creating smaller control problems to solve. As the state-space size grows exponentially with the number of automata, reducing the number of plant components often has a larger effect than synthesizing more supervisors. Experimental results in Sect. 5 confirm this tradeoff.

For multilevel supervisory control synthesis, we analyze the effect of splitting requirements differently than for modular supervisory control synthesis. In multilevel synthesis, the system is decomposed into subsystems. The dependencies between plant models indicate how the system may be decomposed. For the purpose of multilevel synthesis, analyzing the dependencies between plant models induced by the requirement models is valuable, see [8]. Dependencies between two plant models can be formalized as follows. Given $P_i, P_j \in P_s, P_i \ne P_j$, there is a dependency between P_i and P_j if and only if there exists a requirement $R_k \in R_s$ such that both plant models are used in R_k. A plant model is used in a state-event invariant expression if the event in the requirement originates from the alphabet of that plant model or the condition uses a state of that plant model. For example, in $R = P_1.\sigma$ **needs** $P_2.q_2$, where we used the notation $P_1.\sigma$ to indicate that σ is in the alphabet of P_1, plant models P_1 and P_2 are used in R.

Now, consider requirement $R = P.\sigma$ **needs** C where condition C is the conjunction of some state references, that is $C = P_1.q_1 \wedge \ldots \wedge P_l.q_l$. This requirement results in dependencies between plant models P and P_1, P and P_2, and so on, and

---

[1] Here we have a slight abuse of notation of the synchronous product operator, as this one is only formally defined for automata. In case of two requirements modeled with state-event invariant expressions restricting the same event σ, denoted by $R_i = \sigma$ **needs** $C_1, i \in \{1, 2\}$, we define $R_1 \parallel R_2 = \sigma$ **needs** $C_1 \wedge C_2$.

also in dependencies between any pair $(P_i, P_j), i, j \in [1, l], i \neq j$. These dependencies can be visualized with a Dependency Structure Matrix (DSM), see [5]. Figure 1 shows on the left the DSM D for requirement R with $l = 4$. A dependency between plant models is indicated in this DSM with a 1, no dependency is indicated with an empty cell. Such a visualization shows that all plant models are related with each other. Therefore, multilevel synthesis considers plant models $P, P_1, \ldots, P_l$ as a single subsystem and synthesizes a supervisor for control problem $(\{P, P_1, \ldots, P_l\}, \{R\})$.

When requirement R is split into multiple requirements collected in set $R_s = \{R_1, \ldots, R_l\}$ where $R_k = P.\sigma$ **needs** $P_k.q_k, k \in [0, l]$, the dependencies between the plant models reduces. There are still dependencies between plant models P and P_1, P and P_2, and so on till P and P_l, yet there are no longer dependencies between any pair $(P_i, P_j), i, j \in [1, l], i \neq j$, which is the case with the single requirement R. The effect of splitting requirements is visualized in DSM D' in Fig. 1. The number of dependencies has reduced significantly. This reduction allows multilevel synthesis to decompose the system into smaller subsystems, for example into two subsystems where the first is composed of plant models P, P_1, P_2 and the second of plant models P, P_3, P_4. Similar to modular synthesis, smaller subsystems result in smaller control problems to solve, resulting in a reduction of computational effort. Therefore, splitting requirements can be beneficial for multilevel supervisory control synthesis.

D	P_1	P_2	P_3	P_4	P
P_1	-	1	1	1	1
P_2	1	-	1	1	1
P_3	1	1	-	1	1
P_4	1	1	1	-	1
P	1	1	1	1	-

D'	P_1	P_2	P_3	P_4	P
P_1	-				1
P_2		-			1
P_3			-		1
P_4				-	1
P	1	1	1	1	-

Fig. 1. Left the DSM D constructed with the original requirement R and right the DSM D' with the set of splitted requirements R_s.

3.2 Conflicting Supervisors

Similar to modular synthesis, splitting requirements introduces an over-approximation. Synthesizing multiple supervisors for the split requirements may result in conflicting supervisors.

Consider the following example to illustrate the over-approximation induced by splitting requirements. Figure 2 shows the plant models of a door actuator and a door sensor. Requirement R = A_Door.c_off **needs** S_Door.Off $\wedge$ S_Door.On expresses that the actuator may only be turned off when the door sensor is off and

Fig. 2. Examples of two plant models, with an actuator of a door and a sensor of a door. Concentric circles indicate marked locations. Solid arrows indicate controllable events while dashed arrows indicate uncontrollable events.

on. This requirement can be split into the two requirements $R_1 = $ A_Door.c_off **needs** S_Door.Off and $R_2 = $ A_Door.c_off **needs** S_Door.On. Since an automaton cannot be in two locations at the same time, the condition of the original requirement R can never be satisfied, effectively disabling event c_off indefinitely. A supervisor synthesized for the single requirement disables event c_on of the actuator, because location On is not marked. When the single requirement R is replaced by the two requirements R_1 and R_2, conflicting modular supervisors are synthesized. Each local supervisor will not disable event c_on, allowing the actuator to block in location On.

In general, one can perform a nonconflicting check after synthesizing modular or multilevel supervisors for the split requirements. Yet, as discussed in Sect. 2.2, a nonconflicting check should always be performed if modular or multilevel synthesis is applied, even when requirements are not split. It is an interesting question for future research to determine the effect of splitting requirements on the efficiency of the nonconflicting check and on the synthesis of a coordinator.

The example may indicate that splitting 'bad' requirements could induce conflicts. A requirement demanding an automaton to be in multiple states at the same time would probably not be the intention of an engineer. Yet, there is no guarantee that an engineer does not formulate such a requirement. Notwithstanding the general situation, the following conjecture formalizes the situations encountered in cases where requirements can be split which will not introduce conflicting problems.

Conjecture 1. Let $\mathcal{P} = \{P, P_1, \ldots, P_m\}$ be a product system and requirement $R = P.\sigma$ **needs** $C_1 \wedge C_2 \wedge \ldots \wedge C_n$ such that no pair of conditions $C_i, C_j, i, j \in [1, n], i \neq j$ uses the same plant model. Construct the set of split requirements $\mathcal{R} = \{R_1, \ldots, R_n\}$ with each split requirement being $R_i = P.\sigma$ **needs** C_i. Then the set of modular supervisors for $\mathcal{R}$ is nonconflicting.

4   Demonstration with Case Study of Infrastructural System

Splitting state-event invariant requirements is demonstrated with the model of Lock III, located at Tilburg, The Netherlands. Figure 3 shows the lock. The model of Lock III is given in [25]. A lock is an infrastructural system in rivers

Fig. 3. Photo of Lock III, located at Tilburg, The Netherlands. Image from https://beeldbank.rws.nl, Rijkswaterstaat.

and canals with the purpose to maintain different water levels outside the lock while also allowing the vessels to pass from one level to the other. A lock consists primarily of a lock chamber with a lock head on each side. The main subsystems of a lock head are the gates, water leveling systems, and the incoming and outgoing traffic lights. Supervisory control is deployed to ensure safe operation of the system. In this context, safety not only concerns avoiding human injuries or causalities, but also water management as large parts of The Netherlands are located below water level.

For modeling convenience, there is also the state-event invariant expression D **disables** σ, which expresses that event σ is disabled when condition D holds. This expression has the same expressiveness as the form σ **needs** C: D **disables** σ is equivalent to σ **needs** $\neg D$. Following the same splitting mechanism as introduced with the guideline, requirements of the form D **disables** σ can be split if condition D is in disjunctive normal form, i.e., $D = D_1 \vee \ldots \vee D_k$.

The guideline is demonstrated with the following requirement: it is unsafe to open a gate if (1) the water-leveling system at the other side is not closed, or (2) the gate at the other side is not closed, or (3) there is no equal water over the gate, or (4) the incoming traffic light at that lock head is not showing a red or red-red aspect, or (5) the outgoing traffic light at that lock head is not showing a red aspect. For one of the gates this requirement is formalized in the model as

(1) culvert_N.S.flow ∨ culvert_N.A.open ∨ culvert_S.S.flow ∨ culvert_S.A.open ∨

(2) ¬gate_U_N.S.closed ∨ gate_U_N.Dir.opening ∨

     ¬gate_U_S.S.closed ∨ gate_U_S.Dir.opening ∨

(3) s_equal_D.off ∨

(4) ¬(in_D_N.S.red ∨ in_D_N.S.redred) ∨ ¬(in_D_N.A.red ∨ in_D_N.A.redred) ∨

     ¬(in_D_S.S.red ∨ in_D_S.S.redred) ∨ ¬(in_D_S.A.red ∨ in_D_S.A.redred) ∨

(5) ¬out_D_N.S.red ∨ ¬out_D_N.A.red ∨ ¬out_D_S.S.red ∨ ¬out_D_S.A.red

     disables gate_D_N.c_open,

where before the first full stop (.) in every state and event name the letter D is an abbreviation for downstream, U for upstream, N for north, and S for south, and where after the first full stop the letter A stands for actuator and S for sensor. The five unsafe situations in which the gate should not open are indicated in the requirement.

The first option for splitting this requirement is creating five requirements, one for each unsafe situation. This results in the following five requirements:

(1) culvert_N.S.flow ∨ culvert_N.A.open ∨ culvert_S.S.flow ∨ culvert_S.A.open

     disables gate_D_N.c_open,

(2) ¬gate_U_N.S.closed ∨ gate_U_N.Dir.opening ∨ ¬gate_U_S.S.closed ∨

     gate_U_S.Dir.opening

     disables gate_D_N.c_open,

(3) s_equal_D.off

     disables gate_D_N.c_open,

(4) ¬(in_D_N.S.red ∨ in_D_N.S.redred) ∨ ¬(in_D_N.A.red ∨ in_D_N.A.redred) ∨

     ¬(in_D_S.S.red ∨ in_D_S.S.redred) ∨ ¬(in_D_S.A.red ∨ in_D_S.A.redred)

     disables gate_D_N.c_open,

(5) ¬out_D_N.S.red ∨ ¬out_D_N.A.red ∨ ¬out_D_S.S.red ∨ ¬out_D_S.A.red

     disables gate_D_N.c_open.

By specifying these five requirements instead of one, the readability and maintainability of the models also increases. Yet, these requirements can be split even further, as each condition is still in disjunctive normal form. Hence, 17 requirements can be formulated, of which the first four originated from (1) are

     (1a) culvert_N.S.flow **disables** gate_D_N.c_open,

     (1b) culvert_N.A.open **disables** gate_D_N.c_open,

     (1c) culvert_S.S.flow **disables** gate_D_N.c_open,

     (1d) culvert_S.A.open **disables** gate_D_N.c_open.

The other requirements can be split similarly.

Table 1. Experimental results for synthesizing modular and multilevel supervisors with the original and adapted Lock III models. The reported state-space size for modular and multilevel synthesis is the sum of the state-space sizes of the individual supervisors. The number of supervisors refers to the result of multilevel synthesis, monolithic synthesis results in only one supervisor and modular synthesis creates a supervisor for each requirement.

Model	Number of requirements	Monolithic	Modular	Multilevel	Number of supervisors
Original	142	$6.0 \cdot 10^{24}$	$1.60 \cdot 10^{13}$	$1.45 \cdot 10^{19}$	7
Adapted	358	$6.0 \cdot 10^{24}$	$1.32 \cdot 10^{05}$	$4.62 \cdot 10^{09}$	34

Another requirement describes normal closing of a gate and expresses that a gate may only be closed if (1) the command to close the gate is given, and (2) the gate is not yet closed, and (3) the command to stop the gate is not given. The model of this textual requirement for one of the gates is

$$\text{gate\_D\_N.c\_close } \textbf{needs} \text{ cmd\_D\_gate\_close} \wedge \neg\text{gate\_D\_N.S.closed} \wedge$$
$$\neg\text{cmd\_stop\_D\_gate,}$$

where D is an abbreviation for downstream, N for north, S for sensor, and cmd for command. The three terms of the condition are conjunctive, thus this requirement can be split into three smaller requirements as follows:

$$\text{gate\_D\_N.c\_close } \textbf{needs} \text{ cmd\_D\_gate\_close,}$$
$$\text{gate\_D\_N.c\_close } \textbf{needs} \neg\text{gate\_D\_N.S.closed,}$$
$$\text{gate\_D\_N.c\_close } \textbf{needs} \neg\text{cmd\_stop\_D\_gate.}$$

Finally, not all requirements may be split. Consider the requirement expressing that the outgoing traffic light may only switch to a red aspect if the command for showing the red aspect is given or any stop command is given. This requirement is formalized for one of the outgoing traffic lights as

$$\text{out\_D\_N.c\_red } \textbf{needs} \text{ cmd\_D\_out\_r} \vee \text{cmd\_stop.}$$

Experimental results are shown in Table 1. These results have been obtained with the CIF toolset [2] and the models can be accessed at a GitHub repository[2]. For both the original model and the adapted model we show the number of requirements, the controlled state-space size of the monolithic supervisor, the sum of the controlled state-space sizes of each modular and multilevel supervisor, and the number of multilevel supervisors. Splitting the requirements more than doubles the number of requirements and significantly increases the efficiency of both modular and multilevel supervisory control synthesis. Focussing on multilevel synthesis, the gain of using that supervisor architecture for the

---

[2] https://github.com/magoorden/SplittingRequirements.

original model is already substantial comparing to monolithic synthesis. Yet, for the adapted model, the state-space size of the multilevel supervisors approaches the result of modular supervisors by synthesizing only 34 supervisors instead of 358 supervisors, respectively. Also, the number of multilevel supervisors indicates that by splitting the requirements the system can be decomposed into more subsystems, as what is expected from the analysis in Sect. 3.1.

5   Four Case Studies with Experimental Results

In this section, the modeling guideline described in Sect. 3 is applied on several other models of real-life case studies. We first introduce the case studies and show a typical requirement that is split according to the modeling guideline. Subsequently, experimental results are shown after applying modular and multilevel supervisory control synthesis on these models.

5.1   Case Studies Description

Case **Marijke**. In this case study, the Prinses Marijke complex is modeled, see [26]. This infrastructural complex is located in the center of The Netherlands and consists of two waterway locks and a storm surge barrier. In case of high water levels in the Amsterdam-Rhine Canal, the barrier is closed and vessels need to use the waterway locks. In all other conditions, the barrier is opened and vessels can pass under it, without using the waterway locks.

The models of the locks in the Prinses Marijke complex are similar to the model of Lock III, see Sect. 3. Only the modeling level, or abstraction detail, differs. Therefore, the same requirements are specified, which opens the opportunity to split them.

Case **ADAS**. In this case study, an Advanced Driver Assistant Systems (ADAS) is modeled, see [13]. In such an application, a supervisor is synthesized to safely switch in a vehicle between the modes 'no cruise control (NCC)', 'cruise control (CC)', and 'adaptive cruise control (ACC)'. Based on input from the driver as well as vehicle sensors, the vehicle may or may not switch between these different modes of cruise control.

One of the formulated requirements is related to the desired behavior of the CC mode. It expresses that the set-point velocity can be decreased if CC is active **and** the brake sensor is off **and** the set-point velocity is higher than 30 km/h **and** the CC lever is pushed up for longer than 0.5 s **and** a set-point velocity is stored **and** CC is enabled **and** the vehicle velocity is higher than 30 km/h. This single requirement can be split into seven smaller requirements.

Case **FESTO**. In this case study, a production line designed by FESTO is modeled, see [24]. The FESTO production line is designed for vocational training in the field of industrial automation. While no real production takes place, all movements, velocities, and timings are as if it were. The production line consists of six workstations with in total 28 actuators, like DC motors and pneumatic cylinders, and 59 capacitive, optical, and inductive sensors.

In the first workstation, products enter the system from a storage tube. At the bottom of the tube, a pusher is able to push a product out. This pusher is only allowed to push (extend) if the system is initialized **and** the pusher is fully retracted **and** there is a product in the storage tube **and** the output place to push the product to is empty. This example requirement can be split into four smaller requirements formulating together the same desired behavior.

5.2 Results

For each case study, requirements are split as much as possible according to the modeling guideline of Sect. 3, which results in the original model and an adapted model. Subsequently, monolithic, modular, and multilevel supervisory control synthesis are applying with the CIF toolset [2].

Table 2. Experimental results for synthesizing modular and multilevel supervisors with the original and adapted models of the several case studies. The reported state-space size for modular and multilevel synthesis is the sum of the state-space sizes of the individual supervisors. The number of supervisors refers to the result of multilevel synthesis, monolithic synthesis results in only one supervisor and modular synthesis creates a supervisor for each requirement

Model	Variant	Number of requirements	Monolithic	Modular	Multilevel	Number of supervisors
LockIII	Original	142	$6.0 \cdot 10^{24}$	$1.60 \cdot 10^{13}$	$1.45 \cdot 10^{19}$	7
	Adapted	358	$6.0 \cdot 10^{24}$	$1.32 \cdot 10^{05}$	$4.62 \cdot 10^{09}$	34
Marijke	Original	248	$6.68 \cdot 10^{26}$	$1.29 \cdot 10^{7}$	$5.50 \cdot 10^{12}$	26
	Adapted	529	$6.68 \cdot 10^{26}$	$2.24 \cdot 10^{5}$	$4.03 \cdot 10^{11}$	33
ADAS	Original	33	$2.0 \cdot 10^{10}$	$1.5 \cdot 10^{4}$	$1.1 \cdot 10^{8}$	8
	Adapted	72	$2.0 \cdot 10^{10}$	$1.1 \cdot 10^{3}$	$5.2 \cdot 10^{5}$	16
FESTO	Original	78	$2.2 \cdot 10^{25}$	$2.10 \cdot 10^{4}$	$4.00 \cdot 10^{6}$	12
	Adapted	205	$2.2 \cdot 10^{25}$	$2.00 \cdot 10^{3}$	$5.06 \cdot 10^{4}$	24

The results are shown in Table 2. For the three different synthesis techniques, the controlled state space is reported. For monolithic synthesis, the number is the state-space size of the single synthesized supervisor; for modular and multilevel synthesis, the number is the sum of the state-space sizes of the individual supervisors. The number of supervisors in the table refers to the number of supervisors of multilevel synthesis. The number of supervisors for modular synthesis equals the number of requirements and for monolithic synthesis there is only one supervisor. The results from Lock III, discussed in Sect. 4, are added for completeness.

For all four cases, adapting the models by splitting requirements increases the number of requirements significantly, it often more than doubles. The results for modular and multilevel synthesis indicate that splitting the requirements is beneficial for the efficiency of these supervisor architectures. For multilevel synthesis, splitting the requirements allows to decompose the system differently such that more subsystems are identified. Therefore, smaller control problems are defined to be solved, resulting in the reduction of the computational effort.

As expected, the obtained efficiency gain of splitting the requirements differs per model. For example, reformulating the model of Lock III allows multilevel synthesis to formulate an efficient decomposition, indicated by the state-space size and the number of supervisors, while the reduction is minimal for the model of the Prinses Marijke complex. Nevertheless, reformulating the model by splitting the requirements seems to be always valuable for models of real-life cases.

6 Conclusion and Future Work

This paper presents a guideline expressing that requirements should be split into smaller ones, each referring to less plant models than before. Theoretical substantiation is provided for the effectiveness of this guideline. Examples from practice show how the guideline can be used. Experimental results indicate that splitting requirements increases the applicability and efficiency of module-based supervisor architectures.

The examples indicate that automatic model transformation based on this guideline should be possible. Future work includes the design and implementation of such transformations. Furthermore, Sect. 3 showed an example of a requirement that could not be split. In [31], the introduction of new event in the plant is suggested to circumvent this issue. It is worth investigating this suggestion, albeit that also the plant model needs to be adapted. Finally, another direction for future research is considering requirements in the form of state invariant expressions, like the one expressing that actuators A and B may never be both on at the same time, and determining whether, for example, a logically equivalent set of state-event invariant expressions may be more beneficial for module-based supervisor architectures.

Acknowledgments. The authors thank Ferdie Reijnen for providing the models of Lock III and the Prinses Marijke complex. The authors thank Rijkswaterstaat, part of the Dutch Ministry of Infrastructure and Water Management, for providing funding for this research. In particular, the authors thank Maria Angenent, Bert van der Vegt, and Han Vogel for their feedback on the results.

References

1. Basile, D., ter Beek, M.H., Di Giandomenico, F., Gnesi, S.: Orchestration of dynamic service product lines with featured modal contract automata. In: 21st International Systems and Software Product Line Conference , vol. B, pp. 117–122. ACM (2017). https://doi.org/10.1145/3109729.3109741
2. van Beek, D.A., et al.: CIF 3: model-based engineering of supervisory controllers. In: Ábrahám, E., Havelund, K. (eds.) TACAS 2014. LNCS, vol. 8413, pp. 575–580. Springer, Heidelberg (2014). https://doi.org/10.1007/978-3-642-54862-8_48

3. Cai, K., Wonham, W.M.: Supervisor localization: a top-down approach to distributed control of discrete-event systems. IEEE Trans. Autom. Control. **55**(3), 605–618 (2010)

4. Cassandras, C.G., Lafortune, S.: Introduction to Discrete Event Systems, 2nd edn. Springer, Boston (2008). https://doi.org/10.1007/978-0-387-68612-7

5. Eppinger, S.D., Browning, T.R.: Design Structure Matrix Methods and Applications. MIT Press, Cambridge (2012)

6. Fabian, M., Fei, Z., Miremadi, S., Lennartson, B., Åkesson, K.: Supervisory control of manufacturing systems using extended finite automata. In: Campos, J., Seatzo, C., Xie, X. (eds.) Formal Methods in Manufacturing. Industrial Information Technology, pp. 295–314. Taylor & Francis Inc., Boca Raton, February 2014

7. Göbe, F., Ney, O., Kowalewski, S.: Reusability and modularity of safety specifications for supervisory control. In: IEEE 21st International Conference on Emerging Technologies and Factory Automation, pp. 1–8, September 2016. https://doi.org/10.1109/ETFA.2016.7733498

8. Goorden, M.A., van de Mortel-Fronczak, J.M., Reniers, M.A., Rooda, J.E.: Structuring multilevel discrete-event systems with dependency structure matrices. In: 56th IEEE Conference on Decision and Control, pp. 558–564, December 2017. https://doi.org/10.1109/CDC.2017.8263721

9. Greenyer, J., Brenner, C., Cordy, M., Heymans, P., Gressi, E.: Incrementally synthesizing controllers from scenario-based product line specifications. In: 9th Joint Meeting on Foundations of Software Engineering, pp. 433–443. ACM (2013). https://doi.org/10.1145/2491411.2491445

10. Grigorov, L., Butler, B.E., Cury, J.E.R., Rudie, K.: Conceptual design of discrete-event systems using templates. Discret. Event Dyn. Syst. **21**(2), 257–303 (2011). https://doi.org/10.1007/s10626-010-0089-0

11. Jiao, T., Gan, Y., Xiao, G., Wonham, W.M.: Exploiting symmetry of discrete-event systems by relabeling and reconfiguration. IEEE Trans. Syst. Man Cybern.: Syst. **99**, 1–12 (2018). https://doi.org/10.1109/TSMC.2018.2795011

12. Komenda, J., Masopust, T., van Schuppen, J.H.: Control of an engineering-structured multilevel discrete-event system. In: 13th International Workshop on Discrete Event Systems, pp. 103–108, May 2016

13. Korssen, T., Dolk, V., van de Mortel-Fronczak, J.M., Reniers, M.A., Heemels, M.: Systematic model-based design and implementation of supervisors for advanced driver assistance systems. IEEE Trans. Intell. Transp. Syst. **19**(2), 533–544 (2017). https://doi.org/10.1109/TITS.2017.2776354

14. Lin, F., Wonham, W.M.: Decentralized control and coordination of discrete-event systems with partial observation. IEEE Trans. Autom. Control **35**(12), 1330–1337 (1990). https://doi.org/10.1109/9.61009

15. Ma, C., Wonham, W.: Nonblocking Supervisory Control of State Tree Structures. Lecture Notes in Control and Information Sciences, vol. 317. Springer, Heidelberg (2005). https://doi.org/10.1007/b105592

16. Markovski, J., Jacobs, K.G.M., van Beek, D.A., Somers, L.J., Rooda, J.E.: Coordination of resources using generalized state-based requirements, pp. 300–305 (2010)

17. Modarres, M.: Risk Analysis in Engineering : Techniques, Tools, and Trends. CRC Press, Boca Raton (2016). https://doi.org/10.1201/b21429

18. Mohajerani, S., Malik, R., Fabian, M.: A framework for compositional synthesis of modular nonblocking supervisors. IEEE Trans. Autom. Control **59**(1), 150–162 (2014)

19. Mohajerani, S., Malik, R., Fabian, M.: A framework for compositional nonblocking verification of extended finite-state machines. Discret. Event Dyn. Syst. **26**(1), 33–84 (2016). https://doi.org/10.1007/s10626-015-0217-y

20. de Queiroz, M.H., Cury, J.E.R.: Modular supervisory control of large scale discrete event systems. In: Boel, R., Stremersch, G. (eds.) Discrete Event Systems. The Springer International Series in Engineering and Computer Science, vol. 569, pp. 103–110. Springer, Boston (2000). https://doi.org/10.1007/978-1-4615-4493-7_10

21. Ramadge, P.J.G., Wonham, W.M.: Supervisory control of a class of discrete event processes. SIAM J. Control. Optim. **25**(1), 206–230 (1987)

22. Ramadge, P.J.G., Wonham, W.M.: The control of discrete event systems. Proc. IEEE **77**(1), 81–98 (1989)

23. Ramos, A.L., Ferreira, J.V., Barceló, J.: Model-based systems engineering: an emerging approach for modern systems. IEEE Trans. Syst., Man, Cybern., Part C (Appl. Rev.) **42**(1), 101–111 (2012). https://doi.org/10.1109/TSMCC.2011.2106495

24. Reijnen, F.F.H., Goorden, M.A., van de Mortel-Fronczak, J.M., Reniers, M.A., Rooda, J.E.: Application of dependency structure matrices and multilevel synthesis to a production line. In: IEEE Conference on Control Technology and Applications, pp. 458–464, August 2018. https://doi.org/10.1109/CCTA.2018.8511449

25. Reijnen, F.F.H., Goorden, M.A., van de Mortel-Fronczak, J.M., Rooda, J.E.: Supervisory control synthesis for a waterway lock. In: 1st IEEE Conference on Control Technology and Applications, pp. 1562–1568, August 2017. https://doi.org/10.1109/CCTA.2017.8062679

26. Reijnen, F.F.H., Verbakel, J.J., van de Mortel-Fronczak, J.M., Rooda, J.E.: Hardware-in-the-loop set-up for supervisory controllers with an application: the Prinses Marijke complex. In: IEEE Conference on Control Technology and Applications, August 2019 (accepted)

27. Reijnen, F.F.H., Goorden, M.A., van de Mortel-Fronczak, J.M., Rooda, J.E.: Supervisory control synthesis for a lock-bridge combination. Discret. Event Dyn. Syst. (2019, submitted)

28. Rudie, K., Wonham, W.M.: Think globally, act locally: decentralized supervisory control. IEEE Trans. Autom. Control **37**(11), 1692–1708 (1992)

29. Su, R., van Schuppen, J.H., Rooda, J.E.: Synthesize nonblocking distributed supervisors with coordinators. In: 17th Mediterranean Conference on Control and Automation, pp. 1108–1113, June 2009

30. Su, R., van Schuppen, J.H., Rooda, J.E., Hofkamp, A.T.: Nonconflict check by using sequential automaton abstractions based on weak observation equivalence. Automatica **46**(6), 968–978 (2010)

31. Theunissen, R.J.M.: Supervisory Control in Health Care Systems. Ph.D. thesis, Eindhoven University of Technology, Eindhoven (2015). http://repository.tue.nl/786117

32. Wonham, W.M., Ramadge, P.J.G.: Modular supervisory control of discrete-event systems. Math. Control Sig. Syst. **1**(1), 13–30 (1988)

33. Wonham, W.M., Cai, K.: Supervisory Control of Discrete-Event Systems, 1st edn. Springer, Heidelberg (2018). https://doi.org/10.1007/978-3-319-77452-7

34. Zhong, H., Wonham, W.M.: On the consistency of hierarchical supervision in discrete-event systems. IEEE Trans. Autom. Control **35**(10), 1125–1134 (1990)

Incremental Development of a Safety Critical System Combining formal Methods and DSMLs
— Application to a Railway System —

Akram Idani[1,2]([⊠]), Yves Ledru[1,2], Abderrahim Ait Wakrime[2],
Rahma Ben Ayed[2], and Simon Collart-Dutilleul[2,3]

[1] Univ. Grenoble Alpes, CNRS, Grenoble INP, LIG, 38000 Grenoble, France
{akram.idani,yves.ledru}@imag.fr
[2] Institut de Recherche Technologique Railenium, 59300 Famars, France
{abderrahim.ait-wakrime,rahma.ben-ayed}@railenium.eu
[3] Univ Lille Nord de France, IFSTTAR, 59666 Villeneuve d'Ascq Cedex, France
simon.collart-dutilleul@ifsttar.fr

Abstract. In order to assist domain experts, several tools exist for the definition of graphical or textual domain specific modeling languages (DSMLs). The resulting models are useful, but not sufficient, for an overall understanding of the system, especially when formal methods are being applied. Indeed, formal methods failures often result from misunderstandings of the requirements, even if the system is entirely proved. This is confirmed by several industrial experiments which showed that the poor readability of the formal notations is not convenient for communication with domain experts and hence the validation activity is often tedious, time consuming and complex. In order to circumvent this shortcoming, we propose to make domain specific models provable and also executable thanks to the animation of their expected behaviour directly in a dedicated DSML tool. Our approach starts from an intuitive description of the system's operational semantics thanks to high-level Petri-nets which abstract away structural constraints and focus on safety-critical behaviours. Then we take benefit of the B method in order to refine and prove these operational semantics on the one hand, and to merge them with the static semantics of a given DSML, on the other hand. This work is applied to the design of ERTMS/ETCS 3 which is an emergent solution for railway system management.

1 Introduction

Application of formal methods in industrial critical systems became a strong requirement due to their ability to guarantee a zero-fault development. Many well-known success stories can be cited especially in the railway domain [13], like for example Meteor, the automated Paris subway. However, formal methods also suffer from the poor readability of their notations [6] which is not convenient for validation. In fact, failures of formal developments often result from

© Springer Nature Switzerland AG 2019
K. G. Larsen and T. Willemse (Eds.): FMICS 2019, LNCS 11687, pp. 93–109, 2019.
https://doi.org/10.1007/978-3-030-27008-7_6

misunderstandings of the users' needs or errors in the expression of these needs, although the system's correctness is entirely proved.

Petri-nets, introduced in 1962 [16], partially circumvent this shortcoming, since they combine a mathematical notation with an accessible graphical representation based on bipartite directed graphs. They are especially known to be powerful for event-driven systems [10] like distributed and real-time systems, logistic networks, embedded controllers, etc. Several high-level variants of Petri-nets, like coloured Petri-nets or predicate-transition nets, were applied in safety-critical systems and were assisted by formal verification techniques such as animation, model-checking or proofs. Moreover, some experiences like that of the Oslo subway, reported in [8], show that in addition to their formal semantics, high-level Petri-nets facilitated communication with domain experts, because chief engineers from railroad infrastructure and traffic department who are neither specialists in Petri-nets nor in formal methods, were not only able to understand the models, but also to suggest improvements.

Despite the Petri-nets advantages and their suitability for a readable formal description, their main disadvantage is that they miss out the system structure and focus on the system behaviour. Nonetheless, in the real world, structural and dynamic aspects of a system are often interdependent. For example, in train controlling systems the topology of the railroad, which defines position of track sections, orientation of switches and/or automatic train stopping devices with their corresponding signalling mechanisms, impacts the overall safety of train movements and behaviours. In safety critical systems, the system structure as well as critical situations that may arise from this structure are often provided by domain experts using informal graphical representations which may be referenced in the specification documents. We believe that these graphical representations should be defined in dedicated domain-specific languages (DSLs) with tool support, especially as modeling languages development is a well mastered technique today. The emergence of DSL tools in safety-critical systems [9,18,19] allows domain experts themselves to provide useful structural models to the software system engineer who will then develop the operational aspects of the system. However, as far as we know, none of the existing works in the safety-critical domain proposes a way to define proved formal links between the dynamic system description (in Petri-nets or other well known formalisms) and DSL tool development. There exist some attempts in model-driven engineering (MDE) with tools for executable DSLs [2,4,15], however they cannot be applied as is in safety critical systems because they are not assisted by automated reasoning tools and lack well-established verification and validation techniques.

This paper gives practical solutions to address this challenge starting from an intuitive description of a safety critical system where the dynamic aspects are specified thanks to high-level Petri-nets and the structural aspects are designed in a DSL tool. This work allows to enhance the usability of formal methods in industry because it involves domain experts all along the development process for both structural and behavioural modeling. Our approach uses the B method [1] in order to merge both worlds (that of Petri-nets and that of DSLs) and then applies AtelierB in order to prove the correctness of the resulting static and dynamic semantics of the modelled system. We also apply the refinement principle of the B method to incrementally define formal operational semantics by means of refined Petri-net models. In every refinement step we introduce additional conceptual elements with associated safety properties and we prove the preservation of these properties as well as those of the previous level.

Section 2 gives the application context of this work. Sections 3 and 4 separately describe operational and static semantics and can be read in any order; and then, Sect. 5 puts it all together, using the B method, in Meeduse[1] − a tool that we developed in order to mix the formal B method with domain specific languages. Finally, Sect. 6 draws the conclusion and the perspectives of this work.

2 Application Context

This work is funded by the NExTRegio project of IRT Railenium. The project aims at performing a system level analysis of a railway signalling system taking into account emergent solutions for train automation. Indeed, in the last decade, new technologies have been considered in railway systems in order to improve automation on the one hand and to reduce the operating costs on the other hand. In particular, the European ERTMS/ETCS[2] [5,17] has emerged to replace various national signalling systems. There are three levels of ERTMS/ETCS which differ by the used equipments and the operating mode. The first two levels are already operational. However, ERTMS Level 3 is still in design and experimentation phases: it aims at replacing signalling systems with a global european one which is a GPS-based solution for the acquisition of train positions. In 2018, the ABZ conference [3], which gathers several formal methods communities, proposed a case study[3] to model ERTMS/ETCS level 3 and has published several formal models. Unfortunately, these models do not combine the power of formal methods with domain specific approaches and hence they favour verification ("do the system right") rather than domain expert validation ("do the right system"). The application presented in this paper contributes to the design phase of ERTMS/ETCS level 3 by mixing formal techniques and domain specific modeling in a well-known Model Driven Engineering (MDE) paradigm which makes easier domain expert validation without losing sight of the verification activity.

An ERTMS Level 3 solution is based on train position and train integrity confirmation, both transmitted by the on-board train system (called EVC[4]) to the trackside system (called RBC[5]). Given this information, the traffic agent, via RBC, assigns a movement authority to a train allowing it to move to a given

---

[1] http://vasco.imag.fr/tools/meeduse/.
[2] ERTMS: European Rail Traffic Management System.
   ETCS: European Train Control System.
[3] https://www.southampton.ac.uk/abz2018/information/case-study.page.
[4] European Vital Computer.
[5] Radio Block Center.

point. In the RBC, track-circuits exist in a logical form by means of trackside train detection sections (called TTD) which are in turn divided into virtual subsections (called VSS). Figure 1, taken from the ERTMS 3 reference document [5], illustrates a track circuit divided into two TTDs and four VSSs, and where a train is located on VSS23. This simplified view of section conventions, used by railway experts, applies specific domain representations to represent a situation where a train went through TTD2 and reached its ending VSS.

The work proposed in this paper is intended to make domain specific models, provided by domain experts themselves, such as that of Fig. 1, not only provable but also executable thanks to the animation of their expected behaviour directly in the dedicated DSL tool. Operational semantics of these models are described using high-level Petri-nets, especially coloured Petri-nets (CP-nets), which abstract away structural constraints and focus on safety-critical behaviours. Static semantics of these models, together with their graphical representation, are developed in a MDE framework based on EMF[6] and Sirius[7].

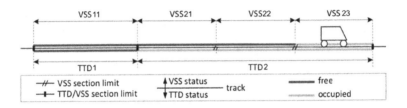

Fig. 1. Section conventions [5]

Figure 2 gives the overall architecture of the resulting models and formal specifications. The DSL meta-model and CP-Net models are automatically translated into B specifications which are enhanced by safety invariants and proved. Then, our approach defines linkage machines allowing to control the functional model and the associated DSL-tool thanks to the CP-Net specifications. Every linkage machine refines a CP-Net model and includes the functional model.

3   Coloured Petri-Nets: From Modeling to Proofs

3.1   Main Concepts

We use coloured Petri-nets (CP-nets) [12] because of their abstraction capabilities and their readability. They combine the strengths of classical Petri-nets with the strengths of high-level programming languages [7], to allow handling data types with pre-defined functions. For a formal description of CP-nets, one can refer to [11]; nonetheless, the main concepts used in this paper are:

---

[6] https://www.eclipse.org/modeling/emf/.
[7] https://www.obeo.fr/fr/produits/eclipse-sirius.

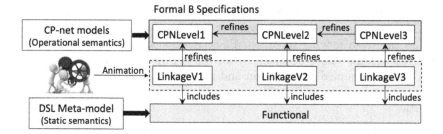

Fig. 2. Overall architecture of a formal DSML semantics

- Data types: can be simple types (*i.e.* Integer, Boolean,...) or complex types (*i.e.* arrays, sequences,...). In this work, we mainly use integer enumerations.
- Places: represent abstractions on data values (called tokens or colours). The place type is called the colour set and it is defined by composing data-types.
- Transitions: they are linked to input and output places. When fired, a transition consumes tokens from its input places such that they match the transition signature. Then, the transition introduces tokens into its output places.
- Predefined functions: describe some computations done by the transitions when they are fired. In this paper, we use three basic functions: calculation of the next (n^{++}) and the previous value (n^{--}) given a token n when n is of type integer, and the negation value $(\neg n)$ when n is of type boolean.

3.2 Level 1: Simple Train Movements

Our first CP-net (Fig. 3) defines simple train movements without train integrity nor movement authorities. This abstract level is mainly intended to guarantee the absence of accidents.

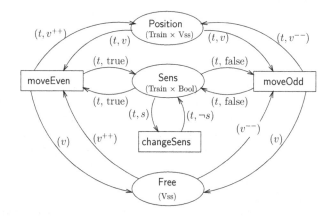

Fig. 3. Simple movement described in a coloured Petri-net

This model describes train movements using transitions moveEven and moveOdd which move the train forward or backward and; and changeSens which switches the train moving direction. Place Position contains pairs (t, v) which record the current VSS v occupied by a train t. Place Free gathers the sections which are not occupied by any train and place Sens registers for every train its current direction. For our first CP-net model, we would like to prove five safety properties:

1. Absence of accidents meaning that at most one train occupies a Vss,
2. Every train is located in one and only one Vss,
3. Absence of overlapping between Vss states free and occupied,
4. Vss states cannot be undefined, they are either free or occupied,
5. The train moving direction is never lost

Transition moveEven is fired given a train t located on section v, whose direction is set to *true*, and such that its next section v^{++} is free (*e.g.* $(t, v) \in$ *Position* $\land (v^{++}) \in$ *Free*). When fired, this transition instantly moves train t from section v to section v^{++}. It consumes tokens (t, v) and (v^{++}) respectively from places Position and Free, and then respectively introduces into these places tokens (t, v^{++}) and (v), meaning that v^{++} becomes the new position of train t, and section v is released. Transition moveOdd applies the same principles to trains in direction *false* but selects the previous section v^{--} if this section is free.

3.3   Extraction of B Specifications

In order to prove the safety properties of our first level CP-net model we translate it into B specifications as follows:

MACHINE	REFINEMENT *CPNLevel1*
CPNData	REFINES *CPNData*
CONSTANTS	VARIABLES
maxTrain, maxVss, CPNTrain, CPNVss	*Free, Position, Sens*
PROPERTIES	INVARIANT
maxTrain $\in$ NAT $\land$ *maxVss* $\in$ NAT	*Free* $\subseteq$ *CPNVss*
$\land$ *CPNTrain* $= 1 .. maxTrain$	$\land$ *Position* $\subseteq$ *CPNTrain* $\times$ *CPNVss*
$\land$ *CPNVss* $= 1 .. maxVss$	$\land$ *Sens* $\subseteq$ *CPNTrain* $\times$ BOOL

First an abstract machine (named CPNData) is generated in order to gather the colour sets together with the transition signatures as defined in the CP-net model. Colour sets Train and Vss, which are integer enumerations, are translated into bounded natural constants CPNTrain and CPNVss. Places Free, Position and Sens become variables in refinement CPNLevel1 because their values evolve during the execution of the CP-net. In this refinement, by default the variable typing applies general functions such as sets' cartesian product and inclusion (*e.g. Position* $\subseteq$ *CPNTrain* $\times$ *CPNVss*).

Every transition leads to a basic operation defined in machine CPNData with a typing precondition and a skip substitution, like the example below of operation moveEven:

```
/* Operation moveEven in machine CPNData */
moveEven(tt, vv) =
    PRE tt ∈ CPNTrain ∧ vv ∈ CPNVss THEN
        skip
    END
```

The skip substitution of the basic operations is then refined in CPNLevel1 by introducing the enabledness guards and the expected actions of the transition. In the following we give the refinement of operation moveEven in CPNLevel1:

```
/* Refinement of the skip substitution in CPNLevel1 */
moveEven(tt, vv) =
    SELECT
        (tt ↦ vv) ∈ Position ∧ (vv + 1) ∈ Free ∧ (tt ↦ TRUE) ∈ Sens
    THEN
        Free := (Free − {(vv + 1)}) ∪ {(vv)} ||
        Position := (Position − {(tt ↦ vv)}) ∪ {(tt ↦ vv + 1)}
    END ;
```

Transitions moveOdd and changeSens are translated by applying the same principles. Regarding the five safety properties, they are manually introduced in machine CPNLevel1 using the following invariants:

```
Position ∈ CPNTrain ⤚ CPNVss /* Properties (1) and (2) */
Free ∩ ran(Position) = ∅ /* Property (3) */
Free ∪ ran(Position) = CPNVss /* Property (4) */
Sens ∈ CPNTrain → BOOL /* Property (5) */
```

These invariants restrict the state space defined by the typing predicates presented above. For example, the typing predicate of relation *Position* defines all combinations of CPNTrain and CPNVss couples, while the invariant restricts these combinations to those where a CPNTrain is linked to one and only one CPNVss while a CPNVss is linked to at the most one CPNTrain. In our methodology, we consider that if the CP-net model is correct, proofs should be done without any enhancement of the corresponding B specifications. Otherwise, we decide whether the CP-net model is wrong or not, given the AtelierB feedbacks. In all cases we do not modify the generated B operations; we either call the interactive prover when the proof fails due to a limitation in the automatic prover, or we correct the CP-net model and translate it again into B. The initial marking substitutions are introduced without invariant violation:

```
INITIALISATION
    Position :∈ CPNTrain ⤚ CPNVss ;
    Free := CPNVss − ran(Position) ;
    Sens :∈ CPNTrain → BOOL
```

Based on machines CPNData and CPNLevel1, and these additional invariants, the AtelierB generated 17 proof obligations and automatically proved 11 amongst them. The 6 other POs were proved using the interactive prover.

4   A Railway Domain-Specific Modeling Language

4.1   Railway Meta-Model

In order to provide a tool for domain experts allowing them to draw models like that of Fig. 1, we apply model-driven engineering tools for DSML creation (EMF, Ecore-Tools and Sirius). In MDE, the creation of a DSML starts by the definition of its meta-model and then for every class in the meta-model a graphical representation is created. Figure 4 gives the meta-model that we use in this work and Fig. 5 gives a screenshot of the resulting DSML-tool in which a model is designed using the proposed graphical representations.

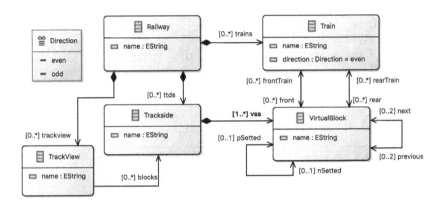

Fig. 4. A railway meta-model

In our meta-model, a railway system is composed of trains (class Train), track sections called TTD in ERTMS/ETCS 3 (class Trackside) and which are divided into portions called VSS (class VirtualBlock). The bottom of Fig. 5 draws an overall railway topology by means of TTD links. Every portion of a given TTD may be linked to two next and previous portions at the most. In practice, there are four kinds of portions: track extremity (*e.g.* VSS11 and VSS62), middle track (*e.g.* VSS12), switch (*e.g.* VSS21 and VSS51) and diamonds. Association pSetted/nSetted provides the currently selected previous/next portion among those to which a portion is linked. This is useful especially for switches and diamonds. For example, the next portions of VSS21 are VSS31 and VSS41, but the position of the switch sets the currently selected next portion of VSS21 to VSS31 and hence the selected previous portion of VSS31 is VSS21 but for portion VSS41 there is no previous selected portion. Portion VSS41 remains then a track limit until the switch position is changed. Note that relation pSetted/nSetted is independent from train direction and a track limit is a portion without a selected next or previous portion.

Class TrackView represents linear views that follow the current next/previous selections and where every view starts and ends with track limits. For example,

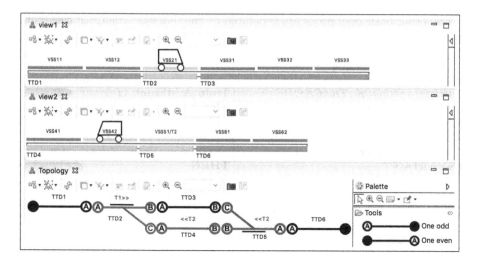

Fig. 5. A railway model (Color figure online)

the topology presented in the bottom of Fig. 5, leads to the two views on the top of the figure. The first view covers sections TTD1, TTD2 and TTD3 and the second view covers the three other sections: TTD4, TTD5 and TTD6. If the switches position changes, these views are changed consequently. For example, if the selected next portion of VSS21 is set to VSS41, then the resulting topology would lead to two different views: one composed of TTD1/TTD2/TTD4/TTD5/TTD6, and an other view dedicated to TTD3 only.

Trains have a direction (even or odd) and their representation depends on the set of portions that their head and rear occupy. In the example of Fig. 5 we consider two trains: T1 whose front and rear occupy the same portion (*i.e.* VSS21), and T2 that stretches from portion VSS42 to VSS51. A TTD is occupied when at least one of its portions are occupied. This is represented by the yellow color in the track views and by the red color in the topology representation. The green color is used to represent free TTD and VSS in the track view.

4.2   Formal Model

As our intention is to provide domain experts with a DSML-tool with formal semantics, we apply the Meeduse platform[8] that we developed in order to automatically translate a meta-model into an equivalent B specification. The resulting formal model gathers the structure of the meta-model (by means of sets, variables and structural invariants) with a set of basic operations such as constructors, getters and setters. For example, we give below the translation of classes Train and VirtualBlock and one basic operation Train_AddFront which adds a virtual block to the set of virtual blocks occupied by the head of a train.

---

[8] http://vasco.imag.fr/tools/meeduse/.

Several other basic operations are generated by the tool like: Train_RemoveFront, Train_AddRear, Train_RemoveRear...

MACHINE *Functional*
SETS
  VIRTUALBLOCK; *TRACKSIDE*
  Direction = {*even,odd*};
VARIABLES
  Train, VirtualBlock, Train_direction,
  frontOfTrain, rearOfTrain
INVARIANT
  Train ⊆ *TRAIN*
  ∧ *VirtualBlock* ∈ *VIRTUALBLOCK*
  ∧ *frontOfTrain* ∈ *Train* ↔ *VirtualBlock*
  ∧ *rearOfTrain* ∈ *Train* ↔ *VirtualBlock*
  ∧ *Train_direction* ∈ *Train* → *Direction*

Train_AddFront(*aTrain,aFront*) =
PRE
  aTrain ∈ *Train* ∧
  aFront ∈ *VirtualBlock* ∧
  (*aTrain* ↦ *aFront*) ∉ *frontOfTrain*
THEN
frontOfTrain :=
  frontOfTrain ∪ {(*aTrain* ↦ *aFront*)}
  END;

The translation of a meta-model into B applies a UML-to-B transformation technique where a meta-class Class is translated into an abstract set named CLASS representing possible instances and a variable named Class representing the set of existing instances such that existing instances belong to the set of possible instances. An enumeration is translated into a enumerated set (*e.g.* Direction). Basic types (*e.g.* integer, boolean) become B types (Z, Bool,...). Attributes and references lead to functional relations depending on multiplicities.

Machine Functional generated by Meeduse is about 500 lines with 38 basic operations from which the AtelierB produced 80 proof obligations that were proved automatically. Proofs associated to this functional specification guarantee that the basic operations do not violate the structural properties of the meta-model such as multiplicities and single-valued and mandatory attributes, etc. Besides the automatic extraction of a correct by-design functional B specification, the interest of Meeduse is that it integrates the ProB [14] animator. Given a model (like that of Fig. 5) Meeduse injects it as valuations in the B specification and calls ProB in order to compute the list of operations that may be animated from these valuations. For example, the following initialization is extracted by Meeduse from our graphical model which leads to an initial state of the B machine which is conformant with the domain model.

INITIALISATION
  Train := {*T1, T2*} ||
  VirtualBlock := {*VSS11, VSS12, ..., VSS62*} ||
  frontOfTrain := {(*T1* ↦ *VSS21*), (*T2* ↦ *VSS42*)} ||
  rearOfTrain := {(*T1* ↦ *VSS21*), (*T2* ↦ *VSS51*)} ||
  Train_direction := {(*T1* ↦ *even*), (*T2* ↦ *odd*)}

Starting from the initial state, when the user asks Meeduse to animate a B operation, the tool calls ProB and gets the new variable valuations and then it translates back these valuations to the graphical model. This technique results in an automatic visual animation[9] of domain models. For example, given the above initial state, the animation of operation Train_AddFront(T1, VSS31) introduces couple (*T1 ↦ VSS31*) into relation *frontOfTrain* and then Meeduse modifies the domain model as presented in Fig. 6 where the head of T1 occupies two virtual blocks VSS21 and VSS31. Since VSS31 is one of the portions of TTD3, then the visual representation of TTD3 automatically changes from green to yellow.

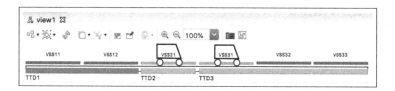

Fig. 6. View 1 after animation of Train_AddFront(T1, VSS31) (Color figure online)

5 Putting It All Together

Section 3 focused on train behaviours with an abstract Petri-net specification that guarantees the absence of accidents, and Sect. 4 focused on domain modeling of structural aspects of a railway DSML. In this section, we combine both concerns in order to provide a railway DSML with a proved safe train behaviour. The B specifications extracted from the meta-model of Fig. 4 represent formal static semantics of our DSML, and those extracted from a coloured Petri-net model introduce its operational semantics. In order to merge static and operational semantics we create machine LinkageV1 which refines CPNLevel1 and includes machine Functional:

> **REFINEMENT** *LinkageV1*
> **REFINES** *CPNLevel1*
> **INCLUDES** *Functional*
> **VARIABLES**
>   *trainMapping, vssMapping, view*
> **INVARIANT**
> $trainMapping \in Train \rightarrowtail CPNTrain$
> $\wedge\ vssMapping \in VirtualBlock \rightarrowtail CPNVss$
> $\wedge\ view \in TrackView$

The refinement guarantees the preservation of the safety invariants of CPN-Level1 and the inclusion allows to redefine the Petri-net transitions and data using the functional variables of the DSML. In this machine the linkage between the DSML and the CP-net model is done via functions *trainMapping* and *vssMapping*. They respectively map variables *Train* and *VirtualBlock* issued from the

---

[9] For place reason we do not develop the animation technique in this paper. Demonstration videos of Meeduse with graphical and textual DSL animation can be found at: http://vasco.imag.fr/tools/meeduse/.

meta-model to sets *CPNTrain* and *CPNVss* issued from the CP-net. In our approach every view in the DSML is controlled by a CP-net since the CP-net defines the VSS set by a sequence of integers. Then, the mapping functions are applied to a given *view* (*view* ∈ *TrackView*). For example, the *vssMapping* relation is computed in the initialisation of LinkageV1 as:

LET *mapVss* **BE** *mapVss* = **ran**(({*view*} ◁ *blocks* $^{-1}$; *theVSSs* $^{-1}$)) **IN**
    ANY *map* **WHERE**
        map ∈ *mapVss* ↣ *CPNVss* ∧
        ∀ *vss* . (*vss* ∈ *mapVss* ∧ *nSetted*[{*vss*}] ≠ ∅
            ⇒ *nSetted*(*vss*) ∈ **dom**(*map*) ∧ *map*(*nSetted*(*vss*)) = *map*(*vss*) + 1)
    THEN
        vssMapping := *map*
    END
END

Note that *blocks* and *theVSSs* represent respectively association blocks between classes TrackView and Trackside, and association vss between classes Trackside and VirtualBlock. Local variable *mapVss* defined by: **ran**((*view* ◁ *blocks*$^{-1}$; *theVSSs*$^{-1}$)) extracts the set of VSS for a given *view* and the mapping is a total injection (↣) that maps every VSS in this view to a unique value from set *CPNVss*. This mapping is done under the condition that if a VSS is not a track extremity (*nSetted*[*vss*] ≠ ∅) then its next selected VSS is mapped (*nSetted*(*vss*) ∈ **dom**(*map*)) and the associated CP-net value is equal to the VSS value plus one. We similarly compute the *trainMapping* relation but under the condition that only trains whose head and rear occupy the same VSS are mapped. In this sense, from the example of Fig. 5 only the first view can be mapped and then controlled by our first level CP-net model.

Given the mapping relations, the safety invariants of CPNLevel1 are rewritten by means of linkage invariants ensuring the relationship between the various B specifications. For example, invariant *Free* ∩ **ran**(*Position*) = ∅ used for Property (3) becomes:

$$(frontOfTrain \cup rearOfTrain)^{-1}[vssMapping^{-1}[Free]] = \emptyset$$

which means that for every free VSS in the CP-net model, the corresponding virtual block in the DSML does not contain any train head or rear. Having the linkage invariants, operation moveEven(tt, vv) in the linkage machine is applied to a train mapped to *tt*, whose head and rear occupy a VSS mapped to *vv*, and whose direction is *even* and such that the next VSS which is mapped to *vv* + 1 is free. Actions of moveEven call basic functional operations issued from machine Functional. They simply remove the head and the rear of the train from *vv* and put them on *vv* + 1. In the following we give the refinement of operation moveEven in LinkageV1:

```
moveEven(tt, vv) =
LET train, vss, nextVss BE
    train = trainMapping⁻¹(tt)
    ∧ vss = vssMapping⁻¹(vv)
    ∧ nextVss = vssMapping⁻¹(vv + 1)
IN
    SELECT
        (train ↦ vss) ∈ frontOfTrain ∩ rearOfTrain
        ∧ nextVss ∉ ran(frontOfTrain ∪ rearOfTrain)
        ∧ Train_direction(train) = even
    THEN
        Train_RemoveFront(train, vss); Train_AddFront(train, nextVss) ;
        Train_RemoveRear(train, vss); Train_AddRear(train, nextVss)
    END
END ;
```

At this stage we are able to do verification and validation. Indeed, verification is done thanks to the 41 POs that were proved by the AtelierB for machine LinkageV1 and which mean that the safety properties (those of CPNLevel1) as well as the structural properties (those of Functional) are preserved. Regarding validation, it is done by railway experts using the animation facility of Meeduse. As we showed previously, Meeduse animation of B operations that impact the functional model automatically animates the corresponding graphical model.

5.1   Incremental Development of Operational Semantics

CPNLevel1 describes simple train movements without train integrity nor movement authorities which are basic concepts of ERTMS/ETCS 3. This specification guarantees the absence of accidents and defines a first abstraction level of our DSML operational semantics. In this section, we show how operational semantics, can be incrementally defined in order to first introduce movement authorities and then the track release mechanism when the train integrity is confirmed.

Machines CPNLevel1, Functional and LinkageV1 of Fig, 2 were discussed in the previous sections. Machines CPNLevel2 and CPNLevel3 are extracted from additional CP-net models and apply a refinement technique where every refinement level introduces new safety properties without violating the properties of the previous levels. In this section we mainly discuss CP-net refinements. Machines LinkageV2 and LinkageV3 will not be discussed since they are defined via the same principles as LinkageV1. They allow the domain expert to animate the domain model for every CP-net refinement and validate the observed behaviours. Thanks to these machines, the domain expert is involved all along the development process.

Level 2: Authorized Train Movements

The assumption made in the first CP-net level, considering that a train moves to the next free virtual section and immediately leaves its current section, is quite simplistic but sufficient in order to model an abstract accident-free behaviour. In this second level we introduce a movement authority mechanism, in order to construct routes to which trains are allowed to move. The movement authority, in the ERTMS/ETCS, is used without visual signals or marker boards. It is sent by the RBC system to a given train via GSM-R.

Our objective is to prove that authorized train movements, no matter how authorizations are assigned to trains, preserve the accident-free behaviour of the previous level. Figure 7 is a CP-net model which includes authorized movements and where we focus on the refinement of transition moveEven and state Free. In addition to transition moveOdd which is analog to moveEven, and transition changeSens which is kept unchanged, this model introduces transition authorize which represents the actions executed by a train when it receives a movement authority signal from the RBC.

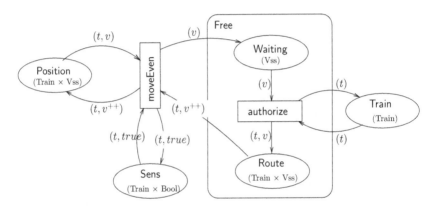

Fig. 7. CP-net for authorized train movements

In this CP-net model, place Free is refined into two places: Waiting and Route. When a train moves away from a given Vss, the Vss is freed but cannot be used before being reserved. The Vss first enters in place Waiting and then transition authorize assigns it to a given train and adds the corresponding movement authority to place Route. The extraction of B specifications follows the same principles as discussed for Level 1, and produces the variables with their typing invariants showed below:

REFINEMENT *CPNLevel2*
REFINES *CPNLevel1*
VARIABLES
 Position, Sens, Waiting, Route
INVARIANT
/* Typing invariant generated from CP-net model */
  $Waiting \subseteq CPNVss \wedge Route \subseteq CPNTrain \times CPNVss$
/* Refinement invariant */
  $Waiting \cup \mathbf{ran}(Route) = Free$

```
/* Refinement of moveEven with authorized movements */
moveEven(tt,vv) =
   SELECT
      (tt ↦ vv) ∈ Position ∧ (tt ↦ vv + 1) ∈ Route ∧ (tt ↦ TRUE) ∈ Sens
   THEN
      Position := (Position − {(tt ↦ vv)}) ∪ {(tt ↦ vv + 1)} ||
      Route := Route − {(tt ↦ vv + 1)} ||
      Waiting := Waiting ∪ {vv}
   END ;
```

The refinement invariant means that the set of tokens of place Free are distributed among places Waiting and Route, and then variable Free is replaced by variables Waiting and Route which are used in the refinement of transition moveEven. The additional safety invariants of this second CP-net level are: (6.) a VSS cannot be waiting and at the same time assigned to a movement authority; and (7.) a movement authority cannot be shared by several trains.

$$Waiting \cap \mathbf{ran}(Route) = \emptyset \text{ /* Property (6) */}$$
$$Route^{-1} \in CPNVss \nrightarrow CPNTrain \text{ /* Property (7) */}$$

Given CP-net of Level 2 and the corresponding safety properties, as well as the refinement invariant, the AtelierB prover generated 32 POs, such that 25 were proved automatically and 7 interactively, which means that CP-net Level 2 guarantees its own properties and also those of CP-net Level 1.

Level 3: Movements with Integrity Confirmation

In the third refinement level we consider a more realistic train representation than that developed in the two previous levels where a train occupies only one VSS. In this refinement, a train is seen as a logical entity defined by the set of VSS that it occupies: its head (place Position), a set of VSS not yet released behind its head (place Wagon) and the safe rear end (place Tail) which is in our case one additional VSS defining the minimal distance between two trains. Thus, a train occupies at least two virtual sections: one for its head and one behind it. When a train moves, its head is advanced from its current VSS v to the next VSS v^{++}, and then v is not freed but a virtual wagon is created over it. Indeed, in ERTMS/ETCS 3, the train must confirm its integrity (*i.e.* it did not lose wagons) before releasing its safe rear end which advances its tail by one VSS and removes the corresponding virtual wagon. Figure 8 provides the refinement of CP-net level 2 introducing integrity confirmation together with the VSS release mechanism. This model introduces places Wagon, Tail and Ready as a refinement of place Waiting, and transition confirmEven which is fired when a train integrity is confirmed. A released VSS becomes ready for reservation and enters in place Ready. Given the B specifications issued from this third level and the associated safety invariants, the AtelierB produced 62 POs and automatically proved 41 among them. The 21 other POs were proved manually.

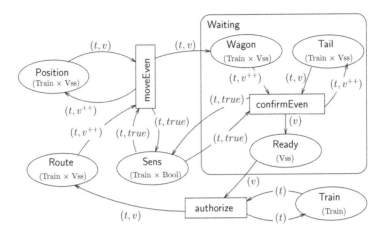

Fig. 8. CP-net for authorized movements and integrity confirmation

6   Conclusion

This paper presented an incremental formal development process that involves domain experts during the modeling activities. First, we use coloured Petri-nets because their graphical notations are more readable than textual mathematical notations. Then, we use DSMLs in order to assist domain experts for the design of the domain models. CP-nets and DSMLs are convenient for validation because they both favour communication complementing each other by focusing on particular concerns: behavioural concerns for CP-nets, and structural concerns for DSMLs. In order to mix the various models we apply the B method which allows a proof-based verification thanks to the AtelierB prover, and domain model animation thanks to Meeduse and ProB. Our approach was successfully applied to a railway safety critical system, the ERTMS/ETCS 3 train automation solution and other case studies (automatic car light regulator, parking-lot controller,...).

Several perspectives araise from this work, especially we plan to develop an automated extraction technique of sub-parts of the linkage machines. In this work, these machines were introduced manually which is still somehow difficult and time consuming when the CP-net scales up such as our third CP-net refinement. We also plan an empirical study with railway experts in order to validate the usability of our tool-set. The validation is currently limited to academic railway experts of the NExTRegio project.

References

1. Abrial, J.-R.: The B-book: Assigning Programs to Meanings. Cambridge University Press, New York (1996)
2. Bousse, E., Leroy, D., Combemale, B., Wimmer, M., Baudry, B.: Omniscient debugging for executable DSLs. J. Syst. Softw. **137**, 261–288 (2018)

3. Butler, M., Raschke, A., Hoang, T.S., Reichl, K. (eds.): ABZ 2018. LNCS, vol. 10817. Springer, Cham (2018). https://doi.org/10.1007/978-3-319-91271-4

4. Deantoni, J.: Modeling the behavioral semantics of heterogeneous languages and their coordination. In: 2016 Architecture-Centric Virtual Integration (ACVI), pp. 12–18, April 2016

5. EEIG ERTMS USERS GROUP ERA, UNISIG. System Requirements Specification, SUBSET-026. Technical report, European Railway Agency, Version 3.6.0 (2016)

6. Gaudel, M.-C.: Advantages and limits of formal approaches for ultra-high dependability. In: Randell, B., Laprie, J.C., Kopetz, H., Littlewood, B. (eds.) Predictably Dependable Computing Systems. ESPRIT Basic Research Series, pp. 241–251. Springer, Heidelberg (1995). https://doi.org/10.1007/978-3-642-79789-7_14

7. Gehlot, V., Nigro, C.: An introduction to systems modeling and simulation with colored petri nets. In: Proceedings of the 2010 Winter Simulation Conference, WSC 2010, USA, 5–8 December 2010, pp. 104–118 (2010)

8. Hagalisletto, A.M., Bjørk, J., Yu, I.C., Enger, P.: Constructing and refining large-scale railway models represented by petri nets. IEEE Trans. Syst. Man Cybern. Part C **37**(4), 444–460 (2007)

9. James, P., Knapp, A., Mossakowski, T., Roggenbach, M.: Designing domain specific languages – a craftsman's approach for the railway domain using CASL. In: Martí-Oliet, N., Palomino, M. (eds.) WADT 2012. LNCS, vol. 7841, pp. 178–194. Springer, Heidelberg (2013). https://doi.org/10.1007/978-3-642-37635-1_11

10. Janczura, C.: Modelling and analysis of railway network control logic using coloured Petri Nets. Ph.D. thesis. University of South Australia (1998)

11. Jensen, K.: Coloured Petri Nets and the invariant-method. Theor. Comput. Sci. **14**, 317–336 (1981)

12. Jensen, K.: Coloured Petri Nets: Basic Concepts, Analysis Methods and Practical Use, vol. 1. Springer, Heidelberg (2010). https://doi.org/10.1007/978-3-662-03241-1

13. Lecomte, T.: Applying a formal method in industry: a 15-year trajectory. In: Alpuente, M., Cook, B., Joubert, C. (eds.) FMICS 2009. LNCS, vol. 5825, pp. 26–34. Springer, Heidelberg (2009). https://doi.org/10.1007/978-3-642-04570-7_3

14. Leuschel, M., Butler, M.: ProB: an automated analysis toolset for the B method. STTT **10**(2), 185–203 (2008)

15. Mayerhofer, T., Langer, P., Wimmer, M., Kappel, G.: xMOF: executable DSMLs based on fUML. In: Erwig, M., Paige, R.F., Van Wyk, E. (eds.) SLE 2013. LNCS, vol. 8225, pp. 56–75. Springer, Cham (2013). https://doi.org/10.1007/978-3-319-02654-1_4

16. Petri, C.-A.: Fundamentals of a theory of asynchronous information flow. In: IFIP Congress, pp. 386–390 (1962)

17. Schn, W., Larraufie, G., Mons, G., Por, J.: Railway signalling and automation, vol. 3. La vie du rail (2014)

18. Svendsen, A., Haugen, Ø., Møller-Pedersen, B.: Synthesizing software models: generating train station models automatically. In: Ober, I., Ober, I. (eds.) SDL 2011. LNCS, vol. 7083, pp. 38–53. Springer, Heidelberg (2011). https://doi.org/10.1007/978-3-642-25264-8_5

19. Vu, L.H., Haxthausen, A., Peleska, J.: A domain-specific language for railway interlocking systems. In: 10th Symposium on Formal Methods for Automation and Safety in Railway and Automotive Systems, pp. 200–209 (2014)

Probabilistic Verification for Reliable Network-on-Chip System Design

Benjamin Lewis[1]([✉])[iD], Arnd Hartmanns[2][iD], Prabal Basu[1][iD],
Rajesh Jayashankara Shridevi[1][iD], Koushik Chakraborty[1][iD],
Sanghamitra Roy[1][iD], and Zhen Zhang[1][iD]

[1] Utah State University, Logan, UT, USA
{benjamin.lewis,prabalb,rajesh.js}@aggiemail.usu.edu,
{koushik.chakraborty,sanghamitra.roy,zhen.zhang}@usu.edu
[2] University of Twente, Enschede, The Netherlands
a.hartmanns@utwente.nl

Abstract. The design of modern network-on-chip (NoC) systems faces reliability challenges due to process and environmental variations. Peak power supply noise (PSN) in the power delivery network of a NoC device plays a critical role in determining reliable operations: PSN typically leads to voltage droop, which can cause timing errors in the NoC router pipelines. Existing simulation-based approaches cannot provide rigorous, worst-case reliability guarantees on the probabilistic behaviors of PSN. To address this problem, this paper takes a significant step in formally analyzing PSN in modern NoCs. Specifically, we present a probabilistic model checking approach for the rigorous characterization of PSN for a generic central router of a large mesh-NoC system, under the Round Robin scheduling mechanism with a uniform random network traffic load. Defining features for PSN are extracted at the behavioral level to facilitate property formulation. Several abstract models have been derived for the central router's concrete model based on the observations of its arbiter's conflict resolution behavior. Probabilistic modeling and verification are performed using the MODEST TOOLSET. Results show significant scalability of our abstract models, and reveal key PSN characteristics that are indicative of NoC design and optimization.

Keywords: Probabilistic model checking · Network-on-chip · Reliability analysis · Power supply noise

1 Introduction

The advancement in probabilistic model checking has enabled its applications in a wide range of domains, including cryptography [11], systems biology [22], network protocols [21], game theory [6], and distributed systems [20]. Likewise, in recent times, the growing demand for robust and secure digital system design has challenged the potential for innovation in formal methods. In this work, we

© Springer Nature Switzerland AG 2019
K. G. Larsen and T. Willemse (Eds.): FMICS 2019, LNCS 11687, pp. 110–126, 2019.
https://doi.org/10.1007/978-3-030-27008-7_7

venture into the probabilistic model checking of the reliability evaluation of a complex and distributed digital system—the on-chip communication network, *network-on-chip* (NoC), deployed in a many-core system.

NoC—the de-facto standard for on-chip communication in modern many-core systems—*generally* comprises of several topologically homogeneous routers operating synchronously in a decentralized control system. Despite the conceptual similarity with conventional computer networks, a NoC is subject to several unique reliability challenges, e.g., process and environmental variations, that are vastly dissimilar to conventional network communication. Over a decade of simulation-based research has gone into NoC design exploration and reliability analysis [1–3,27]. However, simulation-based ecosystems fail to provide worst-case reliability and safety guarantees. Consequently, formal verification is necessary to ensure the correctness of specific functionality of the NoC components.

The primary challenge of applying automated verification, specifically, model checking, is the notorious state explosion issue, as evidenced by a recent work on model checking an asynchronous NoC [31] where the intermediate state space corresponding to only 13 out of the 66 components in a 3×3 NoC consists of several hundred million states. Consequently, accurate modeling of the reliability issues (e.g., power supply noise, quality-of-service guarantees, etc.) is poised to further aggravate its computational complexity.

This paper presents a probabilistic model checking method for the analysis of *power supply noise* (PSN) for a generic central router of a large mesh-NoC system and its impact on the router's reliability under uniform random traffic loads. To enable an accurate and efficient analysis and a convenient formulation of the probabilistic properties, we extract the key characterizing features of the router at the behavioral level. We present formal models for the central router with four full-duplex channels, operated under uniform random packet injection with the starvation-free Round Robin conflict resolution scheduling. To tackle the state space explosion challenge, abstract models have been derived based on critical observations of conflict resolution patterns. Transition probabilities between abstract states are inferred from exhaustive executions of the underlying concrete models with limited steps. We use the high-level formal modeling language MODEST [13] to formulate our models, the state spaces of which are large discrete-time Markov chains (DTMC), and the MODEST TOOLSET's [15] probabilistic model checker MCSTA for the analysis. We check *reward-bounded* properties, for which MCSTA implements scalable analysis techniques [12]; in particular the state elimination approach resulted in significant analysis speedups. The final verification results show significant scalability of our abstract models, and reveal key relations between traffic loads and PSN.

2 Motivation

PSN in the power delivery network of an integrated circuit is composed of two major components: (a) *resistive noise*, which is estimated by the product of the current drawn and the lumped resistance of the circuit; and (b) *inductive noise* that is caused by the inductance the power grid and is proportional to the rate of change of current through the inductance ($\frac{\Delta i}{\Delta t}$). For a distributed system such as a NoC, the latter takes a central component [2].

A high inductive noise is responsible for the intermittent peaks in the cycle-wise noise profile of a NoC. Basu et al. have recently demonstrated that, in an 8 × 8 NoC, the peak PSN can increase from 40% of the supply voltage at the 32-nm technology node to about 80% of the supply voltage at the 14-nm technology node, while running a uniform-random synthetic traffic pattern [2]. Voltage droop due to PSN can radically degrade the delay of various on-chip circuit components. Such increase in the delay has the potential to engender *timing errors* in the pipe-stages of the NoC routers, thus severely impacting the reliability as well as the performance of the overall on-chip communication.

Although recent works [2,27] tackle the PSN problem in NoCs to some extent, they do not guarantee the worst-case peak PSN—a determinant of the NoC reliability—across different operating conditions, realistically conceivable, for any parallel workload. Moreover, these works do not provide any bounds on the temporal PSN profile for a router, given an application execution. Consequently, existing approaches to mitigate PSN are a far cry from a truly reliable NoC design paradigm that can be deployed in mission-critical systems. On the contrary, this work shows that probabilistic model checking, despite its inherent challenges, can offer precise bounds on the performance and reliability with common environment assumptions, leading the way to future reliable NoC design.

3   Related Work

Reliable and energy efficient communication is the backbone of many-core systems. Significant recent research exploring *reactive, proactive* and *predictive* techniques has focused on addressing the challenges of fault tolerance in NoC [4,5,7,17,28]. However, a wide majority of these works are simulation-based analyses, which cannot provide rigorous reliability and performance guarantees.

Formal verification in NoC architectures has largely been focused on functional correctness of routing algorithms [26,31,32]. Zhang et al. investigate properties of deadlock and livelock freedom and tolerance to link failure, and use model checking to enhance an existing routing protocol [31,32]. Based on theorem proving techniques, the DCI2 developed by Verbeek demonstrates significant scalability in proving properties of deadlock and livelock freedom and topology violations of statically determined routing logic [29]. Accurate assessment of NoC reliability has to incorporate quantitative aspects depicting the inherent distributive and reactive nature of NoC. Coste et al. presents in [8] a translation procedure to convert existing functional model into Markov chains for the evaluation of the latency of memory accesses over a *Globally Asynchronous Locally Synchronous* (GALS) NoC. Nevertheless, the scope of existing literature in probabilistic verification of the NoC is minimal.

On the other hand, researchers have extensively employed probabilistic verification to assess and improve reliability, resilience, and security of computer hardware designs [10,24,25,30]. For example, Han et al. demonstrate how to obtain the fundamental error bounds by using bifurcation analysis based on probabilistic models of unreliable gates [14]. Kumar et al. propose an automatic compositional reasoning technique to improve the scalability of probabilistic model checking of hardware systems [19]. Mundhenk et al. propose probabilistic model checking for the security analysis of automotive architectures at the system level [23]. However, the dividends of these works have not yet been carried forward to the NoC domain.

4   Conflict Resolution in Central Routers

Figure 1 depicts the central router of an 8×8, two-dimensional mesh NoC network [2]. It has four full-duplex channels with the bandwidth of one flit of a network packet, where each channel has a buffer with the capability of storing four flits. The router simultaneously transmits and receives flits in all four directions. Assume that each flit carries the next forwarding direction, and that a flit is not diverted back to its incoming direction. The forwarding direction is used for the arbiter in the central

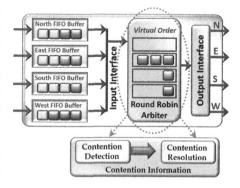

Fig. 1. NoC router model.

router to detect possible conflicts. The arbiter resolves conflicts, created by multiple flits originated from the four buffers attempting the same output direction. The order of conflict resolution relies on the Round Robin scheduling mechanism to guarantee fairness and starvation-free arbitration. The input interface handles flits arrived from all of four directions, and accommodates them in the first available space in the corresponding buffer. The output interface directs flits from the arbiter that are ready to be dispatched to the neighboring routers. The rest of this section describes details of the arbiter's conflict resolution mechanism.

Since the bandwidth of all outgoing channels allows only one flit at a time, conflicts are resolved inside the central router. Conflicts affect the performance of each individual router and hence the entire NoC. During each clock cycle, the arbiter first examines each buffer's front flit's outgoing direction to detect conflicts. If no conflict exists, all the buffers can forward their front flits to their respective outputs in one cycle to maximize the throughput. Otherwise, the arbiter has to resolve all conflicts, requiring one or more additional cycles. Figure 2 demonstrates three representative scenarios of conflicts and their resolution. For simplicity, we ignore the incoming packets to all four buffers at each cycle, and only illustrate conflict resolution. In Scenario A, only one conflict exists between the east and west buffers at cycle t_n, and the east buffer has higher priority. The arbiter, therefore, serves the east buffer at cycle t_n, and

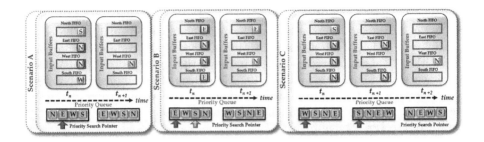

Fig. 2. Conflict scenarios.

it also directs the north and south buffers in this cycle, as their flits do not conflict. In the following cycle t_{n+1}, the priority gets updated by shifting the priority queue, and the west buffer is served. Scenario B demonstrates two pairs of conflicts: the north and south buffers compete for the east output, while east and west compete for the north output in cycle t_n. Following the priority queue, the arbiter serves the east and south buffers in cycle t_n, and the west and north buffers in the next cycle. Scenario C illustrates a three-way conflict: all front flits of the east, west, and south buffers compete for the north output. The arbiter serves the west buffer first, and simultaneously serves the north buffer as it is not conflicting with others. In the following cycle t_{n+1}, the south buffer gets serviced, as it has higher priority than the east, leaving the east buffer to be serviced in cycle t_{n+2}.

5   Formal Model of the Central Router

The formal model implements all potential conflicts in the central router. The MODEST language [13] is used to model the router as shown in Fig. 1. We introduce a datatype `buffer` shown in Listing 1.1. Integer variable `dest` represents the front flit's destination in each buffer: 0 (north), 1 (east), 2 (south), or 3 (west). Value −1 indicates an empty buffer. The field `id` stores the buffer location in the central router, with the same encoding as the flit's destination. Variable `serviced` is `true` if the front flit was serviced in the current cycle, and `false` otherwise. The `priority` field represents the priority position each buffer will occupy in the next clock cycle. Lastly, the actual buffer, `buff`, is modeled as an integer linked list. The size of `buff` is set to four for all models presented in this paper, but its length can be set to any finite integer. The arbiter model `arb` is an array of four `buffer` values. The position of `buffer` in `arb` represents the current priority for servicing all four buffers, array index 0 being the highest priority and 3 being the lowest. For example, if `arb[1]` refers to the east buffer with `id = 1` and `priority = 3`, then at the beginning of the next cycle the buffer will have been moved to position `arb[3]`. Two internal integer variables, namely, `unserviced` and `totalUnserviced`, are used in the Round Robin scheduling mechanism: `unserviced` counts the number of unserviced buffers in one cycle due to

Listing 1.1. Buffer model.

```
datatype buffer = {int(-1..3) dest, int(0..3) id,
   bool serviced, int(0..3) priority, intlist option buff};
buffer north, east, south, west;
buffer[] arb = [north, east, south, west];
int(0..2) unserviced;
int(0..2) totalUnserviced;
```

Listing 1.2. Procedure for updating serviced and unserviced.

```
arb[0].serviced = true;
if (arb[1].dest != -1 && arb[1].dest == arb[0].dest) {
   arb[1].serviced = false;
   unserviced++;
}
else {
   arb[1].serviced = true;
}
if(arb[1].dest != -1 && (arb[2].dest == arb[1].dest || arb
   [2].dest == arb[0].dest)) {
      arb[2].serviced = false;
      unserviced++;
}
else {
      arb[2].serviced = true
}
if(arb[1].dest != -1 && (arb[3].dest == arb[2].dest || arb
   [3].dest == arb[1].dest || arb[3].dest == arb[0].dest)) {
      arb[3].serviced = false;
      unserviced++;
}
else {
      arb[3].serviced = true;
}

totalServiced = unserviced;
```

conflict, and decrements as the unserviced buffer's priority values are calculated; and `totalUnserviced` tracks the total number of buffers unserviced in one cycle.

The `serviced` field for each buffer and `unserviced` are updated by the procedure shown in Listing 1.2. It automatically sets `serviced` to `true` for the buffer in position 0, because the arbiter will definitely serve this buffer in the current cycle. It then moves on to the buffers in all remaining positions. If a buffer is non-empty and is in conflict with another buffer with higher priority, then the latter will be serviced in the current cycle and the former has to wait for its chance in the next cycle. Therefore, `serviced` of the former is set to `false` and `unserviced` is incremented. Otherwise `serviced` is set to `true`. Lastly, the arbiter assigns `totalUnserviced` the updated `unserviced`.

Next, priority for each buffer gets updated using the procedure shown in Listing 1.3. It should be noted that priority update is assumed to strictly follow the order shown in the procedure, starting with the buffer in position 0 of the arbiter array `arb`. If the buffer at `arb[i]` was serviced, its `dest` is updated by peeking the front of the corresponding buffer, followed by an update of the buffer

Listing 1.3. Update priority.

```
for(int i = 0, i < 3, i++) {
    if (arb[i].serviced == true) {
        arb[i].dest = peekFront(arb[i].buff);
        arb[i].buff = dequeue(arb[i].buff);
        arb[i].priority = i + unserviced;
    }
    else {
        arb[i].priority = totalUnserviced - unserviced;
        unserviced--;
    }
}
```

itself. If no element is in `buff`, the `peekFront` function will return -1 to indicate an empty buffer. The `priority` is updated to the sum of its current priority `i` and the number of unserviced buffers, whose priorities have not been updated. Intuitively, buffers not serviced in the current cycle will be given higher priority in the next, and those serviced receive priority corresponding to their position in the arbiter array. If the buffer was not serviced, the `priority` is determined by subtracting `unserviced` from the total number of unserviced buffers in the current cycle, after which the `unserviced` is decremented. We use this method to keep track of the order for buffers that did not get serviced in the current cycle.

As an example, assume `arb=[north, east, south, west]`, and `serviced` are `true`, `false`, `true`, and `false`, respectively. Both `unserviced` and `totalUnserviced` are set to 2, because the east and west buffers were not serviced in the current cycle. Priority updates start with `arb[0]`, i.e., the north buffer. Since it was serviced in the current cycle, its priority is updated to $0 + 2 = 2$. The value of `unserviced` remains at 2. Next, the priority is updated for the east buffer. Because it was not serviced in the current cycle, its priority is set to $2-2 = 0$, giving itself the top priority for the next cycle. The value of `unserviced` then decrements from 2 to 1, indicating that one remaining unserviced buffer is scheduled for the next cycle. Similarly, priorities for the south and west buffers are updated to $2+1 = 3$ and $2 - 1 = 1$, respectively. The variable `unserviced` decrements to 0 after all priory updates. The resulting arbiter array is [`east, west, north, south`].

To model incoming flits to all four buffers, we randomly assign their `dest` fields using the discrete uniform distribution, with the exception that a buffer does not receive a flit destined to its incoming direction. Probabilistic model checking on this routing node model incurs exponential state space growth as cycles increase, quickly becoming too large to be handled. For 100 clock cycles, MCSTA explored 400 million states with another 100 million queued for expansion when 132 GB memory were filled. This is mainly due to the combinatorial explosion of flit values. To address this issue, we present several abstract router models next.

6   Abstract Models and Refinement

Abstract models presented in this paper are based on an ad-hoc method specifically for the central router. The initial abstraction is based on the observation that rather than specific scenarios of conflicts formed by the dest field of four buffers, the arbiter's behavior is *only* determined by a few conflict patterns that can co-exist in one cycle, including non-conflicting scenarios. This observation leads to four abstract states: (1) no conflicts, where all buffers are serviced in the current cycle; (2) one pair of conflicts, where the only unserviced buffer is the one with lower priority in the pair; (3) two pairs of conflicts with two unserviced buffers, both of which have lower priority compared to their conflicting counterparts; and (4) three buffers in conflict, where the two buffers with low priorities are not serviced in the current cycle. Four buffers cannot all be in conflict as it is assumed that a flit is not diverted back to its incoming direction.

Since the abstract model is formulated at the behavioral level without circuit-level details, one has to project the measure of PSN onto the same abstract level. We know that the inductive noise, a major source of PSN, is proportional to the rate of change of current in the circuit. An abrupt change in the router activity in two consecutive cycles directly leads to a high rate of current change [2]. A low router activity is characterized by the arbiter serving no routers in a cycle, as all buffers are empty; while a high router activity is indicated by the arbiter serving three or more buffers in a cycle. The relative frequency of both high-to-low and low-to-high activities over a given timespan can, therefore, accurately reflect the state of the local noise and hence PSN in the NoC routers. For this purpose, we consider the following two probabilistic properties: (1) the probability that the number of high router activity cycles is lower-bounded by $k \cdot N$ within N overall cycles; and (2) the probability that the total number of high-to-low and low-to-high activities is lower-bounded by $k \cdot N$ within N overall cycles, where $k \in (0,1)$. High router activity, as indicated by property (1), can potentially create a high local congestion in the network, leading to a high PSN due to an unbalanced power density [9]. On the other hand, property (2) reflects a large and sudden load change in a router that can lead to a large inductive drop in the power delivery network of the NoC [2]. Collectively, understanding these properties is essential to ascertain the minimum voltage guardband for the NoC, sufficient to ensure a fault-free communication in a many-core system. To facilitate checking of these properties, two variables are created, namely, optimalRuns, which increments if all four buffers are serviced in a cycle, and noiseRuns, which accumulates cycles with high-to-low or low-to-high activities. Formulation of these properties is presented in Sect. 8.

The initial abstract model, however, is incorrect in that after two clock cycles, the accumulation of optimalRuns diverges from that obtained from the concrete model. This is because the probability varies when transitioning between two states with two-pair conflict. Specifically, different scenarios of two-pair conflict result in different probabilities. Table 1 illustrates some examples. Each entry listed under columns arb[i] shows the buffer location and the destination of its front element. For example, "n(e)" under column arb[2] means that the north buffer's front flit is destined for the east output. The entry "w(n, e, s)" in the same column indicates that the west buffer can receive a flit destined to any other three directions. For state "2a", if the arbiter has the two-pair conflict in cycle k, then `arb[0]` and `arb[1]` are serviced, allowing "n(e)" and "e(n)" to move to `arb[0]` and `arb[1]`, respectively, in the next cycle. Observe that at cycle $k+1$, two-pair conflict scenarios include (n(e), e(n), w(n), s(e)) and (n(e), e(n), w(e), s(n)), and the possible three-way conflicts are (n(e), e(n), w(e), s(e)) and (n(e), e(n), w(n), s(n)). For state "2b" with a different two-pair conflict pattern at cycle k, the next cycle can only form the two-pair conflict (w(n), s(e), n(e), e(n)), and no three-way conflict can exist. For state "2c", the only two-pair conflict is (w(s), s(e), n(e), e(s)), and the only three-way conflict is (w(s), s(e), n(s), e(s)). Our analysis reveals that such discrepancies exist in other abstract states.

The four-abstract model is refined based on an analysis of all possible inputs into the arbiter and their respective behaviors. The possible inputs can be grouped into thirteen behaviors which are defined as states as shown in Table 2. Each refined state is conditioned on the number of unserviced buffers at the end

Table 1. History-dependent conflict examples.

State	Cycle	arb[0]	arb[1]	arb[2]	arb[3]
2a	k	w(n)	s(e)	n(e)	e(n)
	$k+1$	n(e)	e(n)	w(n, e, s)	s(n, e, w)
2b	k	n(e)	e(n)	w(n)	s(e)
	$k+1$	w(n)	s(e)	n(e, w, s)	e(n, w, s)
2c	k	n(e)	e(s)	w(s)	s(e)
	$k+1$	w(s)	s(e)	n(e, w, s)	e(n, w, s)

of a cycle and where the flit's destination points, specifically, buffer locations (i.e., the `id` field) the destinations at the arbiter's positions 0 and 1 point to. This table shows predicates defining these refinement conditions. Notations have been simplified as follows: $dest_i$ represents the front flit's destination of the buffer at index i of the arbiter array, i.e., `arb[i].dest`.

To calculate transition probabilities among the thirteen abstract states, we modify the concrete model to include two variables: s_{prev} and s. For every clock cycle, s_{prev} first updates to s and then all predicates in Table 2 are evaluated and s is updated accordingly. Assuming the model starts with no conflicts ($s_{prev} = 0$), we observe that for *up to* two transitions, which corresponds to two clock cycles, *every* one of the thirteen states in Table 2 is reachable. Transition probability emanating from state 0 to an abstract state, say 1b, is calculated by summarizing all probabilities of transitioning from the concrete state 0, which is the same as the abstract state 0, to all concrete states that satisfy the predicate for state 1b, which is *unserviced* $= 1 \wedge dest_0 = id_2$. For this calculation, we added to the model a variable clk that is incremented with every clock cycle. The calculation is then performed by first using MCSTA to query for

$$\mathbf{P}_{=?}(\diamond\, (clk = 2 \wedge s_{prev} = 0 \wedge s = 2)),$$

i.e., the probability to eventually ($\diamond$) reach a state in the model after two clock cycles where $s_{prev} = 0$ and the new abstract state is $s = 2$, i.e., 1b in Table 2. We then divide the result by the sum of probabilities out of state 0. Other transition probabilities are calculated similarly. Another observation is that the next states and transition probabilities from states 2b and 2c are identical, so we combine them into state 2b to form a twelve-state abstract model as shown in Table 3.

Table 2. Refined abstract model with thirteen states.

State	Predicate
0	$unserviced = 0$
1a	$unserviced = 1 \wedge dest_0 = id_1$
1b	$unserviced = 1 \wedge dest_0 = id_2$
1c	$unserviced = 1 \wedge dest_0 = id_3$
2a	$unserviced = 2 \wedge dest_0 \neq dest_1 \wedge dest_0 = id_1 \wedge dest_1 = id_0$
2b	$unserviced = 2 \wedge dest_0 \neq dest_1 \wedge dest_0 = id_2 \wedge dest_1 = id_3$
2c	$unserviced = 2 \wedge dest_0 \neq dest_1 \wedge dest_0 = id_3 \wedge dest_1 = id_2$
2d	$unserviced = 2 \wedge dest_0 \neq dest_1 \wedge dest_0 = id_1 \wedge dest_1 = id_2$
2e	$unserviced = 2 \wedge dest_0 \neq dest_1 \wedge dest_0 = id_1 \wedge dest_1 = id_3$
2f	$unserviced = 2 \wedge dest_0 \neq dest_1 \wedge dest_0 = id_2 \wedge dest_1 = id_0$
2g	$unserviced = 2 \wedge dest_0 \neq dest_1 \wedge dest_0 = id_3 \wedge dest_1 = id_0$
3a	$unserviced = 2 \wedge dest_0 = dest_1 = id_2$
3b	$unserviced = 2 \wedge dest_0 = dest_1 = id_3$

7   Including Idle Cycles in the Abstract Model

The twelve-state abstract model shown in Table 3 assumes that a flit is injected to all buffers in *every* cycle. This is, however, not quite realistic as it is common that one or more buffers do not receive an incoming flit. Such situations change the conflict patterns and hence the arbiter's resolution behavior. From [2], we know that the cycle-wise and intermittent PSN is a direct result of a significant change of buffers served. Precisely three or four buffers are serviced by the arbiter between two consecutive clock cycles. Counting these changes allows us to accurately reflect the state of the local noise and hence PSN in the NoC routers. This implies that change from serving zero to four buffers and vice versa needs to be modeled. This section describes a modified abstract model to include idle cycles for each buffer. Using similar method as described in Sect. 6, refinement is applied to the twelve-state abstract model to account for scenarios with three, two, one, and none serviced buffers in one cycle. This leads to the twenty-five-state abstract model provided in Table 4. The state notation in this table represents the conflict scenario and the number of buffers with incoming flits in a given state. For example state 2_4^b represents the state with the conflict scenario 2b in Table 2 in which four buffers have incoming flits. Note that this refinement does not change the fact that probabilities in this table can be calculated by checking its underlying concrete model for two clock cycles as described in Sect. 6.

Table 3. Twelve-state abstract model with transition probabilities.

	0	1a	1b	1c	2a	2b	2d	2e	2f	2g	3a	3b
0	$\frac{1}{9}$	$\frac{4}{27}$	$\frac{16}{81}$	$\frac{20}{81}$	$\frac{1}{27}$	$\frac{3}{81}$	$\frac{2}{81}$	$\frac{1}{81}$	$\frac{1}{81}$	$\frac{2}{81}$	$\frac{1}{27}$	$\frac{1}{9}$
1a	$\frac{1}{9}$	$\frac{4}{27}$	$\frac{8}{27}$	$\frac{4}{27}$	0	$\frac{2}{27}$	0	$\frac{1}{27}$	0	$\frac{1}{27}$	$\frac{1}{27}$	$\frac{1}{9}$
1b	$\frac{1}{9}$	$\frac{4}{27}$	$\frac{2}{9}$	$\frac{2}{9}$	$\frac{1}{27}$	$\frac{1}{27}$	0	0	$\frac{1}{27}$	$\frac{1}{27}$	$\frac{1}{27}$	$\frac{1}{9}$
1c	$\frac{1}{9}$	$\frac{4}{27}$	$\frac{2}{27}$	$\frac{10}{27}$	$\frac{2}{27}$	0	$\frac{2}{27}$	0	$\frac{1}{81}$	0	$\frac{1}{27}$	$\frac{1}{9}$
2a	$\frac{1}{9}$	$\frac{2}{9}$	$\frac{2}{9}$	0	0	$\frac{2}{9}$	0	0	0	0	$\frac{1}{9}$	$\frac{1}{9}$
2b	$\frac{2}{9}$	$\frac{1}{9}$	$\frac{1}{9}$	$\frac{4}{9}$	$\frac{1}{9}$	0	0	0	0	0	0	0
2d	$\frac{1}{9}$	$\frac{1}{9}$	$\frac{1}{3}$	$\frac{2}{9}$	0	0	0	0	0	$\frac{1}{9}$	0	$\frac{1}{9}$
2e	$\frac{1}{9}$	$\frac{1}{9}$	$\frac{1}{3}$	$\frac{2}{9}$	0	0	0	$\frac{1}{9}$	0	0	0	$\frac{1}{9}$
2f	$\frac{1}{9}$	$\frac{1}{3}$	$\frac{1}{9}$	$\frac{2}{9}$	0	0	0	0	$\frac{1}{9}$	0	$\frac{1}{9}$	0
2g	$\frac{1}{9}$	$\frac{1}{3}$	$\frac{1}{9}$	$\frac{2}{9}$	0	0	$\frac{1}{9}$	0	0	0	$\frac{1}{9}$	0
3a	0	0	$\frac{4}{9}$	0	0	$\frac{1}{9}$	0	0	0	$\frac{1}{9}$	0	$\frac{1}{3}$
3b	0	0	0	$\frac{4}{9}$	$\frac{1}{9}$	0	$\frac{1}{9}$	0	0	0	0	$\frac{1}{3}$

8   Verification Results

All experiments have been performed on the abstract central router models, which are constructed as DTMC models using the high-level compositional modeling language MODEST. The explicit-state probabilistic model checker MCSTA in the MODEST TOOLSET has been used for verification. Properties (1) and (2) are bounded probabilistic reachability queries for the transient behavior up to N clock cycles, with N being a rather large number. Implementing the cycle counter *clk* as a state variable, which we did for the computations in Sect. 6 with bound 2, would *unfold* the model over the cycle count up to the (now large) bound, exacerbating the state space explosion problem. To avoid this problem now, we made *clk* a *transient* variable that is set to 1 when moving from one clock cycle to the next and to 0 otherwise. A transient variable is only "live" during the assignments executed when taking a transition; it is not part of the state vector. In this way, clock cycle progress becomes a *reward* annotation to certain transitions instead of being encoded in the structure of an (unfolded) state space. We can then formalize properties (1) and (2) as reward-bounded reachability queries:

$$(1)\quad \mathbf{P}_{=?}(\diamond^{[\text{accumulate}(clk)\leqslant N]}\ \texttt{optimalRuns} \geqslant k \cdot N)$$

$$(2)\quad \mathbf{P}_{=?}(\diamond^{[\text{accumulate}(clk)\leqslant N]}\ \texttt{noiseRuns} \geqslant k \cdot N)$$

We use the state elimination method [12] implemented in MCSTA for the reward-bounded property checking reported in this section. For our experiments, it provides a significant scalability and efficiency improvement over the classic unfolding-based approaches, but also over the default modified-iteration method, both of which we attempted to use in earlier versions of this model. In this way, our experience mirrors the performance behaviour observed earlier in [12,16,18].

Table 4. Twenty-five-state abstract model with transition probabilities.

	0_4	1_4^a	1_4^b	1_4^c	2_4^a	2_4^b	2_4^c	2_4^d	2_4^e	2_4^f	2_4^g	3_4^a	3_4^b	0_3	1_3^a	1_3^b	1_3^c	3_3^a	3_3^b	0_2	1_2^a	1_2^b	1_2^c	0_1	0_0
0_4	9/256	3/64	1/16	5/64	3/256	1/256	1/128	1/128	1/256	1/256	1/128	3/256	9/256	11/64	15/256	5/64	25/256	1/256	3/256	21/128	3/256	1/64	5/256	1/64	1/256
1_4^a	3/64	1/16	1/8	1/16	0	1/64	1/64	0	1/64	0	1/64	1/64	3/64	11/64	3/64	5/32	1/32	0	1/64	7/64	0	1/32	0	1/64	0
1_4^b	3/64	1/16	3/32	3/32	1/64	0	1/64	0	0	1/64	1/64	1/64	3/64	11/64	3/64	3/32	3/32	0	1/64	7/64	0	1/64	1/64	1/64	0
1_4^c	3/64	1/16	3/32	5/32	1/32	0	0	1/32	0	0	0	1/64	3/64	11/64	3/64	1/64	11/64	0	1/64	7/64	0	0	1/32	1/64	0
2_4^a	1/16	1/8	1/8	0	0	1/16	1/16	0	0	0	0	1/16	1/16	1/32	1/32	1/32	0	0	0	1/64	0	0	0	0	0
2_4^b	1/8	1/16	1/16	1/4	1/16	0	0	0	0	0	0	0	0	1/4	0	0	1/8	0	0	1/16	0	0	0	0	0
2_4^c	1/8	1/16	1/16	1/4	1/16	0	0	0	0	0	0	0	0	1/4	0	0	1/8	0	0	1/16	0	0	0	0	0
2_4^d	1/16	1/16	3/16	1/16	0	0	0	0	0	0	1/16	3/16	1/8	3/16	0	1/8	1/16	0	0	1/16	0	0	0	0	0
2_4^e	1/16	1/16	3/16	1/16	0	0	0	0	1/16	0	0	0	1/16	3/16	0	1/8	1/16	0	0	1/16	0	0	0	0	0
2_4^f	1/16	3/16	1/16	1/16	0	0	0	0	0	1/16	0	1/16	0	3/16	1/8	0	1/16	0	0	1/16	0	0	0	0	0
2_4^g	1/16	3/16	1/16	1/16	0	0	0	1/16	0	0	0	1/16	0	3/16	1/8	0	1/16	0	0	1/16	0	0	0	0	0
3_4^a	0	0	1/4	0	0	0	1/16	0	0	0	1/16	0	3/16	0	0	5/16	0	0	1/16	0	0	1/16	0	0	0
3_4^b	0	0	0	1/4	1/16	0	0	1/16	0	0	0	0	3/16	0	0	0	5/16	0	1/16	0	0	1/16	0	0	0
0_3	9/256	3/64	1/16	5/64	3/256	1/256	1/128	1/128	1/256	1/256	1/128	3/256	9/256	11/64	15/256	5/64	25/256	1/256	3/256	21/128	3/256	1/64	5/256	1/64	1/256
1_3^a	3/64	1/16	1/8	1/16	0	1/64	1/64	0	1/64	0	1/64	1/64	3/64	11/64	3/64	5/32	1/32	0	1/64	7/64	0	1/32	0	1/64	0
1_3^b	3/64	1/16	3/32	3/32	1/64	0	1/64	0	0	1/64	1/64	1/64	3/64	11/64	3/64	3/32	3/32	0	1/64	7/64	0	1/64	1/64	1/64	0
1_3^c	3/64	1/16	3/32	5/32	1/32	0	0	1/32	0	0	0	1/64	3/64	11/64	3/64	1/64	11/64	0	1/64	7/64	0	0	1/32	1/64	0
3_3^a	0	0	1/4	0	0	0	1/16	0	0	0	1/16	0	3/16	0	0	5/16	0	0	1/16	0	0	1/16	0	0	0
3_3^b	0	0	0	1/4	1/16	0	0	1/16	0	0	0	0	3/16	0	0	0	5/16	0	1/16	0	0	1/16	0	0	0
0_2	9/256	3/64	1/16	5/64	3/256	1/256	1/128	1/128	1/256	1/256	1/128	3/256	9/256	11/64	15/256	5/64	25/256	1/256	3/256	21/128	3/256	1/64	5/256	1/64	1/256
1_2^a	3/64	1/16	1/8	1/16	0	1/64	1/64	0	1/64	0	1/64	1/64	3/64	11/64	3/64	5/32	1/32	0	1/64	7/64	0	1/32	0	1/64	0
1_2^b	3/64	1/16	3/32	3/32	1/64	0	1/64	0	0	1/64	1/64	1/64	3/64	11/64	3/64	3/32	3/32	0	1/64	7/64	0	1/64	1/64	1/64	0
1_2^c	3/64	1/16	3/32	5/32	1/32	0	0	1/32	0	0	0	1/64	3/64	11/64	3/64	1/64	11/64	0	1/64	7/64	0	0	1/32	1/64	0
0_1	9/256	3/64	1/16	5/64	3/256	1/256	1/128	1/128	1/256	1/256	1/128	3/256	9/256	11/64	15/256	5/64	25/256	1/256	3/256	21/128	3/256	1/64	5/256	1/64	1/256
0_0	9/256	3/64	1/16	5/64	3/256	1/256	1/128	1/128	1/256	1/256	1/128	3/256	9/256	11/64	15/256	5/64	25/256	1/256	3/256	21/128	3/256	1/64	5/256	1/64	1/256

Results are generated on a desktop computer with an AMD Ryzen Thread-ripper 12-Core 3.5 GHz Processor and 132 GB memory, running Ubuntu Linux. One core is used at any time. All results presented in this section assume uniform random packet arrival at all four buffers. Verification results for property

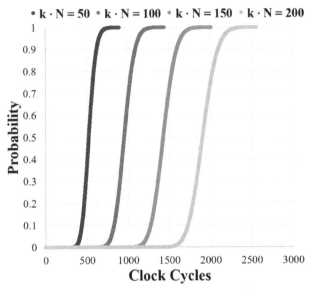

(a) Cumulative probability for **optimalRun**.

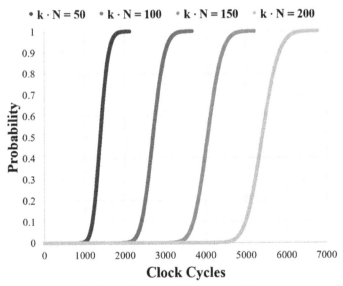

(b) Cumulative probability for **noiseRun**.

Fig. 3. The two probabilistic properties denote high activity (Fig. 3a) and high change in activity (Fig. 3b) in the central router of a mesh NoC, experiencing a uniform-random traffic (Sect. 6). The steep curves reveal a high probability of a heavy congestion, as well as, a sudden and large change in the traffic, which can cause a high PSN in the NoC power delivery network.

(1) are presented for the twelve-state abstract model described in Sect. 6, and it is expected that these results are over-approximations for the abstract model with idle cycles in Sect. 7. For checking property (2), the latter model is used.

Figure 3a shows the cumulative probability for property (1) with several lower bounds. The formal model used for checking this property does not consider any empty buffer, in order to demonstrate the worst case scenario. At the architecture level, a high activity denotes the reception of three or more flits in one cycle. The steep slope of the curves indicates that the central router of a mesh NoC is likely to experience a heavy surge of the traffic load at a relatively short span of time. Such high load of traffic can engender a local hostspot in the network, which in turn, can lead to a large peak PSN.

Figure 3b depicts the cumulative probability for property (2) with several lower bounds. In this case, we consider empty buffers in the formal model of the central router. A high probability of such transitions within a short time span, as seen in this figure, denotes a bursty nature of the traffic encountered by the central router. As a result, there is a large inductive noise in the power delivery network of the NoC. Collectively, these two properties are pivotal in determining the minimum voltage guardband for the central router, because a more conservative guardband marks a power inefficient design, while a smaller one will be prone to intermittent timing errors in the NoC, aggravating its reliability.

Table 5 shows the peak memory usage and the total run-time reported by the MCSTA tool. Model checking property (2) requires significantly more memory than that for property (1). This is due to the increased complexity of the twenty-five-state abstract model depicting idle cycles over the twelve-state model, as well as, that checking property (2) requires more cycles to converge.

Table 5. Performance results.

Property	$k \cdot N$	Peak memory usage (MB)	Total run-time (s)
(1)	50	795	6.6
	100	1393	14.5
	150	2293	24.5
	200	2965	36.3
(2)	50	858	20.7
	100	2993	92.2
	150	6302	249
	200	11522	528.8

9   Conclusion

This paper presents a probabilistic model checking method for the reliability analysis for a generic central router of a large mesh NoC design under uniform random traffic loads. To combat the notorious state explosion problem, abstract models have been derived based on critical observations of conflict resolution using the Round Robin scheduling mechanism. Probabilistic properties are derived by identifying the frequency of abrupt changes in router activities, which causes the inductive noise of PSN. To enable efficient checking, the clock cycle counter variable is set as transient and is treated as a reward annotation only to certain transitions, instead of part of the state space. Verification results reveal crucial PSN behaviors that allow the minimal voltage guardband to be determined for the central router, providing insights in NoC designs with improved reliability.

For future work, we plan to extend the central router model with increased number of channels and variants of Round Robin scheduling mechanisms. Incorporating routing protocols in the router model is also important, as it enables us to model a full NoC and better evaluate its reliability with respect to PSN. Additionally, we plan to investigate probabilistic predicate abstraction techniques to automate the abstraction and refinement of larger NoC models, and evaluate how they may affect the verification of PSN-related properties.

Acknowledgments. Arnd Hartmanns was supported by NWO VENI grant 639.021.754. Benjamin Lewis, Prabal Basu, Rajesh Jayashankara Shridevi, Koushik Chakraborty, and Sanghamitra Roy were supported in part by National Science Foundation (NSF) grants CAREER-1253024, CNS-1421022, and CNS-1421068. Any opinions, findings, and conclusions or recommendations expressed in this material are those of the authors and do not necessarily reflect the views of the NSF.

References

1. Ancajas, D.M., Chakraborty, K., Roy, S., Allred, J.M.: Tackling QoS-induced aging in exascale systems through agile path selection. In: IEEE/ACM International Conference on Hardware/software Codesign and System Synthesis, pp. 1–10 (2014)
2. Basu, P., Shridevi, R.J., Chakraborty, K., Roy, S.: IcoNoClast: tackling voltage noise in the noc power supply through flow-control and routing algorithms. IEEE Trans. VLSI Syst. **25**(7), 2035–2044 (2017)
3. Bhardwaj, K., Chakraborty, K., Roy, S.: An MILP based aging aware routing algorithm for NoCs. In: IEEE/ACM Design Automation & Test in Europe (DATE), pp. 326–331 (2012)
4. Bogdan, P., Marculescu, R.: Hitting time analysis for fault-tolerant communication at nanoscale in future multiprocessor platforms. IEEE Trans. Comput.-Aided Des. Integr. Circ. Syst. (TCAD) **30**(8), 1197–1210 (2011)
5. Chaix, F., Avresky, D., Zergainoh, N.E., Nicolaidis, M.: A fault-tolerant deadlock-free adaptive routing for on chip interconnects. In: IEEE/ACM Design Automation & Test in Europe (DATE), pp. 909–912 (2011)
6. Chen, T., Forejt, V., Kwiatkowska, M., Parker, D., Simaitis, A.: Automatic verification of competitive stochastic systems. Formal Methods Syst. Des. **43**(1), 61–92 (2013)
7. Chou, C.L., Marculescu, R.: FARM: fault-aware resource management in NoC-based multiprocessor platforms. In: IEEE/ACM Design Automation & Test in Europe (DATE), pp. 673–678 (2011)

8. Coste, N., Hermanns, H., Lantreibecq, E., Serwe, W.: Towards performance prediction of compositional models in industrial GALS designs. In: Bouajjani, A., Maler, O. (eds.) CAV 2009. LNCS, vol. 5643, pp. 204–218. Springer, Heidelberg (2009). https://doi.org/10.1007/978-3-642-02658-4_18

9. Dahir, N., Mak, T.S.T., Xia, F., Yakovlev, A.: Modeling and tools for power supply variations analysis in networks-on-chip. IEEE Trans. Comput. (TC) **63**(3), 679–690 (2014)

10. Fang, L., Yamagata, Y., Oiwa, Y.: Evaluation of a resilience embedded system using probabilistic model-checking. arXiv preprint arXiv:1405.1703 (2014)

11. Gay, S., Nagarajan, R., Papanikolaou, N.: Probabilistic model-checking of quantum protocols. arXiv preprint arXiv:quant-ph/0504007 (2005)

12. Hahn, E.M., Hartmanns, A.: A comparison of time- and reward-bounded probabilistic model checking techniques. In: Fränzle, M., Kapur, D., Zhan, N. (eds.) SETTA 2016. LNCS, vol. 9984, pp. 85–100. Springer, Cham (2016). https://doi.org/10.1007/978-3-319-47677-3_6

13. Hahn, E.M., Hartmanns, A., Hermanns, H., Katoen, J.: A compositional modelling and analysis framework for stochastic hybrid systems. Formal Methods Syst. Des. **43**(2), 191–232 (2013)

14. Han, J., Gao, J., Jonker, P., Qi, Y., Fortes, J.A.: Toward hardware-redundant, fault-tolerant logic for nanoelectronics. IEEE Des. Test Comput. **22**(4), 328–339 (2005)

15. Hartmanns, A., Hermanns, H.: The Modest Toolset: an integrated environment for quantitative modelling and verification. In: Ábrahám, E., Havelund, K. (eds.) TACAS 2014. LNCS, vol. 8413, pp. 593–598. Springer, Heidelberg (2014). https://doi.org/10.1007/978-3-642-54862-8_51

16. Hartmanns, A., Junges, S., Katoen, J.-P., Quatmann, T.: Multi-cost bounded reachability in MDP. In: Beyer, D., Huisman, M. (eds.) TACAS 2018. LNCS, vol. 10806, pp. 320–339. Springer, Cham (2018). https://doi.org/10.1007/978-3-319-89963-3_19

17. Hosseini, A., Ragheb, T., Massoud, Y.: A fault-aware dynamic routing algorithm for on-chip networks. In: IEEE International Symposium on Circuits and Systems (ISCAS), pp. 2653–2656 (2008)

18. Klein, J., et al.: Advances in symbolic probabilistic model checking with PRISM. In: Chechik, M., Raskin, J.-F. (eds.) TACAS 2016. LNCS, vol. 9636, pp. 349–366. Springer, Heidelberg (2016). https://doi.org/10.1007/978-3-662-49674-9_20

19. Kumar, J.A., Vasudevan, S.: Automatic compositional reasoning for probabilistic model checking of hardware designs. In: 2010 Seventh International Conference on the Quantitative Evaluation of Systems (QEST), pp. 143–152. IEEE (2010)

20. Kwiatkowska, M., Norman, G., Parker, D.: Probabilistic verification of Herman's self-stabilisation algorithm. Formal Aspects Comput. **24**(4–6), 661–670 (2012)

21. Kwiatkowska, M., Norman, G., Sproston, J., Wang, F.: Symbolic model checking for probabilistic timed automata. Inf. Comput. **205**(7), 1027–1077 (2007)

22. Milazzo, P.: Formal Modeling in Systems Biology: An Approach from Theoretical Computer Science. VDM Verlag (2008)

23. Mundhenk, P., Steinhorst, S., Lukasiewycz, M., Fahmy, S.A., Chakraborty, S.: Security analysis of automotive architectures using probabilistic model checking. In: Proceedings of the 52nd Annual Design Automation Conference, p. 38. ACM (2015)

24. Norman, G., Parker, D., Kwiatkowska, M., Shukla, S., Gupta, R.: Using probabilistic model checking for dynamic power management. Formal Aspects Comput. **17**(2), 160–176 (2005)

25. Norman, G., Parker, D., Kwiatkowska, M., Shukla, S.K.: Evaluating the reliability of defect-tolerant architectures for nanotechnology with probabilistic model checking. In: Proceedings of the 17th International Conference on VLSI Design, pp. 907–912. IEEE (2004)
26. Salamat, R., Khayambashi, M., Ebrahimi, M., Bagherzadeh, N.: A resilient routing algorithm with formal reliability analysis for partially connected 3D-NoCs. IEEE Trans. Comput. **65**(11), 3265–3279 (2016)
27. Shridevi, R.J., Ancajas, D.M., Chakraborty, K., Roy, S.: Tackling voltage emergencies in NoC through timing error resilience. In: ACM International Symposium on Low Power Electronic Devices (ISLPED), pp. 104–109 (2015)
28. Tsai, W.C., Zheng, D.Y., Chen, S.J., Hu, Y.H.: A fault-tolerant NoC scheme using bidirectional channel. In: IEEE/ACM Design Automation Conference (DAC), pp. 918–923 (2011)
29. Verbeek, F.: Formal verification of on-chip communication fabrics (2013)
30. Welke, S.R., Johnson, B.W., Aylor, J.H.: Reliability modeling of hardware/software systems. IEEE Trans. Reliab. **44**(3), 413–418 (1995)
31. Zhang, Z., Serwe, W., Wu, J., Yoneda, T., Zheng, H., Myers, C.: An improved fault-tolerant routing algorithm for a network-on-chip derived with formal analysis. Sci. Comput. Program. **118**, 24–39 (2016)
32. Zhang, Z., Serwe, W., Wu, J., Yoneda, T., Zheng, H., Myers, C.: Formal analysis of a fault-tolerant routing algorithm for a network-on-chip. In: Lang, F., Flammini, F. (eds.) FMICS 2014. LNCS, vol. 8718, pp. 48–62. Springer, Cham (2014). https://doi.org/10.1007/978-3-319-10702-8_4

A Simulator for **LLVM** Bitcode

Petr Ročkai[✉] and Jiří Barnat

Faculty of Informatics, Masaryk University, Brno, Czech Republic
{xrockai,barnat}@fi.muni.cz

Abstract. In this paper, we introduce an interactive simulator for programs in the form of **LLVM** bitcode. The main features of the simulator include precise control over thread scheduling, automatic checkpoints and reverse stepping, support for source-level information about functions and variables in C and C++ programs and structured heap visualisation. Additionally, the simulator is compatible with DiVM (DIVINE VM) hypercalls, which makes it possible to load, simulate and analyse counterexamples from an existing model checker.

1 Introduction

Verification tools are increasingly adopting **LLVM** bitcode as their input language of choice. A frequent reason for implementing **LLVM**-based model checkers (and other analysis tools) is that they can leverage existing compiler front ends, CLang in particular. This in turn enables those model checkers to work with C and even C++ programs without dealing with their irregularity and complexity. Clearly, this tremendously improves the usefulness of any such tool, since C and C++ are widespread implementation languages, and implementation-level model checking is naturally desirable for many reasons.

An additional benefit of the standardisation around the **LLVM** IR [11] (intermediate representation) is that an ecosystem of tools is emerging, where those tools can cooperate through the common input format. Analysis and model checking tools can be used to ascertain correctness of the program with respect to a specification; however, when they find that there is a violation, printing "property violated" is rarely enough. For the result to be genuinely useful, it must somehow convey *how* the specification is violated to the user, so they can analyse the problem and fix their program. One option is to print a *counterexample trace*, which describes the violating execution of the program. In traditional model checkers, for example, it is often sufficient to provide a textual description of the entire execution, since the input model is usually small and its states and transitions can be described compactly.

More advanced tools, however, provide a *simulator*, an interactive tool for stepping through the counterexample, where the user can highlight and investigate particular sections of the counterexample in more detail, and fast-forward through other, uninteresting parts. A simulator is often also useful as

---

This work has been partially supported by the Czech Science Foundation grant No. 18-02177S.

K. G. Larsen and T. Willemse (Eds.): FMICS 2019, LNCS 11687, pp. 127–142, 2019.
https://doi.org/10.1007/978-3-030-27008-7_8

an exploratory tool: the behaviour of the system can be explored by the user, manually navigating through its state space and inspecting variables along the way.

In case of C and C++ programs, it is vitally important that counterexamples can be inspected interactively, since the state of a program is a very complicated structure, often comprising hundreds of kilobytes of structured data. Moreover, violating executions can be quite long, easily hundreds or thousands of distinct states, with non-trivial relationships.

The main contribution of this paper is a reusable simulator for C and C++ code. Since it builds on the LLVM intermediate language, it can be used by multiple different tools which produce counterexamples or otherwise work with LLVM bitcode, and is easily adapted to new high-level languages with LLVM toolchains (like Objective C or Rust). To the best of our knowledge, this work is unique in the sense that no other simulator which would handle C++ programs is available, and simulators which handle C code typically miss important features. Moreover, the simulator is also reusable: while originating from the DIVINE tool set, it can be used standalone, or possibly in combination with other analysis and verification tools.

From a more theoretical standpoint, the *debug graph* (described in Sect. 3.4) represents a new approach to reconciling low-level data as it exists during program runtime with the high-level structure declared in the source code. Another new idea is to build a simulator based on compiled code (as opposed to interpreting the source code directly) and leveraging existing debugger-focused infrastructure (debug metadata in particular), making the implementation especially simple and compact.

The rest of this paper is structured as follows: in Sect. 2 we discuss related work and compare our approach to existing tools. Section 3 describes the LLVM bitcode as it is used by the simulator, how the simulator represents the program state and also introduces the *debug graph*. The focus of Sect. 4 is presentation of the data aspects of a program, while Sect. 5 is concerned with the program's state space. Section 6 mentions some of the more important implementation details. Section 7 wraps the paper up. Additional resources (mainly evaluation-related) are available online[1].

2   Related Work

It is a well-established fact that isolating some bad behaviour of a program in a test is, in itself, not sufficient to easily explain the cause of the problem [1]. The situation is similar in (linear-time) model checking, where a counterexample trace can often be extracted easily enough, but it may not contain sufficient detail, or conversely, may swamp the user in large amount of irrelevant data [15]. The problem also goes beyond the software realm, as witnessed in, for instance, verification of MATLAB Simulink designs [3].

---

[1] https://divine.fi.muni.cz/2019/sim/.

There are basically two orthogonal approaches that attempt to resolve these problems. One is to locate, or at least narrow down, the error automatically, in the hopes that from such a narrowed-down trace, the user will be able to understand the problem by inspection of the source code. In the domain of software verification, this approach is pursued by many tools: counterexamples for violation of temporal properties, generated by the software model checker SLAM [2], for instance, can be analysed and reduced to only cover a small number of source lines, in which the root cause of the error is most likely to lie [1]. An approach to succinctly describe assertion violations (violations of safety properties), based on automated dependency analysis, has also been proposed [4]. Finally, counterexamples from CBMC can be post-processed, in an approach similar to those mentioned above, with a tool called `explain` [6], in this case based on distance metrics.

Unfortunately, even if the problem area is only a few lines of source code, it can be very hard to understand the dynamic behaviour during the erroneous execution. The problem gets much worse when the program in question is parallel, because reasoning about the behaviour of such programs is much harder than it is in the sequential case.

To make understanding and fixing problems in programs (or complex systems in general) easier, many formal verification tools come equipped with a simulator. For instance the UPPAAL tool for analysis of real-time systems provides an integrated graphical simulator [5]. Another example of a formal analysis tool with a graphical simulator would be LTSA [9], based on labelled transition systems as its modelling formalism.

Like many verification tools, the `valgrind` [10] run-time program analyser is primarily non-interactive, but it provides an interface to allow interactive exploration of program state upon encountering a problem, based on `gdb` [13].

Our simulator is based on DiVM [12], an extension of the LLVM language that allows verification and analysis of a wider class of programs (a more detailed description of the DiVM extensions is given in Sect. 3.1). Since pure LLVM is retained as a subset of the DiVM language, the simulator can also transparently work with pure LLVM bitcode.

Besides its relationship to various simulators for modelling and design languages, a simulator for LLVM bitcode is, through its application to code written in standard programming languages like C, related to standard symbolic debuggers. A ubiquitous example on POSIX systems is `gdb`, the GNU debugger [13]. Unlike a simulator, which interprets the program, a debugger instead attaches to a standard process executing in its native environment. A more recent example would be `lldb` [8], which works in essentially the same way, but builds on LLVM components.

2.1 Comparison to Symbolic Debuggers

As outlined above, simulators and debuggers substantially differ in their mode of operation and this leads to very different overall trade-offs. For example, a simulator is much more resilient to memory corruption than a debugger, because the latter has only limited control over the process it is attached to. Both types of tools rely on understanding the execution stack of the program; however, if the program corrupts its execution stack, a debugger must rely on imprecise heuristics to detect this fact and risks providing wrong and possibly misleading information to the user. The simulator can, on the other hand, quite easily prevent such corruption from happening, since it simulates the program at instruction level, and can enforce much stricter memory protections.

On the other hand, the situation is reversed when the program interacts with its surroundings through the operating system. In a debugger, such communication comes about transparently from the fact that the program is a standard process in the operating system and has all the standard facilities at its disposal. In a simulator, communication with the operating system must be specifically relayed and due to imperfections in this translation, some programs may misbehave in the simulation.

Finally, a simulator has a substantial advantage in two additional areas: first, a simulator can very precisely and comfortably control thread interleaving. This allows analysis of subtle timing-dependent issues in the program. Second, since a simulator has a complete representation of the program's state under its control, it can easily move backwards in time or compare variable values from different points in the execution history. While both scheduler locking and reversible debugging exist to a certain degree in traditional debuggers [14], those features are very hard to implement and usually quite limited.

3   LLVM Bitcode

The LLVM bitcode (or intermediate representation) [11] is an assembly-like language primarily aimed at optimisation and analysis. The idea is that LLVM-based analysis and optimisation code can be shared by many different compilers: a compiler front end builds simple LLVM IR corresponding to its input and delegates all further optimisation and native code generation to a common back end. This architecture is quite common in other compilers: as an example, GCC contains a number of different front ends that share infrastructure and code generation. The major innovation of LLVM is that the language on which all the common middle and back end code operates is exposed and available to 3rd-party tools. It is also quite well documented and LLVM provides stand-alone tools to work with both bitcode and textual form of this intermediate representation.

From a language viewpoint, LLVM IR is in a partial SSA form (single static assignment) with explicit basic blocks. Each basic block is made up of instructions, the last of which is a *terminator*. The terminator instruction encodes relationships between basic blocks, which form an explicit control flow graph. An example of a terminator instruction would be a conditional or an unconditional branch or a `ret`. Such instructions either transfer control to another basic block of the same function or stop execution of the function altogether.

Besides explicit control flow, LLVM also strives to make much of the data flow explicit, taking advantage of partial SSA for this reason. It is, in general, impossible to convert entire programs to a full SSA form; however, especially within a single function, it is possible to convert a significant portion of the code. The SSA-form values are called *registers* in LLVM and only a few instructions can "lift" values from memory into registers and put them back again (most importantly `load` and `store`, respectively, plus a handful of atomic memory access instructions).

From the point of view of a simulator, memory and registers are somewhat distinct entities, both of which can hold values. Memory is completely unstructured at the LLVM level, the only assumption is that it is byte-addressed (endianity of multi-byte values is configurable, but uniform). Traditional C stack is, however, not required. Instead, all "local" memory is obtained via a special instruction, `alloca`, and treated like any other memory (memory obtained by `alloca` is assumed to be freed automatically when the function that requested the memory exits, via `ret` or any other way, e.g. due to stack unwinding during an exception propagation). Therefore, a C-style stack is a legitimate way to implement `alloca`, but not the most convenient in a simulator (for more details on how memory is handled in our simulator, see Sect. 3.2).

3.1   Verification Extensions

Unfortunately, LLVM bitcode alone is not sufficiently expressive to describe real programs: most importantly, it is not possible to encode interaction with the operating system into LLVM instructions. When LLVM is used as an intermediate step in a compiler, the lowest level of the user side of the system call mechanism is usually provided as an external, platform-specific function with a standard C calling convention. This function is usually implemented in the platform's assembly language. The system call interface, in turn, serves as a gateway between the program and the operating system, unlocking OS-specific functionality to the program. An important point is that the gateway function itself cannot be implemented in portable LLVM. Moreover, while large portions of the kernel are often implemented in C or a similar portable language, they are also tightly coupled to the underlying hardware platform.

The language of "real" programs is, therefore, LLVM enriched with system calls, which are provided by the operating system kernel. For verification purposes, however, this language is quite unsuitable: the list of system calls is long (well over 100 functions on many systems) and exposes implementation details of the particular kernel. Moreover, re-implementing a complete operating system inside every LLVM analysis tool is wasteful. To reduce this problem, a much smaller set of requisite primitives was proposed in [12] (henceforth, we will refer to this enriched language as DiVM). Since for model checking and simulation purposes, the program needs to be isolated from the outside world, we can skip most of the complexity of an operating system kernel – communication with hardware in particular. Therefore, it is possible to implement a small, isolated operating system in the DiVM language alone. One such operating system is DiOS – the core OS is about 1500 lines of C++, with additional 5000 lines of code providing POSIX-compatible file system and socket interfaces.

Thanks to its support for the DiVM language, our simulator can transparently load programs which are linked to DiOS and its libc implementation. Since a program compiled into the DiVM language is fully isolated from any environment effects, it can be simulated just like a pure LLVM program could be.

Finally, while the simulator uses DiVM to evaluate program instructions and hence relies on correctness of the implementation, errors in DiOS have a smaller impact. The DiOS code is executed in the virtual machine, and is subject to its error checking: therefore, in this case, the most likely outcome is by far a spurious error which can be analysed using the simulator itself.

3.2   Program Memory

Internally, the simulator uses DiVM to evaluate LLVM bitcode, and therefore, how memory is represented in the simulator is directly inherited from DiVM. This means that we can take advantage of the fact that DiVM tracks each object stored in memory separately, and also keeps track of relationships (pointers) between such objects.[2] This way, the simulator precisely knows which words stored in memory are pointers and the exact bounds of each object in memory.

Moreover, DiVM can efficiently store multiple snapshots of the entire address space of the program, both in terms of space (most of the actual storage is shared between such snapshots) and time (taking a snapshot needs time roughly proportional to the total size of modified objects since the last snapshot). Once a snapshot is taken, it is preserved unmodified, regardless of the future behaviour of the program (that is, it becomes persistent).

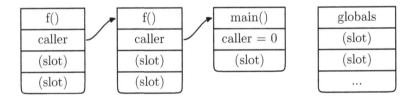

Fig. 1. Execution stack and global variables.

The execution stack of an LLVM program consists of activation frames, one for each active procedure call. In DiVM, activation frames are separate memory objects. Moreover, each memory-stored local variable (i.e. those represented by alloca instructions) is again represented by a distinct memory object. Each frame object contains 2 pointers in its header (one points at the currently executing instruction, the other to the parent frame). Besides the header, the rest of the object is split into *slots*, where each slot corresponds to a single LLVM *register*. An example stack structure is shown in Fig. 1. The correspondence between slots and LLVM registers is maintained by DiVM and is available to the simulator.

---

[2] How this is achieved is described in more detail in [12].

Together, those features of DiVM make it very easy to access the program state in a highly structured fashion. When compared to a traditional debugger, which must work with nearly unstructured memory space, the information our simulator can provide to the user is simultaneously easier to obtain and more detailed and reliable. Finally, since DiVM strictly enforces object boundaries, both the control stack and heap structure in our simulator are very well protected from overflows and other memory corruption bugs in the program. Therefore, the simulated program cannot accidentally destroy information which is vital for the functioning of the simulator, like all too often happens in debuggers.

3.3 Relating Bitcode to Source Code

In native code debuggers, the relationship between the binary and the original source code is often not quite obvious. For this reason, in addition to the executable binary, the compiler emits metadata which describe these relationships. For instance, it attaches a source code location (filename and line number) to each machine instruction. This way, when the debugger executes an instruction, it can display the relevant piece of source code. Likewise, it can analyse the execution stack to discover how the currently executing function was called, and display a *backtrace* consisting not only of function names, but also source code lines. This is important whenever a given function contains two similar calls.

```
struct Point { float x, y; };          binary: 000000000000003f0000e040
                                        .center:
struct Circle                              type:    Point
{                                          .x:
        Point center;                         type: float
        float radius;                         value: 0
};                                         .y:
                                              type: float
Circle c = {                                  value: 0.5
  .center = { .x = 0, .y = 0.5 },       .radius:
  .radius = 7                              type:    float
};                                         value:   7
```

Fig. 2. An example C `struct` type and the corresponding representations: binary and structured (the latter is only possible with debug metadata).

The situation is analogous in LLVM-based tools. Compiler front ends are therefore encouraged to generate *debuginfo metadata* (in a form that reflects the structure of the DWARF debug information format, which is widely used by native source-level debuggers). Besides the vitally important source code locations, the metadata describe local and global variables and their types (including user defined types, like `struct` and `union` types in C). This in turn enables the debugger to display the data in a structured way, resembling the structure which exists in the source code. For example, `struct` types in C have named fields –

the debugger can use the debug metadata to discover the relationship between offsets in the binary representation of the value with the source-level field names (an example is shown in Fig. 2).

3.4 Debug Graph

The memory graph maintained by DiVM is a good basis for presenting the program state to the user, but on its own is insufficient: the only type information it contains is whether a particular piece of memory holds a pointer or not. Therefore, we overlay another graph structure on top of the memory (heap) graph, with richer type information based on debuginfo metadata (more details on how this graph is computed will be presented in Sect. 4). The nodes in the debug graph may be further structured: they have *attributes* (atomic properties, such as an integer or floating point value), *components* and *relations*. While both components and relations are again nodes of the graph, they crucially differ in how they relate to the underlying memory: components of a debug node represent the same memory as their parent node; for example, a debug node which consists of a `struct` C type will contain a *component* for each field of the `struct`. In contrast, *relations* of a debug node correspond to the pointers embedded in the memory it represents (it may, however, point back at the same object it is embedded in). An example debug graph is shown in Fig. 3.

Since memory objects are *persistent* in DiVM (cf. Sect. 3.2), so is the debug graph in our simulator. This means that objects (debug nodes) are immutable, i.e. they always come from a *snapshot* of the memory of the program. Since it would be too expensive to make a copy of the entire memory after every instruction, such snapshots are implemented via copy-on-write semantics.

4   Working with Data

Providing facilities for inspecting data of the program is one of the main functions of an interactive debugger or a simulator. This data can be presented in different forms and from different starting points. In our simulator, heap memory is structured explicitly as a graph, and we can leverage this to greatly improve presentation of data. An example of such a graph is shown in Fig. 3. Each node of the graph corresponds to a single in-memory object, which can have (and often has) additional internal structure. The internal structure reflects the C/C++ type which is deduced from the types of pointers pointing at this particular node.

4.1 Starting Points

For certain memory objects, the type information is directly encoded in the metadata generated by the compiler and does not need to be inferred via pointers. Such objects are the starting point of the type assignment process by which the *debug graph* is obtained.

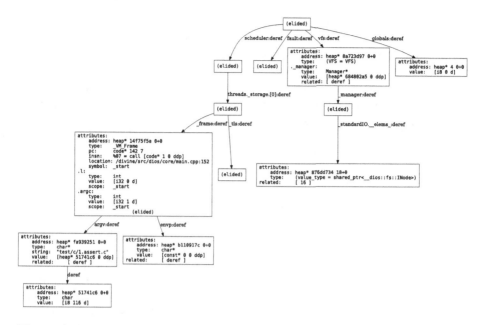

Fig. 3. A debug graph of a simple program. A single memory object may contain multiple *component* debug nodes which are rendered textually. The arrows correspond to *relations*. The depicted graph was obtained directly from the simulator; the only change was that descriptions of some of the nodes were elided for presentation purposes.

In principle, there are 2 types of such objects: *activation frames* and *globals*. Both consist of *slots* which in turn contain values. Values in those slots either correspond to values of (local or global) source-level variables, or contain pointers to variables held elsewhere in memory. In both cases, a *component* debug node is created for each slot, based on the debug information generated by the compiler. These components then form a basis for presenting the data to the user.

Additionally, in DiVM, there is always a single distinguished *root object* in the heap, from which the entire heap is reachable, including the stacks of all threads and any kernel data structures. The address and the C type of this *root object* is also available to the simulator, and is mainly used to discover all the nodes of the 2 abovementioned types.

4.2 Typing the Heap

In all cases, the type information available for the starting points is used to derive type information for the portion of the heap reachable from that starting point. For frames, we can deduce which function the frame belongs to, and obtain information about the frame layout used by that function. That is, for each LLVM register, we obtain a corresponding C type, which is usually either a primitive type or a pointer. If the type is a pointer and it is not null or otherwise invalid, there is an edge in the graph of the heap corresponding to this pointer. The object at the other end of the edge is then assigned the *base type* of the pointer, that is, type of a value obtained by dereferencing the pointer. This procedure is then repeated recursively until all objects where type information exists are assigned a type.

Of course, there is a potential for ambiguity: not all C/C++ programs are consistently typed, therefore, multiple edges pointing at a single object can each carry a different type. In this case, we collect all the applicable types and construct a synthetic *union type*, which is assigned to any such ambiguous debug node. This ambiguity might propagate downstream from an affected node, but for most programs, this does not appear to pose a significant problem.

4.3   Relating Data and Control

The control flow of a C program is reflected in the execution stack and is a part of the program's data. C and C++ are lexically scoped languages: which variables are currently in scope depends on which function (and possibly which block in that function) is currently executing. This is achieved by making local variables part of the execution stack: when a function is entered, an *activation frame* (or activation *record*) is pushed onto the execution stack. In a native execution environment, the frame has space for CPU register spills and for local variables which have their address taken. In DiVM, there are no general-purpose registers as such; instead, LLVM registers are stored inside the frame itself. Any address-taken variables are stored as separate objects (and their address is stored in a register).

Additionally, in a typical implementation of C, the activation frame contains a *return address*, which is a pointer to the `call` instruction that caused the current function to execute. In DiVM, the frame instead contains a *program counter* (in a real CPU, the program counter, also known as instruction pointer, is held in a register). The program counter tells us which function, and which instruction within that function, is currently being executed. Each instruction can in turn be tied, via debug metadata (cf. Sect. 3.3), to a particular source code location (a source file and a line number).

As an example of how this is used in the simulator, if the user requests to list the source code of the currently executed function, the simulator examines the current active activation frame to find the current value of the *program counter*. Then it proceeds to read the corresponding debug metadata to obtain the source code file name, reads the source file, finds the line corresponding to the program counter and prints the surrounding function (example output is shown in Fig. 4).

5   Navigating the State Space

If we treat the data of a program as a spatial dimension, it is natural, then, to treat the state space – the behaviour of program as it executes – as a time dimension. Since the state space is a graph (cf. Fig. 5), the predecessors of a given state (the path from the initial state to the "current" state – the one that is being

```
> show $frame                          > source
  attributes:                             3 int main()
      address: heap* bf24efc5 0+0         4 {
      shared:  0                    >>    5     assert( 0 );
      pc:      code* 1 0                  6     return 0;
      location: test/c/1.assert.c:5      7 }
      symbol:  main
  related:   [ caller ]
```

Fig. 4. An example interaction: listing source code.

examined) constitute the *past* of the computation. The successors, on the other hand, correspond to possible *futures* of the computation (since the behaviour of the program is often non-deterministic[3], there is more than one possible future). In this correspondence of the state-space graph to temporal behaviour of the program, cycles in the state space clearly correspond to behaviours that go on forever.

```
int *mkint()
{
    return malloc( sizeof( int ) );
}

int main()
{
    int *a = NULL;
    while ( !a )
        a = mkint();
    puts( "ok" );
}
```

Fig. 5. An example C program along with its state space.

In a standard debugger, time can only flow in one direction, and which of the potential futures is realised can be influenced, but not controlled. In a simulator, however, it is possible to both go backwards in time (rewind the program state to some past configuration) and to pick exactly which future should be explored. Likewise, it is entirely possible to go back in time and select a different future to explore. These capabilities are derived mainly from the persistent and compact memory representation (see Sect. 3.2).

5.1 Stepping Forward

On the other hand, the state space as explored by model checkers is often too coarse to follow the computation in detail. The states typically correspond to

---

[3] The behaviour of the program may depend on external factors, such as scheduling choices, user inputs, asynchronous events and so on.

locations where threads interleave or where cycles can potentially form. At this level, the edges in the state space correspond, approximately, to atomic actions in the program. Even in heavily parallel programs, though, such atomic actions will span many instructions and possibly multiple source lines. A simulator which works at this level[4] can only present very coarse computation steps to the user and not seeing the intermediate state of the program can prevent users from relating effects to their causes. If the simulator operates with fixed computation steps, the opposite problem can also happen: the user must step through a large number of irrelevant program configurations [7], again frustrating the debugging effort.

In contrast, debuggers give the user very precise control over the forward execution of the program, down to stepping one machine instruction at a time. However, they also make it very easy to fast forward through thousands of lines of code, stopping when a predetermined condition is met, most often a particular source code line is executed (this feature is known as a *breakpoint*).

Building the simulator on top of DiVM, however, gives us execution control at the level of individual LLVM instructions, analogous to a debugger. Building on the instruction stepping mechanism, the simulator also provides all the control functionality common in debuggers: source-line stepping – both into and over function calls – and various breakpoint types (on a source line or a on a function entry).

5.2   Going Back

In general, it is impossible to execute individual instructions backwards. However, if execution is perfectly repeatable (as it is in a simulator), we can reach any earlier configuration of the program by replaying the current execution from the start and stopping right before the instruction of interest executes.

Additionally, the simulator stores intermediate states (automatically at convenient locations, or at a user request). It is then possible to go back to any such stored state and continue execution from that point. This can make the above-mentioned process considerably more efficient: it is enough to replay execution from the most recent stored state that lies on the current execution path.

5.3   Inspecting the Stack

As explained in Sect. 4.3, the control flow of a C program (or, more generally, any LLVM program) is tracked by a simple data structure stored in memory along with other data. This data structure often represents the best means for a user to locate themselves within the execution of a program. A so-called *backtrace* (or *stack trace*) is a fundamental program analysis tool. A backtrace lists each

---

[4] This is often the case in verification-centric tools, partly because it is a simple implementation strategy that builds on the same primitives as the verification tool itself.

```
> start                                      > backtrace
# a new program state was stored as #1         address: heap* fa4b97e2 0+0
# active threads: [0:1]                         pc: code* c49 0
# a new program state was stored as #2          location: _PDCLIB/assert.c:21
# active threads: [0:1]                         symbol: _PDCLIB_assert_dios
# executing main at test/c/1.assert.c:5
> stepi                                         address: heap* 96c75834 0+0
    call @_PDCLIB_assert_dios                   pc: code* 1 1
# executing _PDCLIB_assert_dios                 location: test/c/1.assert.c:5
#          at _PDCLIB/assert.c:21               symbol: main

                                                address: heap* 797b4e39 0+0
                                                pc: code* 1f4 7
                                                location: dios/core/main.cpp:173
                                                symbol: _start
```

Fig. 6. Left: new states are discovered during execution of a program. Right: displaying a backtrace.

activation record in the (reverse) order of activation, and constitutes a description of a location in the computation of the program[5] (an example is shown in Fig. 6).

5.4   Thread Interleaving

As mentioned in Sect. 2.1, a simulator can precisely control thread interleaving: the underlying virtual machine provides means to switch threads at all relevant points. However, many instruction interleavings have equivalent effects, and for this reason, allowing threads to be switched at arbitrary points would be wasteful. For this reason, DiVM explicitly marks points in the instruction stream where threads may be switched, and this behaviour is carried over to the simulator. These *interrupt points* are inserted in such a manner that all possible behaviours of the program are retained in the state space. From a simulation point of view, the downside is that the interleaving may not be the most intuitive, but the reduction in the number of possible states generally outweighs this, since the user needs to consider fewer runs. To further reduce the number of context switches, a model checker may use some form of partial order reduction, but this is not necessary in a simulator, since it doesn't need to explore or store the entire state space.

5.5   Simulating Counterexamples

There are two major tasks for the simulator in the context of program analysis and verification. The first is to allow the user to explore program behaviour and

---

[5] This description is necessarily incomplete, being much more concise than the real representation of the program's state. Including additional information improves completeness, but compromises brevity, which is an important strength of this presentation format.

read off details about its executions. The other is to support verification tools which provide counterexamples to the user. As detailed in Sect. 2, it is a difficult task to analyse problem reports from automated analysis and verification tools, and a simulator can be very helpful in this regard. In case of model checkers, the problem report contains an execution *trace*: a step-by-step description of the problematic behaviour. For tools based on DiVM, this trace is simply a list of 2 types of information:

1. The non-deterministic choices made during the execution of the program (internally, there is only one non-deterministic choice operator and all state-space branching is caused by this operator, including thread interleaving).
2. Which of the *interrupt points* were used in the execution: the model checker may be able to prove that a particular interrupt point is not required, and the simulator needs this information to correctly reproduce the counterexample.

Since the program is isolated from the environment, this list completely and unambiguously describes its entire execution history. When the model checker discovers a problem in the program, it writes this list into a text file, which the simulator can then load along with the program.

When the simulator loads a trace, it locks the outcomes of all non-deterministic choices to follow the trace. In this mode, stepping through the program (backwards or forwards) will simply follow the counterexample, unless a particular choice is overridden by the user. In effect, the user will be guided through the faulty behaviour of the program, and can easily move back and forth to locate the cause of the problem (as opposed to the symptom, which is what the model checker reports and may be distinct from the original cause).

6 Implementation

The ideas presented in this paper are implemented in the simulator component of DIVINE 4, which is available as `divine sim`. All relevant source code is available online[6], under a permissive open source licence. Additional details about the user interface and user interaction in particular can be found in the DIVINE 4 manual[7].

6.1 User Interface

The data structures and most of the code are independent of a particular user interface. In fact, two user interfaces exist for the simulator. The primary interface is command-driven, similar to terminal-based symbolic debuggers like `gdb`. The command-line parser and other interface-specific code entails approximately 800 lines of C++. Additionally, a third-party graphical interface is also available.[8]

---

[6] https://divine.fi.muni.cz/download.html.

[7] https://divine.fi.muni.cz/manual.html.

[8] The source code of the graphical user interface is available from the supplementary materials page at https://divine.fi.muni.cz/2019/sim/.

The command interface uses *meta variables* extensively: each such meta variable holds a reference to a single debug node (cf. Section 3.4). There are two basic types of meta variables, *static* and *dynamic*.

Static variables always point to the same debug node, even as the program executes and the content of its memory changes. Since objects in the DiVM memory are *persistent* (not mutable), this type of variable simply points to such a persistent, immutable object. Static meta variables have names starting with a # sign, e.g. #start.

Dynamic variables reflect the current state of the program at any given time. The debug nodes referenced by those variables are *refreshed* every time the program mutates its memory, so that they always point to an up-to-date copy of the persistent memory object (in other words, they always refer to the current program state). These variables are prefixed with a $ sign, e.g. $frame.

6.2 Programming Language Support

Our simulator design is, to a large degree, independent of the particular high-level language in which the simulated program was developed. The structure of the program is described in the debug info metadata in sufficient detail to provide precise and readable information to the user. This is in contrast to tools like gdb and lldb [8] which mostly rely on evaluating C and/or C++ statements for presenting the program data. That is, the user is allowed to type in a C or C++ expression to be evaluated and the result displayed. The major downside is that if the high-level language support is incomplete (like it is the case with C++ support in gdb), it becomes much harder to obtain certain values without resorting to very low-level means (printing bytes at particular addresses). Consequently, the amount of implementation work required to support a particular programming language in a debugger can be substantial.[9]

On the other hand, the debug graph implemented in our simulator (see Sect. 3.4) is language-neutral, and hence the features derived from this graph are independent of the original programming language. For this reason, we consider the debug graph to be an important contribution: it can be built from LLVM debug metadata in a comparatively small amount of code, but nonetheless provides a very convenient interface.

7 Conclusion

We have described a novel approach to interactive analysis of real, multi-threaded C and C++ programs. The approach plays an important support role in the wider context of automated verification and, in particular, model checking of software. The simulator naturally supports the compact and universal counterexample format used in DiVM. Compared to earlier tools, DIVINE 4

---

[9] We speculate that this is the primary reason why interactive simulators (and debuggers in general) are so scarce.

is substantially more useful in practice, also thanks to the new interactive simulator.[10]

References

1. Ball, T., Naik, M., Rajamani, S.K.: From symptom to cause: localizing errors in counterexample traces. In: POPL, pp. 97–105. ACM (2003)
2. Ball, T., Cook, B., Levin, V., Rajamani, S.K.: SLAM and static driver verifier: technology transfer of formal methods inside Microsoft. In: Boiten, E.A., Derrick, J., Smith, G. (eds.) IFM 2004. LNCS, vol. 2999, pp. 1–20. Springer, Heidelberg (2004). https://doi.org/10.1007/978-3-540-24756-2_1
3. Barnat, J., Beran, J., Brim, L., Kratochvíla, T., Ročkai, P.: Tool chain to support automated formal verification of avionics simulink designs. In: Stoelinga, M., Pinger, R. (eds.) FMICS 2012. LNCS, vol. 7437, pp. 78–92. Springer, Heidelberg (2012). https://doi.org/10.1007/978-3-642-32469-7_6
4. Basu, S., Saha, D., Smolka, S.A.: Getting to the root of the problem: focus statements for the analysis of counter-examples (2012)
5. Behrmann, G., David, A., Larsen, K.G.: A tutorial on UPPAAL. In: Bernardo, M., Corradini, F. (eds.) SFM-RT 2004. LNCS, vol. 3185, pp. 200–236. Springer, Heidelberg (2004). https://doi.org/10.1007/978-3-540-30080-9_7
6. Groce, A., Kroening, D., Lerda, F.: Understanding counterexamples with explain. In: Alur, R., Peled, D.A. (eds.) CAV 2004. LNCS, vol. 3114, pp. 453–456. Springer, Heidelberg (2004). https://doi.org/10.1007/978-3-540-27813-9_35
7. Kleiman, R., Brayshaw, M., Eisenstadt, M., Eisenstadt, M.: Tales of debugging from the front lines (1993)
8. Lee, K.: Using LLDB, pp. 415–434. Apress, Berkeley (2013). ISBN 978-1-4302-5051-7
9. Magee, J.: Behavioral analysis of software architectures using LTSA. In: ICSE (1999)
10. Nethercote, N., Seward, J.: Valgrind: a framework for heavyweight dynamic binary instrumentation. In: PLDI (2007)
11. The LLVM Project. LLVM language reference manual (2016). http://llvm.org/docs/LangRef.html
12. Ročkai, P., Vladimír, Š., Černá, I., Barnat, J.: DiVM: model checking with LLVM and graph memory. J. Syst. Softw. **143**, 1–13 (2018). https://doi.org/10.1016/j.jss.2018.04.026. ISSN 0164-1212
13. Stallman, R., Pesch, R., Shebs, S.: Debugging with GDB (2010)
14. Visan, A.-M., Arya, K., Cooperman, G., Denniston, T.: URDB: a universal reversible debugger based on decomposing debugging histories. In: PLOS 2011 (2011)
15. Groce, A., Visser, W.: What went wrong: explaining counterexamples. In: Ball, T., Rajamani, S.K. (eds.) SPIN 2003. LNCS, vol. 2648, pp. 121–136. Springer, Heidelberg (2003). https://doi.org/10.1007/3-540-44829-2_8

---

[10] Supported by anecdotal evidence from working with students, both individually and in a validation & verification course.

Verification of Decision Making Software in an Autonomous Vehicle: An Industrial Case Study

Yuvaraj Selvaraj[1,2]([✉]), Wolfgang Ahrendt[2], and Martin Fabian[2]

[1] Zenuity AB, Gothenburg, Sweden
yuvaraj.selvaraj@zenuity.com
[2] Chalmers University of Technology, Gothenburg, Sweden
{ahrendt,fabian}@chalmers.se

Abstract. Correctness of autonomous driving systems is crucial as incorrect behaviour may have catastrophic consequences. Many different hardware and software components (e.g. sensing, decision making, actuation, and control) interact to solve the autonomous driving task, leading to a level of complexity that brings new challenges for the formal verification community. Though formal verification has been used to prove correctness of software, there are significant challenges in transferring such techniques to an agile software development process and to ensure widespread industrial adoption. In the light of these challenges, the identification of appropriate formalisms, and consequently the right verification tools, has significant impact on addressing them. In this paper, we evaluate the application of different formal techniques from supervisory control theory, model checking, and deductive verification to verify existing decision and control software (in development) for an autonomous vehicle. We discuss how the verification objective differs with respect to the choice of formalism and the level of formality that can be applied. Insights from the case study show a need for multiple formal methods to prove correctness, the difficulty to capture the right level of abstraction to model and specify the formal properties for the verification objectives.

Keywords: Autonomous driving · Formal verification · Supervisory Control Theory · Model checking · Deductive verification

1 Introduction and Related Work

Significant progress has lately been made in the global automotive industry towards autonomous vehicles. Autonomous vehicles can potentially increase road safety and help reduce road traffic accidents. However, these are extremely complex safety critical systems, and human safety depends on their correctness.

Supported by FFI, VINNOVA under grant number 2017-05519, *Automatically Assessing Correctness of Autonomous Vehicles–Auto-CAV*.

K. G. Larsen and T. Willemse (Eds.): FMICS 2019, LNCS 11687, pp. 143–159, 2019.
https://doi.org/10.1007/978-3-030-27008-7_9

The level of complexity in these systems is manually intractable. Factors like size, structure (level of interaction and communication between different systems), environment (the physical world in the case of autonomous vehicles), application domain etc., all contribute to the complexity. It is imperative that all safety critical parts of an autonomous vehicle are veritably reliable and safe. This is a challenge for the development process due to the complexity needed to be managed not only in the design but also in the verification and validation process.

An autonomous vehicle consists of many software and hardware components interacting to solve different tasks, ranging from sensing, decision making, and planning to actuation and control. The level of complexity involved may lead to subtle but potentially dangerous bugs arising due to unforeseen edge cases, errors in the software design and/or implementation. Coverage based testing is a widely adopted work flow in many large scale software development companies, but exhaustive testing is not tractable. Testing can never guarantee absence of unintended consequences nor provide sufficient certification evidence in all cases. Thus, there is a need for complementary methods to guarantee system safety, and the use of formal methods for this is becoming prevalent [14,23].

The international standard ISO 26262 [16] provides guidance on a risk based approach to manage, specify, develop, integrate, and verify safety critical systems in road vehicles, including various references to formal specification and verification. Adherence to the standard can potentially ensure that system quality is maintained, and unreasonable residual risk is avoided. The standard is based upon the V model of product development [13] and aims at achieving system safety through safety measures implemented at various levels of the development process. However, the standard addresses neither specific challenges inherent to autonomous driving systems, nor the development of safety critical software in an agile development work flow.

Thus, research is needed to solve challenges arising from such interdisciplinary problems, and these challenges are at-least two fold:

1. The application of formal verification to autonomous driving systems;
2. The transfer of formal verification techniques to large scale agile development of safety critical software.

The first challenge is relatively new and is driven by recent developments in autonomous systems. The second challenge relates to a long standing problem of successful industrial adoption of formal techniques in software development. However, the addition of agile methods to safety critical software development has introduced new directions.

Formal methods—with varying levels of formalisation—can be applied at various stages of the software development process. The choice of verification method and the expressive power of the formalism used to specify the properties is an important choice that affects the conclusions drawn from the results of the verification process. In this paper, we evaluate three formal verification methods and their respective formalisms to verify existing software in an autonomous driving vehicle: Supervisory Control Theory with Extended Finite

State Machines [30,34], Model Checking with Temporal Logic of Actions [22], Deductive Verification with contract based programming [4]. We discuss how the verification objective differs in these methods and how multiple formal methods can help tackle the challenges in industrial autonomous driving software development.

A recent survey [23] on formal specification and verification of autonomous robotic systems is a comprehensive study of current state-of-the art literature focused on formal modelling, formal specification, and formal verification of robotic systems. It gives a summary on the challenges faced, current methods in tackling the challenges, and the limitations of existing methods. In [33], an overview of the challenges in designing, specifying and verifying cyber-physical systems, particularly semi-autonomous driving systems with human interaction is provided. [12] presents a model checking framework for verifying autonomous systems with a distinguished rational 'agent', confined to the system architecture level with autonomous driving as one example scenario. There are prior research focused on the development of autonomous systems in a generic sense [14,23], surveys on tool based verification methods and tools [5,9], and the general industrial adoption of formal methods technology [17,18,32,35].

In contrast to the literature cited above, our work is specific to autonomous driving and we discuss a tightly coupled approach to tackle the two-fold challenge with an industrial case study. The problem description is given in Sect. 2, followed by separate sections for the three different verification approaches handled in this paper. Section 6 discusses the evaluation and insights from the industrial case study. The paper concludes with some remarks in Sect. 7.

2   Problem Description

Zenuity is one of the leading companies in the development of safe and reliable autonomous driving software. A significant part of the embedded software developed at Zenuity is safety critical. In [36], formal verification was applied to a small part of the autonomous driving software in development and non-conformance to a few basic specifications was reported. The work presented in this paper is a continuation of the work started in [36].

The focus of this paper is a sub-module of the decision making and planning module, called *Lateral State Manager* (*LSM*), which solves the sub-function of managing modes during a lane change. A simplified overview of the system and the interactions are shown in Fig. 1. The software module is implemented in object-oriented MATLAB-code using several classes, each solving different sub-problems. The interaction of the *LSM* class with a high level strategic planner (*Planner*) and a low level planner (*Path Planner*) is also shown in Fig. 1.

The *Planner* in the lane change module is responsible for strategic decisions and depending on the state of the vehicle, the *Planner* sends lane change requests to the *LSM*, indicating the desired lane to drive in. These requests are in the form of NoRequest, ChangeLeft, and ChangeRight. On receiving a request, the *LSM* keeps track of the lane change process by managing the different modes possible

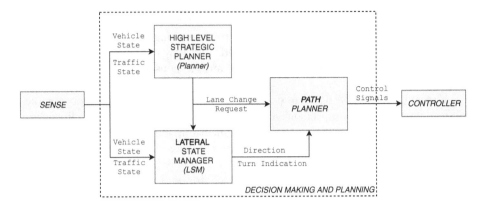

Fig. 1. System overview and interactions.

during the process, and issues commands to the *Path Planner*. If a lane change is requested, the *Path Planner* sends control signals to the low level controller to perform a safe and efficient lane change. Due to the inherent nature of the task to solve, the *LSM* implements a finite state machine. An example of a state in the *LSM* state machine is *State_Finished* that represents the completion of the lane change process.

A call to *LSM* is issued at every execution cycle. During each call, the *LSM* undergoes three distinct execution stages. First, all the inputs are updated according to the function call arguments. Second, depending on the current state, code is executed to decide whether the system transits to a new state or not. This code also assigns outputs and persistent variables. Finally, if a transition is performed, the last stage executes code corresponding to the new state entered and assigns new values to the variables.

Of course, *LSM* is safety critical and its correctness is crucial. In our work, we focus on verifying properties that affect the safety of the system, i.e. a violation of which will result in an unsafe behaviour. From a software development perspective, these properties are typically stated as safety requirements. In [36], one such requirement was modelled to check whether the *LSM* always performs a lane change to the same lane as requested by the *Planner*. This requirement was shown to be violated. Under certain circumstances the vehicle could indicate to go to the right (say), and check for traffic on the right side, but when it was clear to move into the right lane, the vehicle moved to the left. In our work, we further strengthen the property to express definite unsafe behaviours and the strengthened requirement is shown as *Req.1*.

Req.1: If changing lane, the lane change shall always be to the same side as indicated.

In the following sections, we describe how formal verification is performed to show correctness of the *LSM* and to identify the violation of *Req.1* in the three different methods discussed in this paper. While there are several tools and tool based methods that support formal verification [5,9], the choice of the tools discussed in this paper is primarily motivated by prior case studies with Supremica [25,36], TLA$^+$ [20,27], and SPARK [1,7] on software systems similar in nature and scale to autonomous driving systems.

3 Supervisory Control Theory

The Supervisory Control Theory [31] (SCT) provides a framework for modelling, synthesis, and verification of reactive control functions for *discrete event systems* (DES), which are systems that occupy at each time instant a single *state* out of its many possible ones, and transits to another state on the occurrence of an *event*. Given a DES model of a system to control, the *plant*, and a *specification*[1] of the desired controlled behaviour, the SCT provides means to synthesize a *supervisor* that interacting with the plant in a *closed-loop* dynamically restricts the event generation of the plant such that the specification is satisfied.

Though the original SCT focused on synthesising supervisors that by construction fulfil the desired properties, a dual problem of interest here is to, given a model of a plant and specification, verify whether the specification is fulfilled or not. So, in this paper we use ideas from SCT to formally verify *LSM*, and do not focus on the synthesis of supervisors.

A DES modelling formalism appropriate in our context is finite-state machines extended with bounded discrete variables, with guards (logical expressions) over the variables and actions that assign values to the variables on the transitions [34].

Definition 1. *An Extended Finite State Machine (EFSM) is a tuple $E = \langle \Sigma, V, L, \rightarrow, L^i, L^m \rangle$, where Σ is a finite set of events, V is a finite set of bounded discrete variables, L is a finite set of locations, $\rightarrow \subseteq L \times \Sigma \times G \times A \times L$ is the conditional transition relation, where G and A are the respective sets of guards and actions, $L^i \subseteq L$ is the set of initial locations, and $L^m \subseteq L$ is the set of marked locations.*

The current state of such an *Extended Finite State-Machine* (EFSM) is given by its current location together with the current values of the variables. Thus, the state of an EFSM is not necessarily explicitly enumerated, but can be represented symbolically. This richer structure, though with equal expressive power, shows good modelling potential compared to ordinary finite state machines. The expression $l_0 \xrightarrow{\sigma:[g]a} l_1$ denotes a transition from location l_0 to l_1 labelled by event $\sigma \in \Sigma$, and with guard $g \in G$ and action $a \in A$. The transition is enabled when g evaluates to $\mathbf{T}$, and on its occurrence a updates some of the values of the variables $v \in V$, thereby causing the EFSM to change location from l_0 to l_1.

EFSMs naturally interact through shared variables, but they can also interact through shared events, which is modelled by *synchronous composition*, where

---

[1] In the SCT framework, the *specification* is the property of interest to verify with respect to the *plant*.

common events occur simultaneously in all interacting EFSMs, or not at all, while non-shared events occur independently. By this interaction mechanism a supervisor restricts the event generation of the plant; if the supervisor has a specific event in its alphabet but has no enabled transition labelled by that event from its current state, then the closed-loop system cannot execute that event in the current global state. We denote the synchronous composition of two EFSMs E_1 and E_2 by $E_1 \parallel E_2$ [34]. As defined by [34], transitions labelled by shared events but with mutually exclusive guards, or conflicting actions can never occur.

3.1   Nonblocking Verification

Given a set of EFSMs $\mathcal{E} = \{G_1, \ldots, G_n, K_1, \ldots, K_m\}$ where the components G_i ($i = 1, \ldots, n$) represent the plant, and K_j ($j = 1, \ldots, m$) represent the specification, we now want to determine whether the synchronous composition over all the components can from any reachable state always reach some marked state. The straightforward way to do this, called the *monolithic* approach, is intractable for all but the smallest systems, due to the combinatorial state-space explosion problem. Thus, more efficient approaches are needed.

One such approach that pushes the limit of what is tractable is the *abstraction-based compositional verification* [26], which has shown remarkable efficiency and manages to handle systems of industrially interesting sizes and complexity. It can be shown [26] that when $\mathcal{E}$ is blocking, this is due to some *conflict* between the components of $\mathcal{E}$. Thus, the approach of [26] employs *conflict-preserving abstractions* to iteratively remove redundancy and thus to keep the abstracted system size manageable. However, this approach eventually ends up converting the resulting abstracted EFSM system into ordinary finite-state machines, and then doing a monolithic verification of that. This then requires an efficient *explicit* verification algorithm, such as the one presented in [24].

3.2   Verification of *LSM* in Supremica

The software tool Supremica [25] implements the nonblocking verification algorithms mentioned above (as well as various other algorithms, both for verification and synthesis). To verify whether *LSM* presented in Sect. 2 fulfils *Req. 1* or not, we transform *Req. 1* into an EFSM specification in such a way that with an EFSM model of the *LSM* code as the plant, the system will be nonblocking if and only if *LSM* fulfils *Req. 1*.

The manual modelling of the *LSM* as an EFSM, similar to [36], is illustrated with a small excerpt from the actual MATLAB-code, shown in Listing 1.1 with some variable and state names anonymized. Listing 1.1 is a piece of the code that assigns variables and decides whether the system transits to a new state or not. The EFSM corresponding to the code is shown in Fig. 2. As described in Sect. 2, the *LSM* involves three execution stages during each call. The event *update* in the EFSM signifies the first stage: update on the inputs. The event *update*

Listing 1.1. An illustrative excerpt from *LSM* code used for verification.

```
1   function duringStateA(var, laneChangeRequest)
2
3        var.direction = laneChangeRequest;
4        var.x = false;
5        var.y = false;
6        if laneChangeRequest != NoRequest
7             var.state = StateB;
8        end
9
10   end
```

is followed by three transitions to model the possibility for the input variable `laneChangeRequest` to take one of the three values equally likely. Modelling the rest of the lines of code is straightforward. Note that the illustration provided is a minimal example to explain the modelling approach undertaken to manually model the *LSM* source code as an EFSM in Supremica.

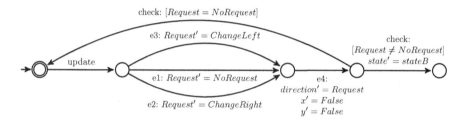

Fig. 2. EFSM of Listing 1.1. Primed variables represent next-state values.

Req. 1 modelled as an EFSM is shown in Fig. 3. The event enterFinished denotes that the *LSM* has reached *State_Finished* completing the lane change process. The guard on the event checks for equality between two variables, Output_Indication and Output_ChangeLane. When these variables differ, the EFSM transits to a blocking state as shown in Fig. 3. Output_Indication and Output_ChangeLane are modelled in a way such that they are set only during specific modes during the lane change process and are reset only when the *LSM* transits back to the initial state, when no lane change is requested. This makes it possible for their use in expressing *Req. 1*. Modelling the *LSM* code in Supremica resulted in an EFSM with 76 locations, 113 events, 144 transitions, and 20 variables. The synchronisation of the *LSM* with the EFSM in Fig. 3 resulted in a model with 1,522,117 reachable states, 113 events, and 2,164,607 transitions. The nonblocking verification of the synchronised model took less than a second and showed that a blocking state can indeed be reached. Supremica also provides a 43 events long counter example that can be analysed in detail to understand the underlying cause.

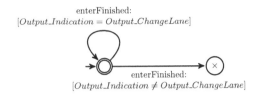

enterFinished:
$[Output\_Indication = Output\_ChangeLane]$

enterFinished:
$[Output\_Indication \neq Output\_ChangeLane]$

Fig. 3. EFSM of the specification to model *Req.1*. The blocking state is represented with a cross inside.

4   Model Checking

Model checking [10, 29] is a framework for verification of finite transition systems using temporal logic [28] as a specification formalism. Several formalisms and powerful model checking tools have emerged over the years [6, 11].

Definition 2. *A finite transition system is a tuple* $T = \langle S, Act, \rightarrow, I, AP, L \rangle$ *where S is a finite set of states, Act is a finite set of actions,* $\rightarrow \subseteq S \times Act \times S$ *is a transition relation, AP is a finite set of atomic propositions, and* $L : S \rightarrow 2^{AP}$ *is a labelling function.*

Given a transition system T, and a temporal logic formula f, the model checking problem is a decision procedure for $T \vDash f$. If $T \nvDash f$, then the model checking algorithm provides a counter example as an evidence for the violation, which can then be used to analyse the issue and the ways to resolve it.

4.1   Temporal Logic of Actions

The Temporal Logic of Actions (TLA) is a logical formalism for specifying and reasoning about concurrent systems [21]. TLA is a variant of temporal logic [28] and uses the notion of states and actions to model behavioural properties of systems. TLA, as a logical formalism provides the expressive power to reason about programs using assertions on states and pairs of states (actions). Actions are predicates that relate two consecutive states and are used to capture how the system is allowed to evolve. This section only presents a brief overview of TLA and the associated formalism for specifying and model checking systems. A more detailed description of the language and other advanced advanced topics is available in [20–22].

The reasoning system in TLA is built around TLA formulas. A TLA *formula* is true or false on a behaviour. A *behaviour* in TLA is an infinite sequence of states. A *state* in TLA is an assignment of values to variables and a *step* is a pair of states. Steps of a behaviour denote successive pairs of states. Given a system S, with the executions of the system represented as behaviours, and a formula f, we can decide whether S satisfies f iff the formula f is true for every behaviour of S.

The elementary building blocks of a TLA formula include state predicates, actions, logical operators (such as $\wedge$, $\neg$, etc.), the temporal operator $\square$ (always) and the existential quantifier $\exists$. A *state predicate* is a boolean valued expression (predicate) on states. An action, $\mathcal{A}$, is a boolean valued expression (predicate) on steps. Actions are formed from unprimed variables and primed variables to represent the relation between old states and new states. The unprimed variables refer to the values of the variables in old states, the first state of the step, whereas the primed variables refer to the variable values in new states, the second state of the step. State predicates have no primed variables. A step is an $\mathcal{A}$-step if it satisfies $\mathcal{A}$. An action is valid, $\vDash \mathcal{A}$, iff every step is an $\mathcal{A}$-step. In TLA, atomic operations of programs are represented by actions.

TLA$^+$ is a formal specification language based on formal set theory, first order logic and TLA. A TLA$^+$ specification, typically denoted *Spec*, is a temporal formula predicate on *behaviours*. All the behaviours satisfying *Spec* constitute the correct behaviours of the system. TLA$^+$ describes a system as a set of behaviours with an initial condition and a next state relation. The initial condition specifies the possible initial states and the next state relation specifies the possible steps. A TLA$^+$ specification is a temporal formula of the form

$$Spec \triangleq Init \wedge \square[Next]_{\langle vars \rangle} \wedge Temporal \qquad (1)$$

where *Init* is a state predicate corresponding to the initial condition, *Next* is an action corresponding to the next state relation, *vars* is a tuple of all variables in the specification, and *Temporal* is a temporal formula usually specifying liveness conditions. Formula *Spec* can be seen as a predicate on behaviours. *Spec* is true for a behaviour σ, iff *Init* is true in the first state of σ and every step in σ is either a step that satisfies *Next* or is a *stuttering* step. A *stuttering* step is one in which none of the variables are changed.

The specification (1) can be model checked using the TLC model checker. TLC takes a TLA$^+$ specification and checks whether the specification satisfies the desired properties by evaluating all possible behaviours of the specification. The TLA$^+$ specification language accompanied by an IDE consisting of TLC and other useful tools can be downloaded from [20].

4.2   Verification of *LSM* in TLA$^+$

The approach we use to formally verify the *LSM* in TLA$^+$ is similar to the approach of Supremica. The *LSM* code is manually translated in TLA$^+$ using the constructs available in the specification language. Listing 1.2 shows the TLA$^+$ translation of the MATLAB-code in Listing 1.1 as a TLA$^+$ formula that relates unprimed variables and primed variables using arithmetic and logical operators. The formula describes the allowed behaviour of the function in Listing 1.1. A call to the function duringStateA is translated to a behaviour where the formula During_StateA is valid.

The TLA$^+$ translation of the entire *LSM* code consists of an initial state predicate, *Init* and *Next*. *Next* is composed of smaller sub-formulae, each corresponding to different functions in the original code, of which one formula is shown in Listing 1.2. With the complete TLA$^+$ translation of the *LSM*, TLC

Listing 1.2. TLA$^+$ translation of the code in Listing 1.1.

```
1   During_StateA ==
2           /\ Lane_Change_Request ' \in ...
                {"NoRequest","ChangeLeft","ChangeRight"}
3           /\ var_state = "StateA"
4           /\ var_direction ' = Lane_Change_Request
5           /\ var_x ' = FALSE
6           /\ var_y ' = FALSE
7           /\ IF Lane_Change_Request # "NoRequest" THEN
8                   var_state ' = "StateB"
9              ELSE UNCHANGED var_state
```

can model check for desired properties, which are described using pre-defined statements and constructs available. More details on the statements and the restrictions on TLC is available in [22]. In order to verify *Req.1* of Sect. 2, we make use of invariant checking in TLC.

An *invariant*, typically denoted as *Inv*, of a *Spec* is a state predicate that should be valid in all reachable states. Invariants can be defined for specifications as well as next-state actions. An invariant of a specification that is also an invariant of a next-state action is sometimes called an inductive invariant of *Spec*. In model checking mode for invariance checking, TLC explores all reachable states and looks for states in which the invariant is not satisfied.

Req.1 is translated to a TLA formula as

$$\text{InvProp} \triangleq \neg(\text{var\_state} = \text{``State\_Finished''}$$
$$\wedge \text{Output\_Indication} \neq \text{Output\_Change\_Lane}). \quad (2)$$

Reaching a state where InvProp is violated means that the state predicate evaluate to false, i.e. a behaviour where the lane change is finished and the outputs for showing indication and changing lane differ, is allowed in our specification, thereby showing the presence of an error in our code. The complete TLA$^+$ translation was 250 lines with 20 variables. In model checking mode using breadth-first search, TLC shows the violation of InvProp with a 5 step long error trace for analysis.

5   Deductive Verification

Model checking is well suited to establish (temporal) properties of state traces, but mostly requires *abstractions* over the real source code. In contrast to that, deductive verification [15] techniques are well suited for fully precise reasoning about the computation on the *source code level*. Often, first order-logic is used to characterise conditions on the data in specific states, in pre and post-conditions of procedures, or invariants. Deductive verification typically uses a compositional methodology, specifying and verifying one procedure at a time. Verification tools exist for common programming languages such as C [19], Java [3], or Ada [7].

5.1   SPARK

Ada [8] is a high level imperative programming language targeting the development of large scale safety critical software. Ada is suited to meet the high integrity software requirements and has been used in several industrial embedded software development projects [1]. SPARK is a subset of Ada with additional features to support formal verification [7]. SPARK uses property specifications in the form of program annotations described inline with the source code to perform static program analysis and build automated proofs to show the correctness of the software. In that sense, SPARK uses the correct by construction philosophy through contract based programming to develop software.

A SPARK program is made up of one or more program units. Subprograms and packages are two examples of SPARK program units. A subprogram execution is invoked by a call and subprograms express a sequence of actions. Procedures and functions are the two types of subprograms in SPARK. Procedure calls are standalone statements, whereas function calls occur in an expression and return a value. Packages group together entities like data types, subprograms, etc., and can be considered to be the equivalent of header files in an object oriented programming language like C++. A program unit consists of two structures, a specification and a body. The specification contains the variables, types and the subprogram declarations with their annotations. The body of a program unit contains the details of the implementation.

Properties are in SPARK specified using subprogram contracts (pre and post-conditions), loop invariants, and data dependencies. The formal verification toolset in SPARK can perform program analysis on the source code at various levels. Flow analysis capabilities ensure the program correctness with respect to data flow and information flow. Errors arising due to uninitialized variables, data dependencies between inputs and outputs of subprograms, well-formedness of programs, etc., are checked by this level of analysis. A higher level of analysis is to perform automated proofs to check for run time errors and conformance of the program with the specifications. The program annotations specified are used to generate *verification conditions*, which can then be discharged using the proof tools to show program correctness.

5.2   Verification of *LSM* in SPARK

SPARK 2014 [1] and its associated tools are used to formally verify the *LSM*. With the use of packages and subprograms in SPARK, the code structure of the original implementation of *LSM* using classes and methods in MATLAB-code is preserved. Listing 1.3 shows how the code in Listing 1.1 is built in SPARK. The implementation is done as a procedure (subprogram). Lines 1–6 represent the specification part of the subprogram and lines 8–19 represent the body. The specification consists of the subprogram declaration and its contract in the form of pre and post-conditions. The parameter mode in out permits both read and write operations on the values of the associated parameter.

Listing 1.3. SPARK implementation of the code in Listing 1.1.

```
1    procedure During_StateA
2        (Var                    : in out Var_Type;
3         Lane_Change_Request   : in Lane_Change_Direction_Type)
4    with Pre  => Var.State = StateA,
5         Post => ((Var.Direction = Lane_Change_Request) and
6                  (Var.State in StateA | StateB));
7    - - - - - - - - - - - - - - - - - - - - - - - - - - - - - - - - - - - - - - - - - - -
8    procedure During_StateA
9        (Var                    : in out Var_Type;
10        Lane_Change_Request   : in Lane_Change_Direction_Type)
11   is
12   begin
13       Var.Direction := Lane_Change_Request;
14       Var.X := False;
15       Var.Y := False;
16       if Lane_Change_Request /= NoRequest then
17           Var.State := StateB;
18       end if;
19   end During_StateA;
```

SPARK has a set of core annotations as predefined rules that can be checked without user defined contracts. However, here we are interested in verifying functional properties like *Req.1* and therefore SPARK needs stronger annotations to perform formal analysis. The contract specified in Listing 1.3 is an illustrative example of type of contracts used to show correctness of *LSM* with respect to *Req.1*. The preconditions, denoted Pre, are assertions that are satisfied when the procedure is called and the postconditions, denoted Post, are the conditions that should be satisfied as a result of the procedure call. These contracts are used by the analysis tools to generate verification conditions, which are mathematical expressions relating a number of hypotheses (obtained from preconditons) and conclusions (from postconditions). Providing a correctness proof of the program then boils down to showing that the conclusions always follow from the hypotheses. Detailed information on the the analysis tools is available in [2,7].

With this general idea, the initial approach to prove correctness of the *LSM* was to specify one global contract to capture *Req.1*. This global contract was specified on the complete *LSM* code implemented as a package in SPARK. However, results from the analysis showed that one global contract was insufficient to show correctness of *Req.1*. Subsequent annotations were added to the different subprograms. *Req.1* was specified as a postcondition (3) of a subprogram responsible for execution on the completion of a lane change.

$$\text{Post} \Rightarrow (\text{Var.State = Finished) and}$$
$$(\text{Output\_Indication = Output\_ChangeLane}) \tag{3}$$

Although the proof checks for most of the subprogram contracts were automatically proved by SPARK analysis tools, error messages from proof checks reported that a few postconditions including (3) might fail. The unproved checks could possibly indicate incorrectness of the code (implementation and specification) or the need for stronger annotations for the tools in the form of intermediate assertions and better code organisation. In order to conclusively decide the cause for the failed proof checks, more manual reviews, analysis of the execution paths corresponding to the failed checks and possibly stronger contracts were needed. However, the undertaken approach of implementing the code first and then incrementally annotating the subprograms in order to satisfy the property turned out to be inefficient. A better work flow in our case would be the reverse approach, where the property is formally broken down into suitable subprogram contracts followed by the implementation to show correctness.

6 Insights and Discussion

This section provides a discussion and the insights gained from this case study. The discussion is focused on how the verification methods aid in addressing the challenges mentioned in Sect. 1, and does not aim to compare the performances or the algorithms of the tools.

Describing the System. Autonomous driving systems are often categorised as Cyber-Physical Systems (CPS) or reactive systems in literature, depending on the focus of research. Irrespective of the classification, modelling and observing the system and its *environment* is a known challenge. The expressive power is limited to the choice of formalism. In our case, describing *LSM* as extended finite state machines and transition systems (although not too different) was sufficient to capture—and reason about—correctness due to its discrete nature. However, correctness of *Path Planner, Controller, Sense* in Fig. 1 is just as crucial as *LSM* and the formalism discussed in this paper might not be sufficient as they have continuous dynamics and probabilistic behaviour. Choosing task specific formalisms and tools for different software development teams complicates the industrial adoption of such techniques. In this respect, having subtle and necessary extensions to the existing formalisms so as to capture a wider spectrum of abstractions, while still being decidable, can be invaluable.

Modelling the observable behaviour of the environment faces the risk of statespace explosion. Defining the operating boundaries of the environment with respect to the system is very crucial in successfully addressing the challenge. For example, in our case of the lane change software module, the traffic state (position, behaviour of other vehicles,...) could serve as a definition of the environment for the decision making component in Fig. 1. However, using the same definition for environment to model and reason about *LSM* or *Path Planner*, would neither help tackle the challenge nor be an efficient use of any of the formal technique discussed in this paper. The use of deductive verification in SPARK decouples from such problems by applying verification techniques on the source code. Nevertheless, the challenge then manifests in the need to write complex functional specifications to have the formal analysis done, as it turned out in our case.

From our experience, the key to address these challenges is to use formal approaches with different levels of abstractions to *divide and conquer* in a modular way, similar to classical large scale software development. Higher level abstractions could be used to define logical boundaries between the systems and their environments and lower level abstractions to reason about the systems within their boundaries. Compositional verification can then be used to reason about systems in a modular way. Supremica, TLA$^+$ and SPARK have features to support such compositional verification of systems. This work flow could also be used to formally obtain subprogram annotations in the deductive verification framework to show correctness of source code.

Requirements and Properties. In this paper, the focus is to verify one requirement that affects the safety of the system. In the SCT framework, EFSM is used as the specification language. A violation of the requirement is modelled as an event leading to a blocking state and nonblocking verification is performed to check for errors. This is similar to checking whether in all computations, we eventually reach a state from where a marked state can be reached. While nonblocking cannot be directly translated in linear-time temporal logic, the use of invariants is exploited in TLA$^+$ to check for the desired property. In SPARK, the use of pre/post conditions to look for the particular unsafe behaviour did not prove to be an efficient work method. While TLA$^+$ and Supremica provided counter examples that could help in the analysis of the bug, the counter example generation in SPARK was not sufficient to draw concrete conclusions in our particular case. This could be attributed to the fact that for efficient use of automated reasoning in contract based programming, operational completeness, meaning contracts for normal, error and exceptional behaviour should be included in the specification. The reverse approach of implementing the source code first and then annotating with contracts to check for a particular unsafe behaviour proved very inefficient. However, a program crashing is just as unsafe as compared to the behavioural safety property discussed in this paper. For such software program malfunction due to run time errors (such as division by zero, overflow, etc.), modelling and specifying in Supremica and TLA$^+$ is complicated and will greatly increase the complexity. SPARK is efficient in this regard.

Type of Analysis and the Scope of Correctness. Formal methods can be applied to all levels of the software development process. While acknowledging the individual strengths of each of the methods discussed in this paper, no method on its own is sufficient to prove correctness for the *LSM*. Supervisory control and TLA$^+$ are abstract methods that are best suited for verification at the system level, software architectural level and software design level of the ISO 26262 standard. Deductive verification methods give the most benefit at the software unit (program) verification, the lowest level (source code) of the V-model. SPARK is developed to suit the needs of high integrity safety critical applications and therefore provides better evidence for compliance to several clauses of the standard at the software unit verification level. The abstraction based approaches discussed in this paper involves manual modelling of the system and therefore requires additional effort to ensure that the right detail is captured in the modelling as well as in specifying the properties. The occurrence of false alarms in such methods is of course an implicit trade-off.

Leveraging Formal Methods in an Industrial Setting. The verification approaches discussed in this paper are all performed after the software was implemented. A software to solve an intended function was written in a programming language and then verified for correctness. Although, better use of the methods described in this paper could be made in the earlier stages of the development process (correct by construction approach), the situation where software is verified for correctness in the later stages seems more common in the industrial setting. In our experience, the challenging task encountered while working with the abstract methods is the lack of interoperability with the other tools used in the development. Supremica and TLA$^+$ are stand alone methods and currently, the only way to use them is for engineers to have parallel activities, one with the formal tools and the other with the conventional development tools. While this might be justified for high integrity applications, the need for manual effort to synchronise the parallel activities to obtain a concrete impact is often a drawback. Work on suitable intermediary plug-ins to have traceability between the informal requirements management activity and the formal specification methods would definitely work in favour of increased adoption in the software specification stages. Counter-example generation in the abstract methods discussed in this paper is easily the highest return on investment in an industrial setting. This could further be enhanced by work on using counter-examples to generate test scenarios in the preferred testing framework in the development routine. This will also suit well within the continuous development and continuous integration principles of agile development. In this regard, SPARK is well suited for easier integration. However, the use of SPARK as an after development verification tool without formal specification in the earlier stages, is still inefficient.

7   Conclusion

In this paper, we have applied formal verification based on Supervisory Control Theory, Model Checking and Deductive Verification to verify correctness of a decision making software in an autonomous vehicle. Discussion on how the verification scenario differs in each of the methods is presented. We also provide insights on how the different approaches can address the challenges in industrial development of safe autonomous driving software. The difficulty in working with all these tools is not in learning them but in capturing the right level of abstraction for the verification objectives and stating the formal properties. Although this paper deals with the verification of one safety requirement of a decision making software module, the insights gained are valuable to address the challenges. Future work includes the investigation of integrating multiple formal approaches to tackle the challenges mentioned in this paper also to scale the approaches to different types of systems in an autonomous vehicle for larger classes of properties with more software requirements.

References

1. Adacore. https://www.adacore.com/. Accessed 26 Apr 2019
2. Spark 2014 reference manual. https://docs.adacore.com/spark2014-docs/html/lrm/index.html. Accessed 26 Apr 2019
3. Ahrendt, W., Beckert, B., Bubel, R., Hähnle, R., Schmitt, P.H., Ulbrich, M. (eds.): Deductive Software Verification-The KeY Book. LNCS, vol. 10001. Springer, Cham (2016). https://doi.org/10.1007/978-3-319-49812-6
4. Apt, K.R., de Boer, F.S., Olderog, E.: Verification of Sequential and Concurrent Programs. Texts in Computer Science. Springer, London (2009). https://doi.org/10.1007/978-1-84882-745-5
5. Armstrong, R.C., Punnoose, R.J., Wong, M.H., Mayo, J.R.: Survey of existing tools for formal verification. SANDIA REPORT SAND2014-20533 (2014)
6. Baier, C., Katoen, J.P.: Principles of Model Checking. MIT Press, Cambridge (2008)
7. Barnes, J.: SPARK: The Proven Approach to High Integrity Software. Altran Praxis (2012)
8. Barnes, J.: Programming in Ada 2012. Cambridge University Press, Cambridge (2014)
9. Beckert, B., Hähnle, R.: Reasoning and verification: state of the art and current trends. IEEE Intell. Syst. **29**(1), 20–29 (2014)
10. Clarke, E.M., Emerson, E.A.: Design and synthesis of synchronization skeletons using branching time temporal logic. In: Kozen, D. (ed.) Logic of Programs 1981. LNCS, vol. 131, pp. 52–71. Springer, Heidelberg (1982). https://doi.org/10.1007/BFb0025774
11. Clarke, E.M., Henzinger, T.A., Veith, H., Bloem, R.: Handbook of Model Checking. Springer, Cham (2018). https://doi.org/10.1007/978-3-319-10575-8
12. Fisher, M., Dennis, L.A., Webster, M.P.: Verifying autonomous systems. Commun. ACM **56**(9), 84–93 (2013)
13. Forsberg, K., Mooz, H.: The relationship of system engineering to the project cycle. In: INCOSE International Symposium, vol. 1. Wiley Online Library (1991)
14. Guiochet, J., Machin, M., Waeselynck, H.: Safety-critical advanced robots: a survey. Robot. Auton. Syst. **94**, 43–52 (2017)
15. Hoare, C.A.R.: An axiomatic basis for computer programming. Commun. ACM **12**(10), 576–580, 583 (1969)
16. ISO: Road vehicles - Functional safety. Technical report, ISO 26262 (2011)
17. Kasauli, R., Knauss, E., Kanagwa, B., Nilsson, A., Calikli, G.: Safety-critical systems and agile development: a mapping study. In: 2018 44th Euromicro Conference on Software Engineering and Advanced Applications (SEAA). IEEE (2018)
18. Kemmerer, R.A.: Integrating formal methods into the development process. IEEE Softw. **7**(5), 37–50 (1990)
19. Kosmatov, N., Prevosto, V., Signoles, J.: A lesson on proof of programs with Frama-C. Invited tutorial paper. In: Veanes, M., Viganò, L. (eds.) TAP 2013. LNCS, vol. 7942, pp. 168–177. Springer, Heidelberg (2013). https://doi.org/10.1007/978-3-642-38916-0_10
20. Lamport, L.: The TLA$^+$. https://lamport.azurewebsites.net/tla/tla.html. Accessed 22 Apr 2019
21. Lamport, L.: The temporal logic of actions. ACM Trans. Program. Lang. Syst. (TOPLAS) **16**(3), 872–923 (1994)

22. Lamport, L.: Specifying Systems: The TLA$^+$ Language and Tools for Hardware and Software Engineers. Addison-Wesley Longman Publishing Co., Inc., Boston (2002)
23. Luckcuck, M., Farrell, M., Dennis, L., Dixon, C., Fisher, M.: Formal specification and verification of autonomous robotic systems: a survey. arXiv preprint arXiv:1807.00048 (2018)
24. Malik, R.: Programming a fast explicit conflict checker. In: 2016 13th International Workshop on Discrete Event Systems (WODES), pp. 438–443. IEEE (2016)
25. Malik, R., Akesson, K., Flordal, H., Fabian, M.: Supremica-an efficient tool for large-scale discrete event systems. IFAC-PapersOnLine 50(1), 5794–5799 (2017). https://doi.org/10.1016/j.ifacol.2017.08.427. 20th IFAC World Congress
26. Mohajerani, S., Malik, R., Fabian, M.: A framework for compositional nonblocking verification of extended finite-state machines. Discrete Event Dyn. Syst. **26**(1), 33–84 (2016)
27. Newcombe, C.: Why Amazon chose TLA$^+$. In: Ait Ameur, Y., Schewe, K.D. (eds.) ABZ 2014. LNCS, vol. 8477, pp. 25–39. Springer, Heidelberg (2014). https://doi. org/10.1007/978-3-662-43652-3_3
28. Pnueli, A.: The temporal logic of programs. In: 18th Annual Symposium on Foundations of Computer Science (SFCS 1977), pp. 46–57. IEEE (1977)
29. Queille, J.P., Sifakis, J.: Specification and verification of concurrent systems in CESAR. In: Dezani-Ciancaglini, M., Montanari, U. (eds.) Programming 1982. LNCS, vol. 137, pp. 337–351. Springer, Heidelberg (1982). https://doi.org/10.1007/3-540-11494-7_22
30. Ramadge, P.J., Wonham, W.M.: Supervisory control of a class of discrete event processes. SIAM J. Control Optim. **25**(1), 206–230 (1987)
31. Ramadge, P.J., Wonham, W.M.: The control of discrete event systems. Proc. IEEE **77**(1), 81–98 (1989)
32. Saiedian, H., Hinchey, M.G.: Challenges in the successful transfer of formal methods technology into industrial applications. Inf. Softw. Technol. **38**(5), 313–322 (1996)
33. Seshia, S.A., Sadigh, D., Sastry, S.S.: Formal methods for semi-autonomous driving. In: 52nd ACM/EDAC/IEEE Design Automation Conference (DAC). IEEE (2015)
34. Skoldstam, M., Akesson, K., Fabian, M.: Modeling of discrete event systems using finite automata with variables. In: 2007 46th IEEE Conference on Decision and Control, pp. 3387–3392. IEEE (2007)
35. Wolff, S.: Scrum goes formal: agile methods for safety-critical systems. In: Proceedings of the First International Workshop on Formal Methods in Software Engineering: Rigorous and Agile Approaches, pp. 23–29. IEEE Press (2012)
36. Zita, A., Mohajerani, S., Fabian, M.: Application of formal verification to the lane change module of an autonomous vehicle. In: 2017 13th IEEE Conference on Automation Science and Engineering (CASE), pp. 932–937. IEEE (2017)

Author Index

Printed in the United States
By Bookmasters